PRENTICE-HALL BIOLOGICAL SCIENCE SERIES
William D. McElroy and Carl P. Swanson, *Editors*

Concepts of Modern Biology Series

Behavioral Aspects of Ecology, PETER H. KLOPFER
Concepts of Ecology, EDWARD J. KORMONDY
Ecological Development in Polar Regions, MAXWELL J. DUNBAR
Euglenoid Flagellates, GORDON F. LEEDALE
Introduction to the Structure of Biological Molecules, J. M. BARRY and E. H. BARRY
The Organism as an Adaptive Control System, JOHN M. RINER
Processes of Organic Evolution, G. LEDYARD STEBBINS

**To all ecologists—
in spirit and in fact**

Nearer the coasts are the giant forests of the redwoods extending from near the Oregon line to Santa Cruz. . . . these withdrawn gardens of the woods—long vistas opening to the sea—sunshine sifting and pouring upon the flowery ground in a tremulous, shifting mosaic, as the light-ways in the leafy wall open and close with the swaying breeze . . .

JOHN MUIR

Lying out at night under those giant sequoias was lying in a temple built by no hand of man, a temple grander than any human architect could by any possibility build, and I hope for the preservation of the groves of giant trees simply because it would be a shame to our civilization to let them disappear. They are monuments in themselves.

THEODORE ROOSEVELT

I went to the woods because I wished to live deliberately, to front only the essential facts of life, and see if I could not learn what it had to teach, and not, when I came to die, discover that I had not lived.

HENRY DAVID THOREAU

Redwood Stand, Del Norte County, California. (*U. S. Forest Service.*)

CONCEPTS OF MODERN BIOLOGY SERIES
William D. McElroy and Carl P. Swanson, Editors

EDWARD J. KORMONDY

Professor of Biology
Oberlin College
Director
Commission on Undergraduate Education in
the Biological Sciences, Washington, D. C.

concepts

of

ecology

PRENTICE-HALL, INC., Englewood Cliffs, New Jersey

PRENTICE-HALL INTERNATIONAL, INC., *London*
PRENTICE-HALL OF AUSTRALIA, PTY. LTD., *Sydney*
PRENTICE-HALL OF CANADA LTD., *Toronto*
PRENTICE-HALL OF INDIA PRIVATE LTD., *New Delhi*
PRENTICE-HALL OF JAPAN, INC., *Tokyo*

© 1969 by Prentice-Hall, Inc. Englewood Cliffs, New Jersey.

All rights reserved. No part of this book may be reproduced in any form or by any means without permission in writing from the publisher.

Current printing (last digit):
10 9 8 7 6 5 4 3 2

Library of Congress Catalog Card Number: 75-77664

Printed in the United States of America

preface

It has been my hope to present the significant concepts of modern ecology in a readable and intelligible way, and to develop these concepts in a manner that reflects the way in which they have in fact developed—not as truth revealed or *fait accompli* but as a searching into the nature of things, asking questions, analyzing data, generalizing, and predicting. I have not been completely consistent in this approach, any more than any scientist is in his day-to-day research. He builds on the store of previous work and hence must master established facts and formulas; it would be imprudent and ludicrous for him to search out everything from scratch. Little, if any, progress would ever be made. Thus, in treating some ideas I have been more descriptive than developmental, more assertive than investigatory. At the least, however, I would hope to have portrayed ecology as both very old and very new, very secure on some concepts and very open on others, and very much of an exciting cross- or inter-disciplinary field, as is much of contemporary biology.

I have aimed for an audience of post-general biology students but there is little reason for anyone to avoid the book just because he has not been exposed to Mendelism, Darwinism, fetal pigs, or glycolysis. I have consciously minimized jargon, hopefully without sacrificing accuracy, and I have tried to write about ideas rather than things. I would really hope thereby that concerned and interested laymen of a non-scientific orientation might also find this effort worth their time, particularly the final chapter.

To start, it seems appropriate to indicate what ecology is about, because the subsequent chapters are not concerned with such a matter *per se*. As a term, ecology appears to have first been used in the middle-nineteenth century. On January 1, 1858, the New England transcendentalist-naturalist Henry David Thoreau wrote to his cousin George Thatcher, of Bangor, Maine, "Mr. Hoar is still in Concord, attending to Botany, Ecology, etc. with a view to make his future residence in foreign parts more truly profitable to him." According to Paul Oehser, Edward Hoar was Thoreau's Concord neighbor and companion on several trips including the famous journey to the Maine woods in 1857.

Although the original coining of the term is an uncertainty, there is consensus that the German biologist Ernst Haeckel first gave substance to it in the following statement:

> By ecology we mean the body of knowledge concerning the economy of nature—the investigation of the total relations of the animal both to its inorganic and to its organic environment; including above all, its friendly and inimical relation with those animals and plants with which it comes directly or indirectly into contact—in a word, ecology is the study of all the complex interrelations referred to by Darwin as the conditions of the struggle for existence. The science of ecology, often inaccurately referred to as "biology" in a narrow sense, has thus far formed the principle component of what is commonly referred to as "Natural History." As is well shown by the numerous popular natural histories of both early and modern times, this subject has developed in the most close relations with systematic zoology. The ecology of animals has been dealt with quite uncritically in natural history; but natural history has in any case had the merit of keeping alive a widespread interest in zoology.

This quotation appeared in a work by Haeckel in 1870 although he appears to have first used the term in 1866. Some seven years previously, the French zoologist Isodore Geoffroy St. Hilaire had proposed the term *ethology* for, "the study of the relations of the organisms within the family and society in the aggregate and in the community." At about the same time the English naturalist, St. George Jackson Mivart, coined the term *hexicology*, which he defined in 1894 as, "devoted to the study of the relations which exist between the organisms and their environment as regards the nature of the locality they frequent, the temperatures and the amounts of light which suit them, and their relations to other organisms as enemies, rivals, or accidental and involuntary benefactors."

Ernst Haeckel carried considerable influence in his day, much more so than either Mivart or St. Hilaire; this may be, in part, the explanation for the eclipsing of the alternate terms ethology and hexicology, and the adoption, by common usage, of Haeckel's term *ecology*. As you are probably aware, St. Hilaire's term ethology has subsequently become a synonym for the study of animal behavior.

Haeckel's definition, involving the concept of interrelationships of organisms and environment, has had somewhat different and perhaps more incisive interpretations placed upon it by investigators since 1900. The British ecologist Charles Elton, for example, defined ecology as "scientific natural history" concerned with the "sociology and economics of animals." An American plant ecologist, Frederick Clements, considered ecology to be "the science of the community," and the contemporary American ecologist Eugene Odum has defined it, perhaps too broadly, as "the study of the structure and function of nature."

Regardless of precise definition, the substance of ecology is found in the myriad of abiotic and biotic mechanisms and interrelations involved in moving energy and nutrients, regulating population and community structure and dynamics. Like many fields of contemporary biology, ecology is multidisciplinary and almost boundless in its concern. This point has been well stated by the British ecologist A. Macfadyen:

> "Ecology concerns itself with the interrelationships of living organisms, plant or animal, and their environments; these are studied with a view to discovering the principles which govern the relationships. That such principles exist is a basic assumption—and an act of faith—of the ecologist. His field of inquiry is no less wide than the totality of the living conditions of the plants and animals under observation, their systematic position, their reactions to the environment and to each other, and the physical and chemical nature of their inanimate surroundings. . . . It must be admitted that the ecologist is something of a chartered libertine. He roams at will over the legitimate preserves of the plant and animal biologist, the taxonomist, the physiologist, the behaviourist, the meteorologist, the geologist, the physicist, the chemist and even the sociologist; he poaches from all these and from other established and respected disciplines. It is indeed a major problem for the ecologist, in his own interest, to set bounds to his divagations."
>
> *Animal Ecology: Aims and Methods* (1957)

I would suppose that the investigator would pass beyond the bounds of ecology when he was no longer directly concerned with interrelationships of the physical and the biological but with any particular process in its own right. It has been my intent here to delve into these processes *per se* but always in the context of the whole picture of the ecosystem. If I have not succeeded in this intention it is no reflection on the many upon whom I've depended for the development of my ideas and the execution of this book. Like any venture, this book is of the "OTSOG" sort; because I too have stood "*on the shoulders of giants*"—the many investigators who have given the substance from which I've drawn heavily, the few really creative idea men who have given direction to the discipline, my students who have provided a critical audience against which my thoughts and presentations have been tested over the years, and finally, my several ecologist-colleagues who have had the onus of reviewing portions of the manuscript: Francis Evans, Gene Likens, Robert Whittaker, and George Woodwell. I am especially grateful for a review of the entire manuscript by a nonecologist, my Oberlin colleague Thomas F. Sherman, for the cooperation of various publishers and authors to reproduce material, and for the typing of several revisions of the manuscript by Marie Cook. Finally, but foremost, my forbearing and, of necessity, forgiving wife has been a most vital ingredient of this project—thanks, Peg.

EDWARD J. KORMONDY

contents

CHAPTER 1 the nature of ecosystems — 1

CHAPTER 2 energy flow in ecosystems — 7

Energy Fixation by Autotrophs — 10
Energy Beyond the Producers — 21

CHAPTER 3 biogeochemical cycles and ecosystems — 35

The Hydrologic Cycle — 36
Gaseous Nutrient Cycles — 40
Sedimentary Nutrient Cycles — 48
Nutrient Budgets and Ecosystems — 54

CHAPTER 4 ecology of populations — 62

Characteristics of Population Growth — 64
The "Equilibrium Level" of Populations — 84

CHAPTER 5 the organization and dynamics of ecological communities — 113

The Major Terrestrial Ecosystems — 115
Structural Aspects of the Deciduous Forest — 129
Functional Aspects of the Deciduous Forest — 140
Ecological Succession — 154

CHAPTER 6 ecology and man — 165

Human Population — 166
Pollution — 178
Epilogue — 195

index — 199

There are a substantial number of general textbooks and references in the field of ecology of which the interested reader may wish to be aware. Because of their general application, I have not included them in individual chapter references since many would have had to be repeated in virtually each instance. It does seem appropriate to bring such titles to the attention of the reader. This list includes those which I personally have found to be particularly valuable.

Allee, W. C., Emerson, A. E., Park, O., Park, T. and Schmidt, K. P. 1949. *Principles of Animal Ecology.* Philadelphia: W. B. Saunders Company.

Andrewartha, H. G. and L. C. Birch. 1954. *The Distribution and Abundance of Animals.* Chicago: University of Chicago Press.

Billings, W. D. 1964. *Plants and the Ecosystem.* Belmont, California: Wadsworth Publishing Company.

Clarke, G. L. 1965. *Elements of Ecology* (rev. printing). New York: John Wiley and Sons, Inc.

Daubenmire, R. F. 1947. *Plants and Environment.* New York: John Wiley and Sons, Inc.

Elton, C. S. 1927. *Animal Ecology.* New York: The Macmillan Company.

Odum, E. P. 1959. *Fundamentals of Ecology* (2d ed.). Philadelphia: W. B. Saunders Company.

Oosting, H. J. 1956. *The Study of Plant Communities* (2d ed.). San Francisco: W. H. Freeman and Company.

Smith, R. L. 1966. *Ecology and Field Biology.* New York: Harper and Row.

postscript

the nature of ecosystems

CHAPTER 1

Besides the relationship which all organisms share because of their evolutionary history, there are kinships that develop from satisfying the requisites for the continuance of life and kind—food, shelter, moisture, respiratory gases, mates, etc. The array of interactions which serve to meet these environmental dependencies is bewildering, surpassing both expectation and wildest imagination. It is the intent of this book to enable the reader to gain some understanding of the ecological relationships that exist between organism and organisms of the same and of different kinds, and of those relationships that exist between organism and environment.

Ecological relationships are manifested not in a vacuum but in physico-chemical settings, sets of nonliving or *abiotic* environmental substances and gradients. These include basic inorganic elements and compounds such as water and carbon dioxide, calcium and oxygen, carbonates and phosphates, and an array of organic compounds, the by-products of organism activity or death. They also include such physical factors and gradients as moisture, winds, currents, and solar radiation with its concomitants of light and heat. It is against this abiotic backdrop that the *biotic* components—plants, animals, and microbes—interact in a fundamentally energy-dependent fashion. The abiotic physico-chemical environment and the biotic assemblage of plants, animals, and microbes comprise an ecological system, or *ecosystem*, in which ecological kinship is demonstrated. Ecosystems are perforce, then, the province of ecology, and an understanding of their structure and dynamics is the concern of the ecologist.

Ecosystems are real—like a pond, or a field, a forest, an ocean, or even an aquarium; they are also abstract in the sense of being conceptual schemes developed from a knowledge of real systems. In spite of the great diversity in types of actual ecosystems—from small to large, terrestrial to aquatic, laboratory to field—and in spite of the unique combinations of particular abiotic and biotic components in any particular one, there are certain general structural and functional attributes that are recognizable and to which attention can be directed.

Inasmuch as ecological kinship is in the final analysis energy-oriented, consideration of the nature of the ecosystem may well begin with the influx of energy. Radiant energy, in the form of sunlight, is the ultimate and only significant source of energy for any ecosystem; it is used in the photosynthetic process whereby carbon dioxide is assimilated into energy-rich carbon compounds. The organisms that perform this vital function are the *producers;* typically these are the chlorophyll-bearing plants, the algae of a pond, the grass of a field, the trees of the forest. Of considerably less significance in most ecosystems are the carotenoid-bearing purple bacteria that also assimilate carbon dioxide with the energy of sunlight, but only in the presence of organic compounds, compounds initially produced through photosynthesis. Finally, producers also include chemosynthetic bacteria, all of which obtain energy by oxidizing simple inorganic compounds. Chemosynthetic producers are relatively insignificant in the energy relations of an ecosystem but play a substantial role in the movement of mineral nutrients in ecosystems.

The term producer, in an energy context, is misleading and misrepresentative. Producers produce carbohydrates, not energy; since they convert or transduce radiant energy into a chemical form, they might better be referred to as converters or transducers. However, the term "producer" is so widely employed and firmly entrenched that it would be futile to try to dislodge it.

Since the energy incorporated in the producer by photosynthesis is subsequently synthesized into other molecules that serve the nutritional requirements of the producer's own growth and metabolism, one can speak of the producer as being *autotrophic* (= self-feeding). By the same token, organisms whose nutritional needs are met by feeding on other organisms can be referred to as *heterotrophic* (= other feeding). A primary consumer, or, more commonly, a herbivore, is a heterotroph that derives its nutrition directly from plants; a carnivore, or secondary consumer, is a heterotroph deriving its energy indirectly from the producer by way of the herbivore. Some ecosystems contain tertiary consumers—carnivores that feed on other carnivores. A simple but nonetheless actual example of this autotroph-heterotroph relationship is seen in the reindeer moss-reindeer-human food chain in Lapland. Energy captured by the photosynthesizing reindeer moss (which is actually a lichen, not a moss) serves as the food base for reindeer, and the latter in turn for the Laplander. In this chain, the reindeer moss is the producer, and is an autotroph; the reindeer and the Laplander are heterotrophs, the former a primary consumer or herbivore, the latter a secondary consumer or carnivore.

Implicit in this autotroph→heterotroph, producer→consumer, or producer→herbivore→carnivore relationship is the direction of energy movement through the ecosystem. It is unidirectional and noncyclic. In part, one could reason this *a priori,* for plants do not consume animals except for the unusual carnivorous plants such as sun-dew, pitcher plant, Venus flytrap and a number of bromeliads. The rationale for the noncyclic, unidirectional flow of energy, however, is to be found in the energy losses that occur at each transfer along the chain and in the efficiency of energy utilization which occurs within each link of the chain, matters to be considered at length in the next chapter. For the moment, however, let it suffice to state that a one-way flow of energy constitutes one of the most important if not the cardinal principle of the ecosystem.

But there is another major group of heterotrophs in ecosystems, a group of organisms collectively referred to as *decomposers* and consisting chiefly of bacteria and fungi. For the most part, decomposers do not consume food in the ingestive manner of a herbivore or carnivore; they do so by absorption. Enzymes produced within their bodies are released into dead plant and animal material, and some of the degraded and digested products are then absorbed. As a concomitant of supplying their own growth and metabolism requirements, however, decomposers perform an invaluable service to the ecosystem, the mineralization of organic matter. By their exo-enzyme digestive activity, basic elements bound in protoplasm are released to the environment and thereby made available for reuse by producers. It now becomes evident that two processes have been proceeding concurrently, the movement of energy and of nutrient elements. The former of these has been seen to be unidirectional and noncyclic; the implication of decomposer mineralization activity is that the movement of nutrients is cyclic. This point needs further clarification.

In the process of converting radiant energy into chemical energy by photosynthesis, the green plant also incorporates into its protoplasm a variety of inorganic elements and compounds. Among the important ones are the direct components of the photosynthetic reaction, carbon dioxide and water, and those that are critical to protoplasmic synthesis, notably nitrogen, phosphorus, sulfur, and magnesium as well as some fifteen other essential nutrients. As the green plant is grazed upon, not only is chemical energy in the form of carbohydrates, fats, and proteins transferred to the herbivores, but a host of nutrients as well. Similarly, there is a transfer of both energy and nutrients from herbivore to carnivore and from all the preceding levels to the decomposers. Although, as already noted, there is a progressive diminution of energy in this trophic or feeding chain, the nutrient component is not diminished; in fact, some may even become concentrated in certain steps of the chain. In any event, nutrients are not lost in the manner of energy, for when nutrient-containing protoplasm is eventually subjected to decomposer activity they are released to the environment and here they are potentially available for reuse, for recycling. The peculiarities of the cycling

THE NATURE OF ECOSYSTEMS

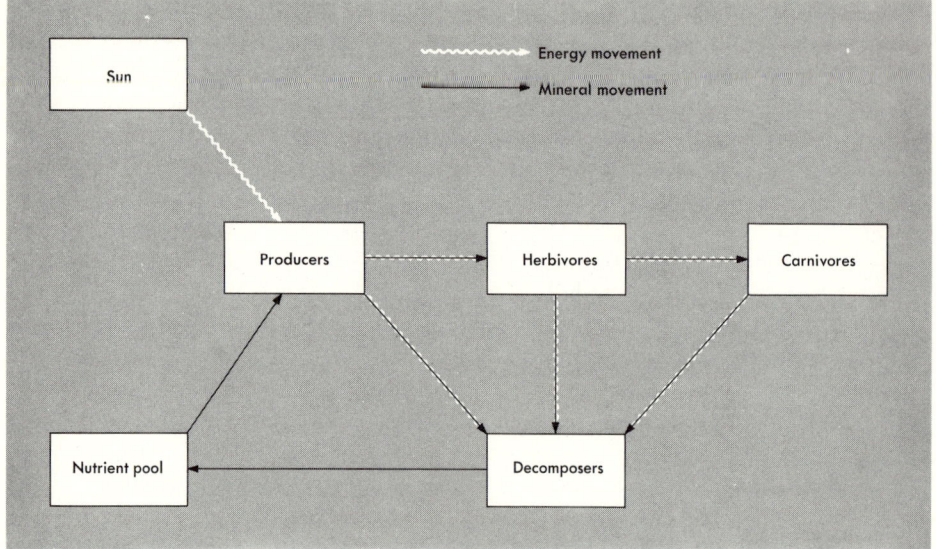

Fig. 1-1. A simplified model of energy and mineral movement in ecosystems. Note that energy flow is noncyclic, whereas nutrient movement is cyclic.

process and the interaction of physical, chemical, and biotic factors in it will be discussed in detail in Chapter 3.

These two ecological processes of energy flow and mineral cycling, involving interaction between the physico-chemical environment and the biotic assemblage, lie at the heart of ecosystem dynamics. They are the *raison d'être* of both ecosystems and the myriad complex processes which take place within them. It is the purpose of this book to substantiate this claim. For the moment, however, we may represent these two processes by an oversimplified model (Figure 1-1) for purposes of codifying the discussion to this point. The inadequacy of this model will become apparent subsequently and will relate to two major matters. First, energy not only flows unidirectionally as shown, but is also lost irretrievably from the system in several ways. Second, although minerals circulate within an ecosystem with an initial input from the environment as shown, there is net loss in several ways. But these serious and acknowledged deficiencies of the present model do not obviate its immediate usefulness in providing a general overview; modifications will be easily accomplished and more readily understood in the fuller discussion of subsequent chapters.

These two major processes have significance of considerable magnitude in the contemporary scene. Meeting the food requirements of an expanding human population demands a more intimate knowledge of the efficiency and output of producers. Of no less consequence is the efficiency of energy flow through man-oriented ecosystems and the dependence of those systems on the availability and abundance of essential nutrients. Further, the introduction into the environment of radioactive forms of nutrients and of toxic substances such as detergents and pesticides typically results in their incorporation into man-oriented food chains as a result of natural cycling processes, constituting thereby one of the major problems facing man today. Such considerations, as we shall see, involve a thorough and basic understanding of these two major ecological processes beyond what we now fully possess.

Although the processes of energy flow and mineral cycling are indeed fundamental, they are not the whole of ecology. The manifestation of these processes, as we have already seen, is through the vehicle of living organisms—plants, animals, and microbes. These terms, like the term ecosystem, have objectivity in actual populations of specific organisms, each of which plays a role that is characteristic of the species and unique in any given ecosystem. Each species has not only unique morphological, physiological, and behavioral attributes, but, because of them, unique ecological attributes as well. Given plant species, as we shall see, are considerably more efficient in energy capture at particular altitudes or at particular depths in aquatic systems than are other species; some are more tolerant of excesses and minima of particular nutrients and less tolerant of extremes in others. Because of this, one expects *a priori* that no two ecosystems would likely have precisely the same biological composition but rather ecological equivalents performing comparable functions. Further, it should follow that as physical and chemical factors show gradation, species populations sensitive to those gradations should correspondingly increase or decrease in abundance as well as importance. And it should also follow that these shifts in any given population would bear on the relationships that become established between populations of different species. The consequences of varying specificities of organisms and environment ramify quickly and affect the growth, size, and distribution of populations. We shall need to consider in some detail, then, both general patterns of growth and regulation of populations and some of the unique aspects of particular species populations.

These comments on environmental tolerances of species populations, when coupled with the acknowledged differences in physical and chemical parameters of the environment, raise several significant implications. In the first instance, although no two ecosystems would be expected to be exactly alike, some, like members of the same species population, would be expected to be more alike than others. Thus one groups together fields, or ponds, or forests; or, in turn, evergreen forests as distinct from deciduous ones, and within the latter, oak-hickory forests as different from beech-maple forests. The ecologist can have in his purview the general ecosystem (e.g., forest) or any of its subdivisions (beech-maple or oak-hickory forests) or any of its particular manifestations (the beech-maple woods north of town). These assemblages, large or small, geographically limited or expansive, are the actual ecosystems in which energy flows, minerals cycle, and populations grow and interact. A consideration of the structure and dynamics of these ecological communities will be undercurrent throughout this book but will receive especial focus in Chapter 5.

There is yet another and significant aspect of ecosystems which needs to be made explicit. As no organism is sufficient unto itself, so too an ecosystem. Ecosystems are not discrete entities delimited sharply from other ecosystems. What pond exists that is not surrounded by another ecosystem, perhaps a field, from which organic matter may be added, or that is not connected by a stream to another pond to which it contributes organic or nutrient matter? What of the often complex feeding relationships that result in biological transfer of energy and nutrients from one system to another? The existence of contiguity and/or continuousness at once complicates the study of ecosystems, requiring the investigator to take into account the influences of surrounding and connecting systems.

Thus, whereas the biologist likes to have as an object of study something discrete, like a cell or cell organelle that can be isolated into a test tube, the ecologist in studying natural systems is confronted by the complexities of almost unlimited variables. He seeks, then, systems that are either more delimited, or in which interrelationships can be more sharply defined—or he moves into the laboratory. A good deal of very sound ecology has, in fact, taken place in the laboratory; here ideas and concepts can be tested with a limitation of variables and variability that nature otherwise seldom provides; the ultimate test of laboratory pronouncement, however, is to be found in nature.

SUGGESTED READINGS

Kormondy, E. J., 1965. *Readings in Ecology.* Englewood Cliffs, New Jersey: Prentice-Hall, Inc.

Evans, F. C., Ecosystem as the basic unit in ecology, p. 166.

Forbes, S. A., The lake as a microcosm, p. 168.

Leopold, A., Lakes in relation to terrestrial life patterns, p. 200.

Möbius, K., An oyster-bank is a biocönose, or a social community, p. 121.

energy flow in ecosystems

CHAPTER 2

Biological activity involves the utilization of energy, energy that comes ultimately from the sun, and which is transformed from the radiant to the chemical form in photosynthesis and from the chemical to mechanical and heat forms in cellular metabolism. These conversions and sequential dependencies are at once both elementary in conception and fundamental to the energetics of organisms and ecosystems.

The sun, essentially a thermonuclear or so-called hydrogen bomb, has a temperature and composition such that hydrogen is transmuted to helium with a concomitant release of considerable energy in the form of electromagnetic waves. Although this radiation extends from shortwave X- and gamma rays to long-wave radio waves, about 99 per cent of the total energy is in the region of wavelengths from 0.2 to 4.0 microns (μ), the region of the ultraviolet through the infrared. Significantly, about half of this energy is in the region that encompasses the visible spectrum (0.38 to 0.77 μ)! If you pause to consider how small a target the Earth is in the solar system, it is not surprising to learn that only about one fifty-millionth of the sun's tremendous energy output reaches the Earth's outer atmosphere, and it does so at a constant rate. This constant is referred to as the *solar flux,* the amount of radiant energy of all wavelengths that cross a unit area or surface per unit of time; from available meteorological data this value is estimated to be 2 calories per square centimeter per minute (cal/cm^2/min), for a total income of 13×10^{23} cal/year. Because of the elliptical orbit of the Earth around the sun, the flux at any given spot varies seasonally with latitude (Figure 2-1); and, of course, because of the Earth's rotation, the flux at a given place varies diurnally.

Of significance for biological systems, however, is the fact that half or more of this

ENERGY FLOW IN ECOSYSTEMS

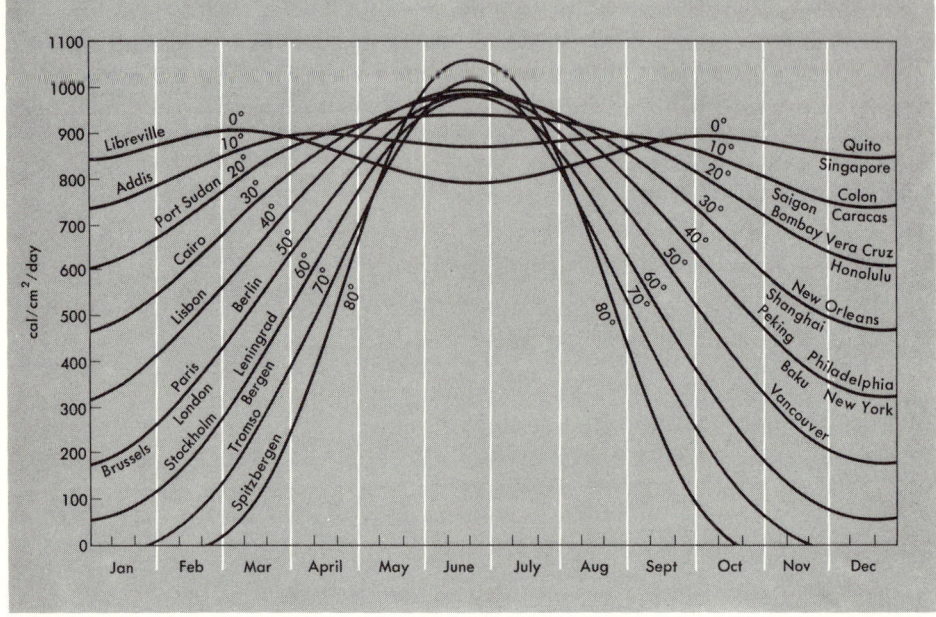

Redrawn by permission from D. M. Gates. 1962. *Energy Exchange in the Biosphere*. New York: Harper and Row.

Fig. 2-1. Daily totals of solar radiation received on a horizontal surface for different geographical latitudes at different times of the year and based on a solar constant value of 1.94 g cal/cm^2/yr.

flux is depleted as it passes through the troposphere (Figure 2-2). In the northern hemisphere, according to the German meteorologist Dr. Rudolf Geiger, about 42 per cent of incoming solar radiation is reflected back—some 33 per cent from clouds and 9 per cent from dust. This reflecting power, or albedo, of the Earth would make it about as bright for an inhabitant of space as Venus is for us, according to Dr. Geiger. An additional 10 per cent of the solar flux is absorbed by ozone, oxygen, water vapor, and carbonic acid, or is diffusely scattered by air molecules and small particles. This leaves only about 48 per cent of the total solar output that actually reaches the Earth's surface, some of which, in turn, may be reflected back into the atmosphere from light surfaces. For example, as much as 80 per cent is reflected from clean bright sand, as the soles and eyes of many beachcombers well recognize. On cloudy days, of course, much less light reaches the Earth's surface, the actual amount being inversely related to the density of the cloud cover.

Radiant energy absorbed in the troposphere is radiated outward in all directions in the infrared portion of the electromagnetic spectrum; some of this strikes the Earth from whence some of it is, in turn, reradiated. The two energy-income components, direct solar radiation and indirect infrared radiation, heat the lower air, the soil and water at the surface and

ENERGY FLOW IN ECOSYSTEMS

the organisms living there, but, in addition, the visible light component of direct radiation is requisite to initiating the ecosystem dynamo via the photosynthetic machinery. A variety of instruments have been designed to measure the rate and amount of solar radiation, but a discussion of them would take us afield. Pragmatically, an ecologist needs to know the limita-

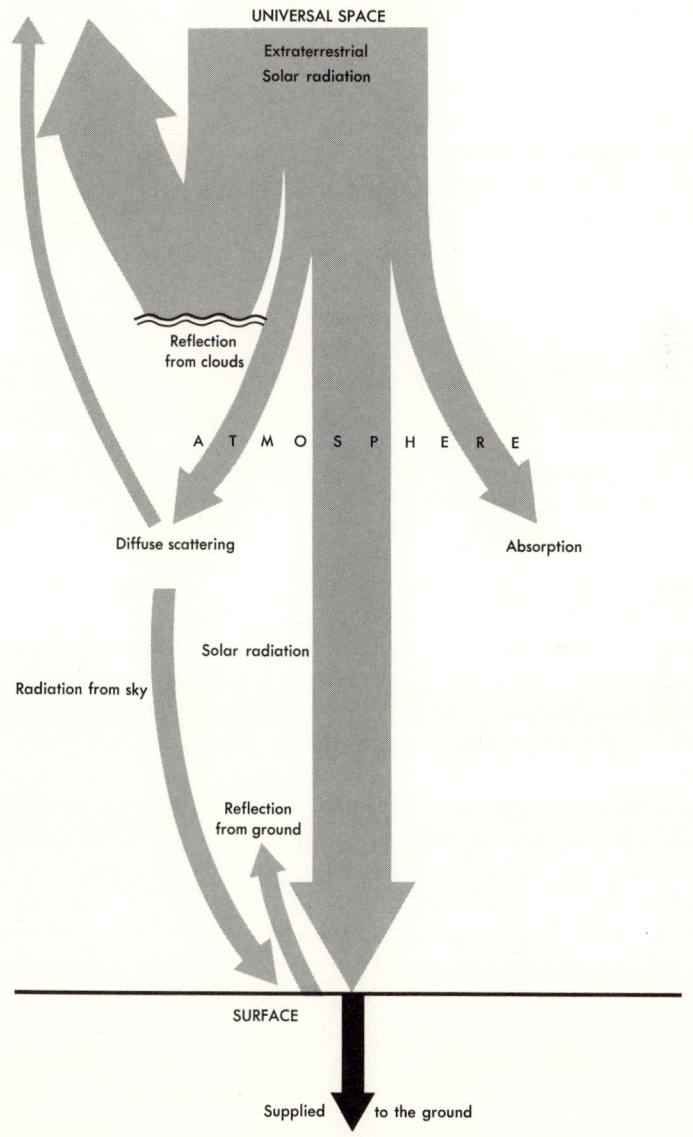

Redrawn by permission of the publishers from Rudolf Geiger. The Climate Near the Ground. Cambridge, Mass.: Harvard University Press, Copyright 1950, by the President and Fellows of Harvard College.

Fig. 2-2. Energy intake at the earth's surface at mid-day.

tions of particular instruments, but what he really wants to know is how much visible light radiation has been or is being received in order to consider the efficiency with which a given ecosystem utilizes that energy. That is, it is the fate of solar radiation as it becomes incorporated and passes through an ecosystem that is the ecologist's concern.

ENERGY FIXATION BY AUTOTROPHS

Since radiant energy is converted by autotrophs in photosynthesis, measurement of the amount and rate of energy fixation is predicated on the photosynthetic equation:

$$6\ CO_2 + 12\ H_2O \xrightarrow[\text{chlorophyll (or other pigment)}]{673\ \text{kilocalories}} C_6H_{12}O_6 + 6\ O_2 + 6\ H_2O$$

The stoichiometry of the equation is such that if the amount of one of the components is known, other components of the equation can be computed. For example, in some situations, it may be more appropriate and convenient to measure the amount of carbon dioxide utilized in a given period of time than it would be to measure the amount of carbohydrate produced. Having done so, the investigator could then compute the amount of carbohydrate produced because of the relationship that for each six units of carbon dioxide assimilated one unit of carbohydrate is produced. Precise calculations involve certain qualifications of these equivalences; however, for purposes of developing the general principle the basic equation is adequate.

Although the various methods developed to date are beset with technical and/or interpretational limitations, they do provide approximations of a process that is difficult to measure under both field and laboratory conditions. Because it is important to recognize some of these difficulties, as well as to gain an understanding of some of the methodology of ecological study and to recognize the limitations inherent in the data to be discussed subsequently, a brief consideration of the major techniques of measuring primary production, i.e., the amount and rate of energy fixation, is in order.

Measuring Primary Production

Harvest Methods. One of the most commonly employed methods of measuring autotroph or primary production, and historically one of the oldest, is that of harvesting. For many years farmers have used the harvest method in reporting their yields as so many bushels of wheat, so many pounds of beef, or so many gallons of milk. The ecologist also employs the harvest method by removing vegetation at periodic intervals and weighing the material. The part of the plant harvested varies with the intent of the study; in harvesting grasses, for example, plants are typically clipped at ground level. Aquatic vegetation has been sampled in the same way, but recent studies show that a considerable error is introduced by failing to harvest the roots as well, particularly the large rootstocks common to many aquatic plants, let alone the roots of trees (Figure 2-10). After drying to constant weight, the harvest can be expressed in terms of the biomass as mass per unit area per unit time, for example, as grams per square meter per year. If the exact caloric content of the material is known, biomass can be converted and expressed in energy terms. Although the caloric content of many species is known, a harvest more often than not is a mixture of many kinds; for thumbnail purposes, a gross estimate can be reached on the basis that each gram of dried plant material has an energy content of about 4 to 5 kilocalories (kcal).

One of the major limitations of the harvest method is that it fails to account for the amount of material (or energy) consumed by herbivores; no less crucial is its failure to account for the energy utilized by the autotroph in its own metabolism, growth, and development. What is actually measured is the standing crop, the amount of autotroph at a given time, or at given time intervals, which has been in excess of the demands of its own metabolism or of the herbivores that depend on it. If this harvest is corrected for the amounts lost by respiration (metabolism), as well as any other avenues of loss (e.g., herbivory), an estimate of the total or *gross production* will have been made. In some instances the ecologist is interested in gross production, sometimes in net production (total production less plant respiration), and sometimes in both. The significance of these two ways of considering production will be apparent later in this chapter.

Although the harvest approach is widely used in ecological studies, particularly in terrestrial situations, there are other methods which are more sophisticated, but often no more precise, and certainly no less beset with methodological limitations. These methods are directed at other components of the photosynthetic equation and at measurements of CO_2 assimilation, O_2 release, and chlorophyll production among others.

Carbon Dioxide Assimilation. The uptake of CO_2 in photosynthesis or its loss in respiration under natural conditions has been determined by use of infrared gas analysis. Such analyzers measure the amount of CO_2 entering and leaving an airtight enclosure of a known area or volume constructed of a light-transmitting substance such as plexiglass, glass, or plastic. It is assumed that any CO_2 removed from the incoming air has been incorporated into organic matter during the period of observation, thereby indicating both the amount and rate of photosynthesis. However, while photosynthesis has been going on, so has metabolic or respiratory activity; hence, what has again been measured is a short-term aspect of net production. If a comparable study area is established using a light-tight container, no photosynthesis will take place but respiration will; therefore, the amount of CO_2 released from the chamber in a given period, or at periodic intervals, will be a measure of the amount and rate of respiratory activity. This value, added to that obtained in the light-exposed chamber, can be used to approximate the total or gross production of the system. Although the technique usually employs small enclosures, Howard Odum has enclosed a large section of tropical rain forest in an airtight canopy.

Oxygen Production. Infrared gas analysis of carbon dioxide is not feasible in an aquatic ecosystem, and other carbon dioxide-based methods have been developed. However, the measurement of oxygen evolution has been one of the most widely used procedures, partly because of its relative simplicity. Samples of water containing the autotrophs (and almost invariably some heterotrophs, too) are taken from a given depth of a pond, lake, or ocean and are distributed into pairs of smaller sample bottles, typically of 125 to 300 milliliters (ml) capacity. One of the paired bottles is of light-transmitting material, typically glass, permitting photosynthesis to take place; the other bottle is darkened to preclude photosynthesis but not respiratory activity. The setup is then comparable to that employed in the study of CO_2 assimilation. The bottles are resuspended usually at the level from which the samples were taken and allowed to incubate for a given period of time. At the end of this time the oxygen content is determined either by standard chemical titration or with one of the newer electromagnetic devices. This value can be plugged into the photosynthetic equation to determine the amount and rate of photosynthesis. By using the dark bottle data, the normal respiratory consumption of oxygen can be accounted for; by combining this amount with the value obtained in the light bottle, total or gross production can be approximated.

In another variant of the oxygen-evolution method, an aquatic ecosystem is sampled every two to three hours for a period of twenty-four hours; by use of an electromagnetic sensor attached to a recording device, it is also possible to sample the system continuously for a 24-hour period. The natural photoperiod thus substitutes for the nighttime simulation achieved in the dark-light bottle technique, and the total ecosystem instead of only subsamples is evaluated. By various calculations, it is possible to determine the net production of oxygen (i.e., the excess over that consumed in respiration) and then in turn to determine, by the photosynthetic equation, the gross production in the system. In Chapter 5 we shall see how such diurnal information is significant in assessing the dynamic state of an ecosystem.

Radioisotope Methods. Considerable precision and sensitivity can be gained in measuring primary production by using a radioisotope tracer in the photosynthetic process. Although other isotopes have been employed, the radioactive form of carbon known as carbon-14 (^{14}C) has been the most fruitful; it can be used in a method similar to the light-dark bottle technique for measuring oxygen. Water samples are taken from a desired level and distributed in paired light and dark bottles. A known quantity of ^{14}C, usually in the form of a bicarbonate such as $NaH^{14}CO_3$, is then introduced into the bottles, and they are resuspended to incubate, usually for about 6 hours. During the time of exposure, both the stable carbon, which is present as CO_2 or as HCO_3, and the unstable ^{14}C are assimilated into carbohydrate and incorporated in the protoplasm of the autotrophs. At the conclusion of the incubation period, the samples are filtered, the stable and radioactive carbon that has been incorporated biologically being captured on the filter. The filters are dried and placed in a counting chamber to determine their level of radioactivity, and thereby the amount of radioactive carbohydrate produced. Calculations are then made from the photosynthetic formula based on the assumption that the uptake of radioactive carbon is proportional to the stable carbon (actually, it is not exact and is corrected by multiplying the amount of radioactive carbohydrate by 1.06),

$$\frac{6^{14}CO_2}{6CO_2} = \frac{^{14}C_6H_{12}O_6}{C_6H_{12}O_6}$$

It should be obvious that both the ^{14}C and dark-light O_2 methods are almost necessarily restricted to the study of aquatic autotrophs that can be confined in relatively small containers.

Other Methods. Among other major methods is one based on a determination of chlorophyll, the premise being that there is a close correlation between the amount of chlorophyll and the amount and rate of photosynthesis. The procedure involves periodic sampling of aquatic systems and the subsequent extraction of chlorophyll in a suitable organic solvent, the concentration being determined by spectrophotometric means. On the assumption of given rates of photosynthesis per unit of chlorophyll, it is then possible to give dimension to the production of the area sampled. As an advantage over some of the other methods, samples do not have to be confined in dark or light containers. It is well adapted to and has been used quite extensively in the study of aquatic systems but has not received much application in terrestrial situations. However, the basic assumptions of this method are questionable, since the process of photosynthesis is contingent on many factors besides chlorophyll, and, moreover, direct causal relationships between amounts of chlorophyll and rates of photosynthesis are yet to be confirmed absolutely.

ENERGY FLOW IN ECOSYSTEMS

TABLE 2-1. Energy Budget of an Acre (= 0.405 hectare) of Corn During One Growing Season of 100 Days

	Glucose (kg)	Kilocalories (millions)	Solar Energy Utilized (%)
Incident solar radiation		2043	100.0
Biological utilization			
Energy incorporated			
Net production (NP)	6687	25.3	1.2
Respiration (R)	2045	7.7	0.4
Gross production (GP) (= NP + R)	8732	33	1.6
Energy used in transpiration	—	910	44.4
Energy not utilized	—	1110	54.0

Data of E. N. Transeau, 1926, Ohio Journal of Science 26: 1–10.

Estimates of Primary Production

In a study published in 1926, and one which proved to be considerably in advance of its time, Edgar Transeau estimated the accumulation of energy by a midwestern corn field in a single growing season (Table 2-1). His calculations were based on an estimated harvest of 10,000 plants per 0.405 hectare* weighing 6000 kilograms (kg)* and on available information on the chemical composition of the plants. From these premises he calculated that there were 2675 kg of carbon in the 10,000 corn plants; since this carbon entered the plants only through photosynthesis, it would be equivalent to 6687 kg of glucose. To this net production, Transeau added the equivalent amount of glucose which had been metabolized in cellular respiration during the growing season, 2045 kg, to obtain the total or gross production of 8732 kg. Since 3760 kilocalories (kcal)* are required to produce one kilogram of glucose, 33 million kcal would have been incorporated in gross production of which 7.7 million kcal was used in metabolic activities. He also estimated that 1.5 million kg of water was transpired from the area—this is about 408,000 gallons, sufficient to cover the area to a depth of 15 inches. This would have required an expenditure of 910 million kcal of energy.

Since the total solar energy available to the corn field was known, it was possible for Transeau to calculate the efficiency of energy utilization. It may be surprising to learn that the field of corn incorporated only 1.6 per cent of the total energy available:

* Hectare = 10,000 m^2 or 2.471 acres.
  Kilogram = 1000 grams.
  Kilocalorie = 1000 gram-calories.

$$\frac{\text{Gross production}}{\text{Solar radiation}} \times 100 = \frac{33 \text{ million kcal}}{2043 \text{ million kcal}} \times 100 = 1.6 \text{ per cent}$$

Transeau noted, however, that since only about 20 per cent of the solar radiation measured by the instrument used was actually effective in photosynthesis, the actual efficiency would be somewhat higher, namely about 8 per cent.

Another matter of interest is the efficiency of the autotroph with respect to utilization of the energy it has incorporated. The energy utilized in growth, development, and maintenance is reflected, of course, in cellular respiration, and is measured as the loss via respiratory activity. In the case of the corn field, the energy loss by respiratory activity, the converse of which might be termed metabolic or assimilation efficiency, is 23.4 per cent:

$$\frac{\text{Energy of respiration}}{\text{Energy of gross production}} \times 100 = \frac{7.7 \text{ million kcal}}{33.0 \text{ million kcal}} \times 100$$
$$= 23.4 \text{ per cent}$$

Thus, although relatively little of the total available energy was utilized in photosynthesis, the plants are quite efficient (76.6 per cent) in converting the captured energy to biomass.

This study shows, in some ways, how information on primary energy fixation can be interpreted to direct attention to at least two major aspects of primary production—amount and rate. The amount for the growing season is what has been discussed so far. Since the growing season for corn is assumed to be 100 days in the region Transeau considered, a rough approximation to a daily rate of energy fixation might be made. However, since there are differences in rate of photosynthesis per unit of leaf area by age and since the total amount of photosynthetic surface in a plant varies with age, only the crudest of approximations to a daily rate can be made. Transeau himself estimated the average daily increment to be in the neighborhood of 8 per cent. Periodic measurement, utilizing one of the nonharvest methods described above, would have to be employed to be more confident of daily or even hourly rates of energy fixation.

Transeau's study was based on managed agricultural land in northern Illinois; in the same general temperate region, Frank Golley investigated an old field ecosystem in southern Michigan. The harvest and respiratory data for the perennial grass-herb vegetation of the field is shown in Table 2-2. By calculation, the efficiency of energy utilization by the grass-herb component is seen to be 1.2 per cent (i.e., $5.83 \times 10^6 \div 471.0 \times 10^6$), and the percentage of energy lost in plant respiration is 15.1 per cent ($0.88 \times 10^6 \div 5.83 \times 10^6$).

Although the efficiency of energy capture in this terrestrial ecosystem is about three-fourths that of the corn field (1.2 vs. 1.6 per cent), the respira-

TABLE 2-2. Annual Energy Budget for Perennial Grass-herb Vegetation in Southern Michigan

	gcal/m^2/yr
Incident solar radiation	471.0×10^6
Plant utilization	
Net production (NP)	4.95×10^6
Respiration (R)	0.88×10^6
Gross production (GP)	5.83×10^6

Data of F. B. Golley, 1960. Ecological Monographs 30: 187–206.

tory loss is only about two-thirds (15.1 vs. 23.4 per cent). Hence, although the efficiency of energy capture is less, the utilization of that energy (i.e., the amount conserved in plant tissue) is greater in the natural old field than in the managed corn field. In a comparable old field study in South Carolina, Golley found that during the 1960 growing season, 48 per cent of gross production was lost in respiration by the dominant plant, broom sedge. And finally, in a wet marine grassland, a salt marsh, John Teal found that 77 per cent of gross production was consumed in respiration by plants. In these last two instances, then, a substantial portion of the initial energy captured was dissipated out of the ecosystem at the first trophic level.

Now, let us consider energy capture in two aquatic ecosystems in the same general latitude—a lake in Wisconsin and one in Minnesota. The date from Lake Mendota, Wisconsin shown in Table 2-3 were collected by Chancey Juday, one of the significant figures in the early development of scientific investigation of aquatic ecosystems. According to these data, only

TABLE 2-3. Annual Energy Budget of Lake Mendota, Wisconsin

	gcal/cm^2/yr
Incident solar radiation	118,872
Plant utilization	
Phytoplankton	
Net production (NP)	299
Respiration (R)	100
Gross production (GP)	399
Bottom flora	
Net production	22
Respiration	7
Gross production	29
Gross production by autotrophs	428

Data of C. Juday, 1940. Ecology 21: 438–450.

ENERGY FLOW IN ECOSYSTEMS

TABLE 2-4. Annual Energy Budget of Cedar Bog Lake, Minnesota

	gcal/cm^2/yr
Incident solar radiation	118,872.0
Plant utilization	
Net production (NP)	87.9
Respiration (R)	23.4
Gross production (GP)	111.3

Data of R. Lindeman, 1942. Ecology 23: 399–418.

0.35 per cent of the solar flux is incorporated in gross production at the autotroph level (428 ÷ 118,872); this is about one-fourth that found by Transeau and one-third that found by Golley. For maintenance and growth, Lake Mendota phytoplankton utilize 25 per cent of their energy intake in metabolism and the bottom flora utilize 24 per cent—results virtually identical to those obtained for corn by Transeau and higher than that found by Golley for the grass-herb community of the old field in Michigan.

Juday, however, failed to account for energy lost to herbivores as well as to decomposers; thus, these efficiencies are in error. Several years after Juday's study, Raymond Lindeman computed the loss due to herbivory to be 42 gcal/cm^2/yr and to decomposition, 10 gcal/cm^2/yr; by adding the components, the gross autotroph production rises from 428 to 470 gcal/cm^2/yr with a consequent increase in energy fixation efficiency, from 0.35 to 0.39 per cent, and decrease in loss due to respiration, from 25 to 22.3 per cent.

With the same incident solar radiation as Lake Mendota, Cedar Bog Lake in Minnesota is only one-fourth as efficient according to the data assembled by Lindeman (Table 2-4). Gross production, including losses due to herbivory and decomposition, was 111 gcal/cm^2/yr for an efficiency of energy capture of 0.10 per cent. Energy lost in respiration at the autotroph level amounted to 23.4 gcal/cm^2/yr, or 21 per cent.

In both of these aquatic ecosystems, energy capture is considerably less than in the two terrestrial systems already discussed (0.10 and 0.39 per cent vs. 1.2 and 1.6 per cent). This difference in primary energy capture is in large measure related to diminished light penetration in water. That is, the incident solar radiation is measured at the surface rather than the amount that is transmitted through the water to the actual sites of photosynthesis. Thus, actual efficiency is somewhat higher than indicated by Lindeman and Juday and perhaps in the order of 1 to 3 per cent respectively. On the other hand, respiratory losses at the autotroph level in the two aquatic ecosystems (21.0 and 22.3 per cent) is about the same as in the corn field (23.4 per cent) but more than in the old field grass-herb community (15.1 per cent).

ENERGY FLOW IN ECOSYSTEMS

Comparison of Primary Energy Capture

The data on primary energy capture in these two terrestrial and two aquatic ecosystems indicate that only 0.1 to 1.6 per cent of the incident solar radiation is initially incorporated into protoplasm. From a large number of studies, largely since the 1940's, it appears that the efficiency of energy capture under natural conditions is seldom more than 3 per cent and more typically about 1 per cent. It is important to note that in these calculations investigators have employed total incident radiation and have not discriminated between the wavelengths utilized in photosynthesis, 0.38 to 0.77 μ, and the wavelengths of visible light, nor has compensation been made for the reduced light penetration in aquatic ecosystems. Had these adjustments been made, efficiency would be increased to perhaps a range of about 2 to 6 per cent.

Energy expenditure in self-maintenance and growth and loss via respiration also varies considerably, from 15 to 24 per cent, as we have already seen, but in temperate forests this expenditure reaches 50 to 60 per cent, and in tropical forests, 70 to 75 per cent. On the basis of a large number of studies, it appears that, in general, autotroph respiration accounts for 30 to 40 per cent of gross production; only about 60 to 70 per cent and often less of the initial energy captured generally results in net production.

Generalizations of this sort are tentative, subject to revision based on subsequent data, and tenuous when one is considering any particular ecosystem. It is well recognized that there are various factors which influence the rate and amount of photosynthesis; for our purposes here, we need briefly mention only two—season and age. Jacob Verduin showed a ninefold seasonal increase in gross primary production by phytoplankton in Lake Erie, from a winter low of 4 kcal/m^2/day to 36 kcal/m^2/day in summer. The influence of age is evident in the annual net production in a plantation of Scots pine (*Pinus sylvestris*) in England (Figure 2-3). According to the investigator, J. D. Ovington, net production increases to a maximum of about 52 × 10^6 kcal/hectare (i.e., 5200 kcal/m^2) at about 30 years of age.

In our consideration of community ecology (Chapter 5), shifts in productivity with age will be given further consideration. At the moment, we need to give attention to the amount and rate of primary energy capture in a variety of ecosystems. Table 2-5 is modified from one prepared by the British ecologist D. F. Westlake based on 31 fertile ecosystems. The data, given originally in metric tons (1 metric ton = 1000 kg), were converted to kilocalories. As already mentioned, as a rule of thumb, one gram of dry protoplasm has a caloric value of about 4 kcal; this is the conversion value used for the table. There is in fact, however, wide variation in caloric values; for example, protoplasm that is largely carbohydrate, like sugar beets, will be of lower caloric content than that rich in oils, like peanuts. Also, if the material is dried and the amount of mineral ash is determined and sub-

ENERGY FLOW IN ECOSYSTEMS

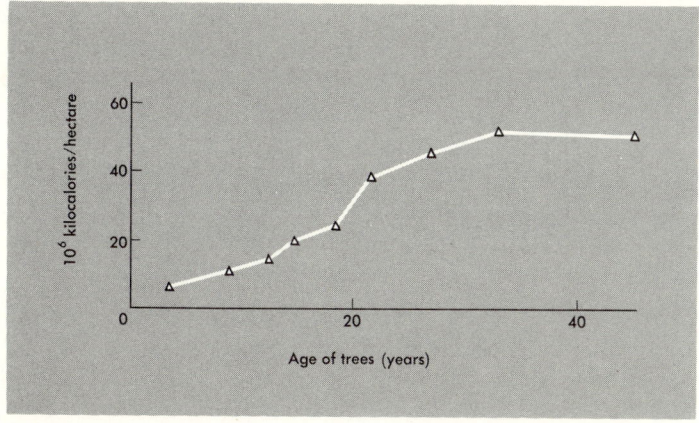

Adapted, by permission, from J. D. Ovington. 1962. *Advances in Ecological Research*, Vol. 1. New York: Academic Press.

Fig. 2-3. Annual mean productivity of trees and understory vegetation in a Scots pine (*Pinus sylvestris*) plantation in England.

TABLE 2-5. Estimates of Annual Net Primary Productivity of Fertile Sites

Type of Ecosystem or Producer	Climate	Productivity (kcal/m² /yr)
Desert	arid	400 ± 200
Phytoplankton		
Ocean	—	800 ± 400
Lake	temperate	800 ± 400
Polluted lake	temperate	2400 ± 1200
Submerged macrophytes		
Freshwater	temperate	2400 ± 480
Freshwater	tropical	6800 ± 1700
Marine	temperate	11,600 ± 1740
Marine	tropical	14,000 ± 2100
Forest		
Deciduous	temperate	4800 ± 1200
Coniferous	temperate	11,200 ± 2800
Rain forest	tropical	20,000 ± 4000
Agricultural plants		
Annuals	temperate	8800 ± 1320
Perennials	temperate	12,000 ± 2400
Annuals	tropical	12,000 ± 2400
Perennials	tropical	30,000 ± 4500
Swamps and marshes		
Salt marsh	—	12,000 ± 2400
Reedswamps	temperate	17,100 ± 3400
Reedswamps	tropical	30,000 ± 4500

Modified, by permission, from D. F. Westlake, 1963. *Biological Reviews* **38**: 385–425.

tracted to give the true organic weight, the caloric equivalent would be higher than 4 kcal/g. A number of determinations suggest a normal range of 4.1 to 5.2 kcal/g of dry organic weight, but some algae have values of up to 8.7! Any selected conversion is thus arbitrary, and I have chosen to err on the low side by using the value of 4 kcal/g.

Before examining the data, it is important to underscore the fact that the communities Westlake selected were all fertile sites; hence, the production values are no doubt much higher than normal ecosystems. With this admitted limitation, examination of these data shows that the most productive communities are in the tropics; tropical marine macrophytes are more productive than their temperate counterparts, tropical perennials are more productive than their temperature counterparts, etc. The effect of latitude on incident solar radiation is one of the significant variables here (see Figure 2-1). The most productive temperate communities are the reed swamps, swamps dominated by cattail (*Typha*), rushes (*Scirpus*), and sedges (*Carex*); this category would also include rice paddies. Deciduous forests come off a poor second to coniferous forests, but both are nearly only half or less as productive as tropical rain forests. It must be noted, however, that under ordinary conditions there does not appear to be much difference in production in coniferous and deciduous forests, and the productivity of tropical forests is not yet adequately known—they may prove to be not very different from their temperate counterparts. In aquatic systems, both freshwater and marine phytoplankton are considerably less productive than submerged macrophytes.

Although there are various limitations to the data accumulated to date on primary production, there are certain patterns that are evident when assembled graphically (Figure 2-4); this figure was initially developed by Eugene Odum, one of the foremost proponents of studying ecology from the viewpoint of the ecosystem; it has been modified to express the units in energy terms by the same conversion factor used for Table 2-5, 4 kcal/g. The data of Table 2-5 (which are *net* production) and those in the figure (which are *gross* production) are in substantial agreement, although Westlake has suggested that the upper limit of the most productive communities might be raised slightly.

It is apparent that the oceans and deserts are much less productive when compared to the ocean-land interface regions such as the continental shelf and coral reefs. Since the oceans constitute 75 per cent of the Earth's surface and deserts about 28 per cent of the land area, about 80 per cent of the Earth's surface falls in the least productive ecosystems. For the most part, low production in the sea is a function of nutrient limitation, as we shall see in the next chapter; in the desert, lack of moisture is the primary factor. Periodically, availability of nutrients in the ocean or rain in the desert results in daily rates of production comparable to those of the higher productive

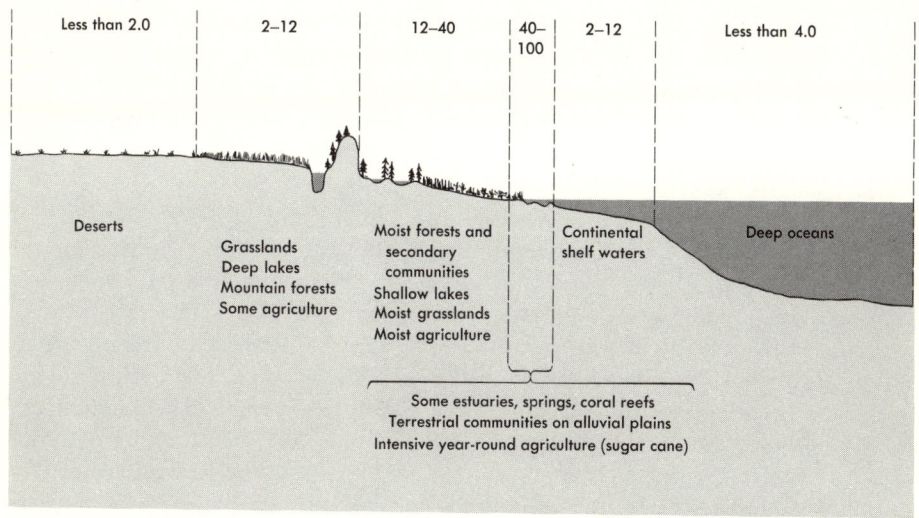

Adapted, by permission, from E. P. Odum. 1959. *Fundamentals of Ecology*, 2d ed. Philadelphia: W. B. Saunders Co.

Fig. 2-4. World distribution of gross primary production in kilocalories per square meter per day.

regions, but these are transitory and as a result, the daily rate based on annual data is much lower.

The large surface of the sea compensates, in part, for the low production on a unit area basis. Doctor J. R. Vallentyne has estimated the total annual net productivity of the marine area of the earth to be 2.2 to 6.0 $\times$ 10^{10} metric tons of carbon (1 metric ton = 1000 kg) compared to 2.2 to 3.2 $\times$ 10^{10} metric tons of carbon for the total land area. Since we have been considering production in energy units, it will be more meaningful to convert these numbers. Various analyses of dry organic matter show it to be about 49 per cent carbon; if we assume this and a caloric equivalent of 4 kcal/g of dry organic matter, we obtain about 4.3 to 11.8 $\times$ 10^{16} kcal/yr for the oceans and 4.3 to 6.3 $\times$ 10^{16} kcal/yr for the land.

ENERGY BEYOND THE PRODUCERS

Up to this point we have considered only the initial incorporation and utilization of energy by the autotrophs; we need now to turn attention to the fate of energy beyond this initial trophic level. To do so, let us consider the flow of energy in Cedar Bog Lake, Minnesota, developing further the data (Table 2-4) discussed earlier in this chapter. There is good historical reason for using these data, for the investigator responsible for them, Raymond Lindeman, was perhaps the most significant person in developing the concept of the energy dynamics, or, as he termed it, the "trophic-dynamics" of ecosystems.

Autotroph-based Ecosystems

The fate of energy incorporated by the autotrophs is shown diagrammatically in Figure 2-5. We have already noted that gross production (net production plus respiration) was 111 gcal/cm^2/yr with an efficiency of energy capture of 0.10 per cent; also we noted that 21 per cent of this energy, or 23 gcal/cm^2/yr, is consumed in the myriad biological reactions occurring at the cellular level, reactions that allow the growth, development, and reproduction of the autotrophs. From the diagram, we can see that 15 gcal/cm^2/yr are consumed by the herbivores as the latter graze or feed on autotrophs—this amounts to 17 per cent of net autotroph production. Decomposition accounts for about 3.4 per cent of net production (3 gcal/cm^2/yr). The remainder of the plant material, 70 gcal/cm^2/yr, or 79.5 per cent of net production, is not utilized at all and becomes part of the accumulating sediments. It is obvious, then, that much more energy is available for herbivory than is consumed, and that this ecosystem is especially prodigal in energy utilization beyond the autotroph level.

A further observation about Figure 2-5: you will note that the various pathways of loss are equivalent to and account for the total energy capture of the autotrophs, i.e., gross production. Also, collectively the three upper "fates" (decomposition, herbivory, and not utilized) are equivalent to net production. Since similar diagrams will be used in developing the fate of energy at subsequent levels, recognition of this basic pattern is important to understanding what follows.

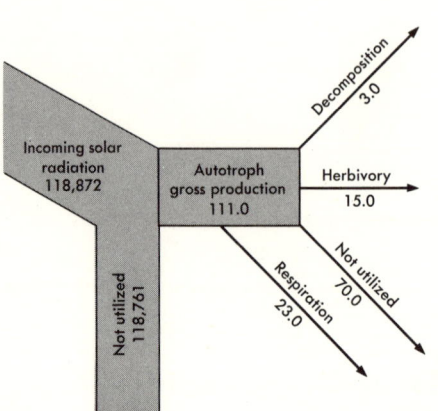

Data of R. Lindeman. 1942. Ecology 23: 399–418.

Fig. 2-5. Fate of energy incorporated by autotrophs in Cedar Bog Lake, Minnesota in gram calories per square centimeter per year.

ENERGY FLOW IN ECOSYSTEMS

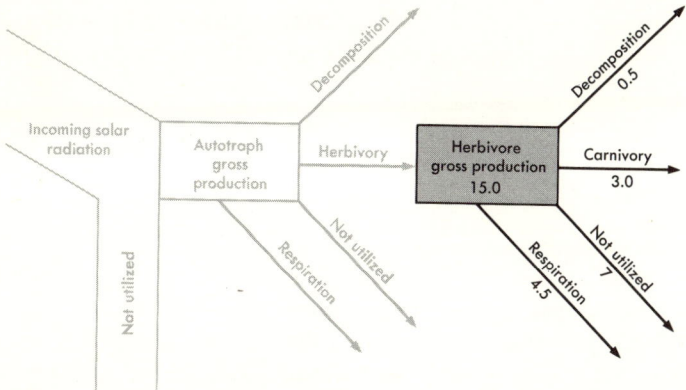

Data of R. Lindeman. 1942. Ecology 23: 399–418.

Fig. 2-6. Fate of energy incorporated by herbivores in Cedar Bog Lake, Minnesota in gram calories per square centimeter per year.

Of the total energy incorporated at the level of the herbivore, namely 15 gcal/cm^2/yr, 30 per cent or 4.5 gcal/cm^2/yr is used in metabolic activity (Figure 2-6). There is then considerably more energy lost via respiration by herbivores (30 per cent) than by autotrophs (21 per cent). Again there is considerable energy available for the carnivores, namely 10.5 gcal/cm^2/yr or 61 per cent, which is not entirely utilized; in fact, only 3.0 gcal/cm^2/yr or 28.6 per cent of net production passes to the carnivores. This is more efficient utilization of resources than occurs at the autotroph→herbivore transfer level, but nonetheless is still quite profligate.

At the level of the carnivore (Figure 2-7), about 60 per cent of the carnivore's energy intake is consumed in metabolic activity and the re-

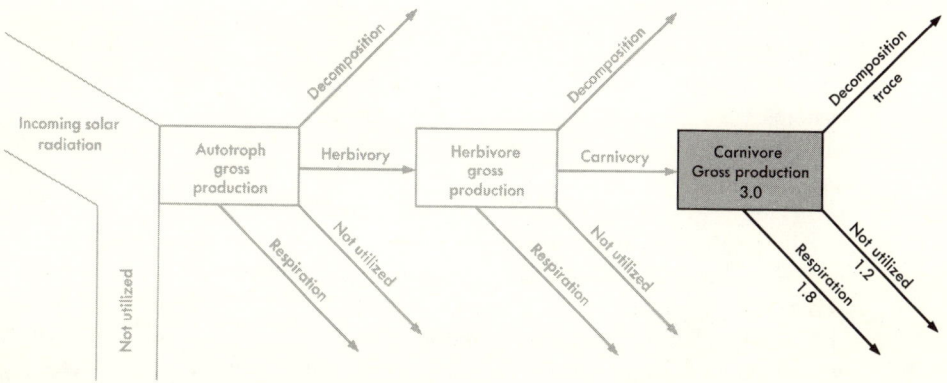

Data of R. Lindeman. 1942. Ecology 23: 399–418.

Fig. 2-7. Fate of energy incorporated by carnivores in Cedar Bog Lake, Minnesota in gram calories per square centimeter per year.

ENERGY FLOW IN ECOSYSTEMS

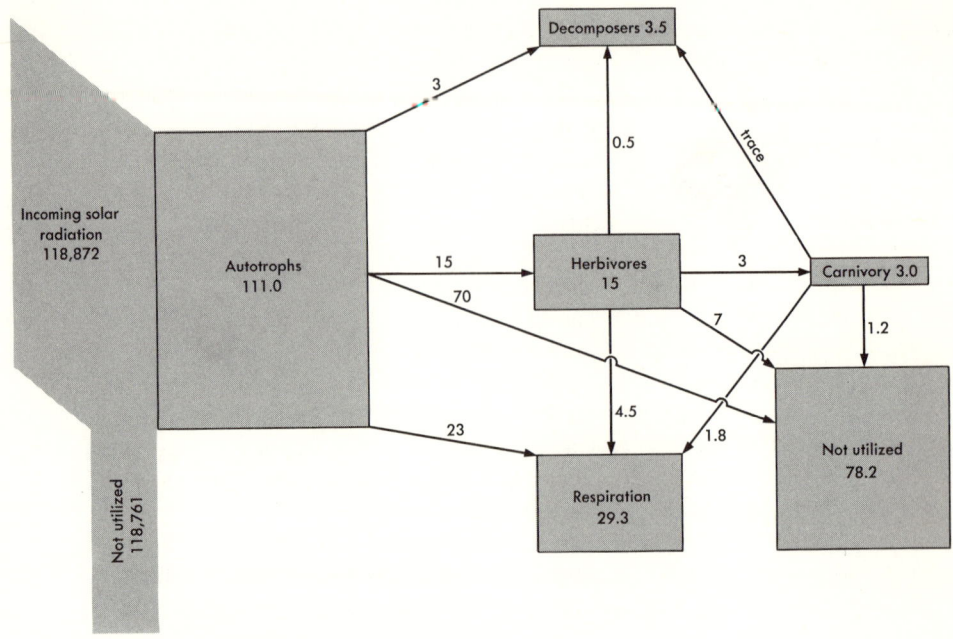

Data of R. Lindeman. 1942. Ecology 23: 399–418.

Fig. 2-8. Energy flow diagram for Cedar Bog Lake, Minnesota in gram calories per square centimeter per year.

mainder becomes part of the nonutilized sediments; only an insignificant amount is subject to decomposition yearly. This high respiratory loss compares with 30 per cent by herbivores and 21 per cent by autotrophs in this ecosystem. A number of factors are involved in this greater energy utilization, but among the more significant is the generally greater locomotor activity of carnivores—in effect, they have to expend considerable energy to get their energy.

Having developed in stepwise fashion the fate of energy in this ecosystem, we can now look at it in a composite way (Figure 2-8), slightly modified from the diagram previously employed. Using this as a model, we find that several points are immediately evident. Most important of these is the one-way street along which energy moves. The energy that is captured by the autotrophs does not revert back to solar input; that which passes to the herbivore does not pass back to the autotrophs, etc. As it moves progressively through the various trophic levels it is no longer available to the previous level. The immediate implication of this unidirectional energy flow in an ecosystem is that the system would collapse if the primary energy source, the sun, were cut off.

The next major thing to be noted is the progressive decrease in energy at each trophic level. This is accounted for largely by the energy dissipated as heat in metabolic activity and measured here as respiration coupled with energy that is not utilized. Even if more of the nonutilized energy were used in a more efficient system, there would still be a considerable loss in respiration. For example, if all the nonutilized plant material were consumed by herbivores, there would be 85 gcal/cm^2/yr gross production at the herbivore level; however, about 30 per cent, or 25 gcal/cm^2/yr, would still be lost via respiration at this trophic level. And by the same token, if there were 100 per cent efficiency of energy transfer to the carnivore level, of the approximately 60 gcal/cm^2/yr gross production at that level, some 36 gcal/cm^2/yr would be lost via respiration. Hence, even with a higher efficiency of energy utilization, considerable energy would still be required to maintain the system.

These factors—unidirectional flow and efficiency of energy utilization—account for the requirement of a continual source of energy to preclude collapse of an ecosystem. An ecosystem simply cannot maintain itself if deprived of energy income for any extended period.

The model of energy flow in Cedar Bog Lake is, of course, highly diagrammatic and greatly oversimplified; hopefully, it will enable an understanding of a more sophisticated representation of energy flow as developed

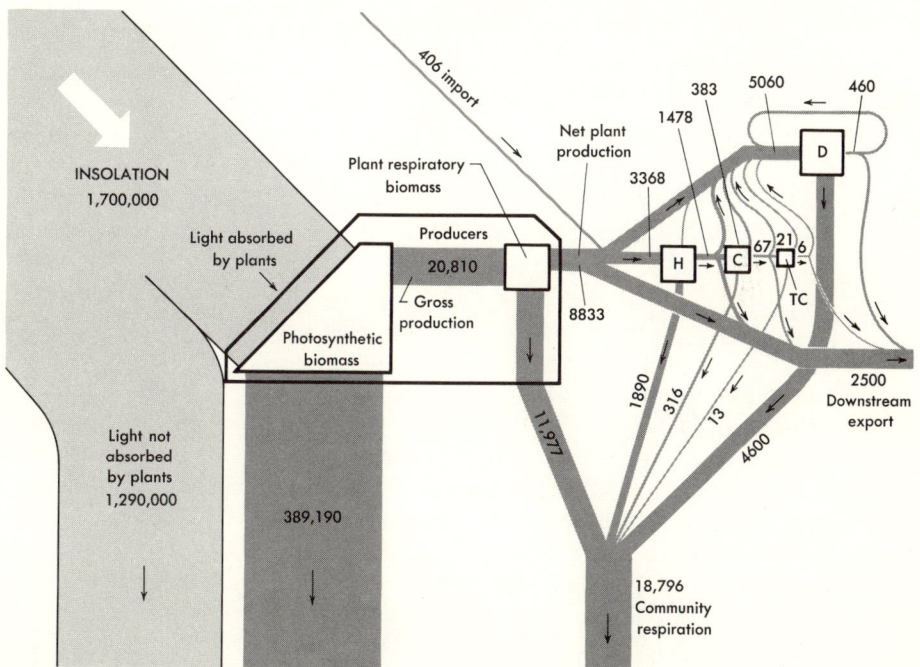

Redrawn, by permission, from H. T. Odum. 1957. Ecological Monographs 27: 55–112.

Fig. 2-9. Energy flow diagram for Silver Springs, Florida in kilocalories per square meter per year.

ENERGY FLOW IN ECOSYSTEMS

by Howard T. Odum from a study on a river system, the famous tourist attraction of Silver Springs, Florida (Figure 2-9). There are several elegant refinements over the Cedar Bog Lake diagram. For example, the light actually absorbed by the plants is the basis for considering autotroph efficiency, not the total incident solar radiation; also there is an accounting of material (=energy) entering the system from contributory streams or the

TABLE 2-6. Comparison of Energy Flow in a Bog Lake[1] and a River[2]

	Cedar Bog Lake, Minnesota (kcal/m²/yr)	(%)	Silver Springs, Florida (kcal/m²/yr)	(%)
Incoming solar radiation (S)	1,188,720		1,700,000	
Effective solar radiation (ES)	?		410,000	
Producers (autotrophs)				
Gross production (GP)	1113		20,810	
Efficiency $\left(\dfrac{GP}{S \text{ or } ES}\right)$		0.10		1.2 or 5.1
Respiration (R)	234		11,977	
Respiratory loss $\left(\dfrac{R}{GP}\right)$		21.0		57.6
Net production (NP$_A$)	879		8833	
Decomposed or not utilized		83.1		61.9
Herbivores				
Gross production	148		3368	
Efficiency $\left(\dfrac{GP}{NP_A}\right)$		16.8		38.1
Respiration	44		1890	
Respiratory loss		29.7		56.1
Net production (NP$_H$)	104		1478	
Decomposed or not utilized		70.2		72.7
Carnivores				
Gross production	31		404	
Efficiency $\left(\dfrac{GP}{NP_H}\right)$		29.8		27.3
Respiration	18		329	
Respiratory loss		58.1		81.4
Net production	13		73	
Decomposed or not utilized		100.0		100.0
Total loss via respiration	296	26.6	14,196	68.2
Total loss via decomposition	310	27.9	5060	24.3
Total loss via nonutilization	507	45.5	1554	7.5

[1] Data of R. Lindeman, 1942. *Ecology* **23**: 399–418.
[2] Data of H. Odum, 1957. *Ecological Monographs* **27**: 55–112.

surrounding terrain (labeled "import"). And most significantly, the large energy loss by way of decomposer respiration is considered.

A comparison of these two systems (Table 2-6) is in order for several reasons: both are classic studies in modern ecology; they represent two quite different ecosystems, one a bog-water lake, the other a clear-water river; and, as can be seen, the amounts, rates, and efficiency of energy movement are quite different. Among the differences which may be noted, the autotrophs in Silver Springs are at least ten times more efficient in capturing solar energy than their counterparts in Cedar Bog Lake; but subsequent to initial capture, about two and a half times more energy is lost in respiration in Silver Springs, the higher loss being observed at all trophic levels. Although the percentage of energy lost to decomposition and nonutilization combined appear more or less comparable at each trophic level, the actual percentage loss to each of these is quite different (see totals). Of the total, only about a third is decomposed yearly in Cedar Bog; this accounts for the progressive accumulation of sediments typical of boreal bog lakes, sediments known as peat. By contrast, most of the nonutilized material in Silver Springs is exported downstream.

Detritus-based Ecosystems

The ecosystems that have been discussed are directly dependent on an influx of solar radiation—they are characterized by a dependency on autotroph energy capture and secondarily by movement of that captured energy through the system initiated by grazing herbivores. A number of ecosystems function in just this way. However, there are others that are less dependent on direct solar energy incorporation and more on the influx of organic material produced in another system. At the outset one might wish to argue that such a system is not self-contained and hence not an ecosystem strictly considered, or that it is only a subcomponent of another ecosystem. Lest definition deny search, let us consider two such ecosystems; one is a spring in Massachusetts, the other a forest in England.

Root Spring, 2 m in diameter and 10 to 20 cm deep, is located in Concord, Massachusetts not far from another aquatic locale of significance to naturalists, Thoreau's Walden Pond. While at Harvard University, John Teal determined that of the total energy income, photosynthesis accounted for 710 kcal/m^2/yr. By contrast, terrestrial plant debris falling on the spring accounted for 2350 kcal/m^2/yr; hence, more than three times as much energy entered the system in the form of dead organic material, or *detritus*. Of this total income (3060 kcal/m^2/yr), the herbivores consumed about 75 per cent (2300 kcal/m^2/yr), the remainder being deposited in the system. Thus, in Root Spring, most of the energy supporting the higher trophic levels is

ENERGY FLOW IN ECOSYSTEMS

neither produced within the system nor is it derived from living material; the energy is largely of external origin and in the form of detritus.

Comparable situations certainly occur in the soil component of forest ecosystems. In the young forest ecosystem, energy initially stored in plant material becomes part of the litter on the forest floor either by continuous (coniferous) or periodic (deciduous) leaf and branch fall. This detritus serves as the energy source for an interacting system of herbivores, carnivores, and decomposers in the litter and upper soil layers. It is obvious that in the absence of living plant material in such systems, the herbivore-detritus food chain is of greater significance than the herbivore-grazing chain. On the basis of a forest study by J. D. Ovington in England and one conducted by himself and his colleagues in the United States, Eugene Odum concluded that ten times as much energy flows through the detritus chain as through the grazing chain. The detritus chain cannot then be disregarded in energy flow studies—and there is considerable evidence accumulating to suggest that it is of greater importance in energy flow in many ecosystems than grazing chains. In fact, some authors suggest that as much as 90 per cent of the energy flow may be through detritus feeders.

In a recent review of energy flow, the British soil ecologist A. MacFadyen has noted that in plankton-based ecosystems, nearly all the energy flows through herbivorous grazers and little accumulates as detritus. In contrast, the greater amount of annual grass and forest production is never eaten by grazers; it accumulates and that which dies becomes available to the detritus feeders. For example, in his study in the broom sedge field

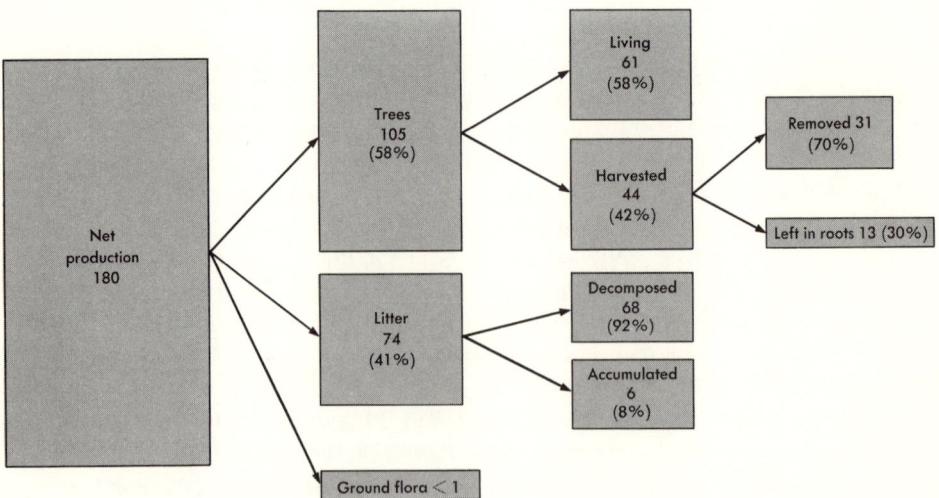

Based on data of J. D. Ovington. 1962. Advances in Ecological Research, Vol. 1. New York: Academic Press.

Fig. 2-10. Fate of energy in a Scots pine (*Pinus sylvestris*) plantation over 18 years, in 10^7 kilocalories/hectare.

in South Carolina, Golley reported that of the 1960 net production of 2692 kcal/m^2/yr, about 53 per cent (1419 kcal) remained unconsumed as standing dead vegetation and about 9 per cent (237 kcal) became part of that year's litter. Most significantly, he noted that less than 2 per cent of the year's net plant production passed through the grazing herbivores; this figure is comparable to the 1.6 per cent he obtained in his old field study in Michigan (Table 2-2) and is consistent with limited data available from other studies.

For the forest situation let us consider energy flow over an 18-year period in a mature, managed Scots pine plantation in England between 17 and 35 years after planting (Figure 2-10). These data of J. D. Ovington show that (1) a substantial proportion of the energy initially incorporated in the system passes through a detritus food chain, and (2) relatively little of the living material is grazed by herbivores but rather is harvested by man. Whereas such harvesting is certainly performed by a consumer, it is scarcely grazing in an energy flow sense. Another significant factor to be recognized is that 30 per cent of the harvested tree production is not actually harvested but remains in roots. Earlier in the chapter we noted that harvest measurements of plant production have typically by-passed analysis of roots—for the very good reason that they are so very difficult to remove. However, the kind of information presented here, and that now available elsewhere, indicates that this is a component that must be reckoned in assessing the energy budget of an ecosystem.

An Energy Flow Model

It should be obvious by now that the various ecosystem models used so far (Figures 1-1, 2-8, and 2-9) need to be modified further. The model shown in Figure 2-11 attempts to recognize the various inputs and fates of energy. For purposes of the model, there is assumed to be an equal flow of energy from the two primary sources, imported living and dead organic matter, and from photosynthesis; further, the contribution from each in the rest of the chain is assumed to be about equal. To apply the model to any given system one need merely expand or contract the amount of shading to correspond to the energy recruitment by organic matter and to expand or contract the diameter of the energy channels and dimensions of the trophic level boxes. For example, a model of Cedar Bog Lake and the Scots pine plantation would have a large "storage" box, whereas Root Spring would have a much greater diameter for the organic matter import channel.

It should be readily obvious that the type of information required to construct an energy flow diagram for any particular ecosystem is extremely difficult to come by. For this reason, relatively few systems have been studied in detail; in such studies as have been done, the critical reader as well as the investigator himself is well aware of the limitations of the data.

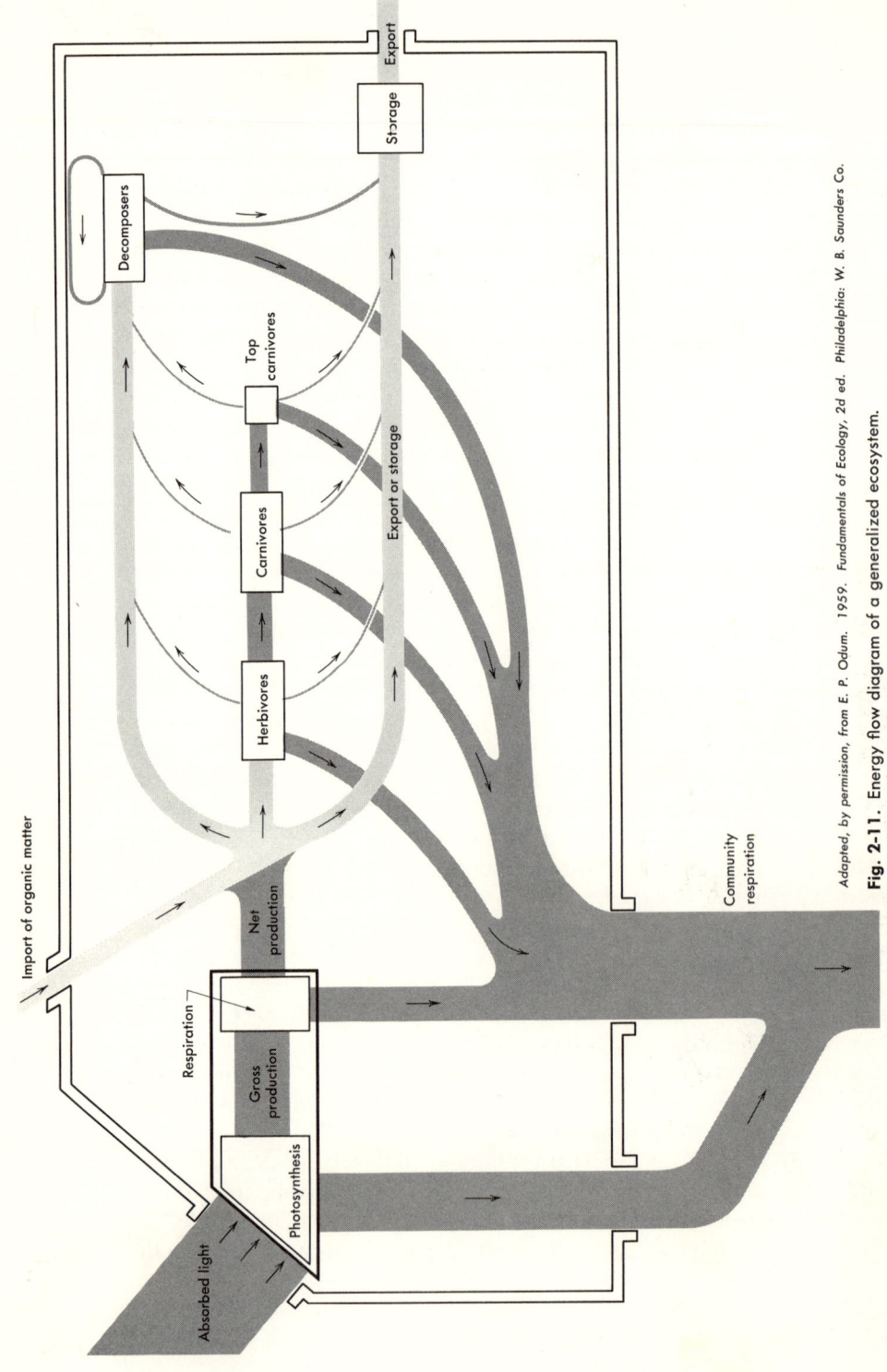

Adapted, by permission, from E. P. Odum. 1959. Fundamentals of Ecology, 2d ed. Philadelphia: W. B. Saunders Co.

Fig. 2-11. Energy flow diagram of a generalized ecosystem.

There are not only many parameters to be assessed simultaneously; there are numerous variables inherent in the material being studied. Young trees undergo photosynthesis at a rate different from old trees (Figure 2-5), and young as well as smaller animals metabolize at higher rates than older and larger ones, etc. Seasonal shifts in quality and amount of sunlight must be accounted for (Figure 2-1), and, of no small consequence, the inevitable question of adequate sampling to assure replicability is a continual thorn in the ecologist's (and any scientist's) side. Hence, some ecologists have taken to the sanctity of the laboratory, where some of the variables can be more limited or at least regulated. From such studies, often done concurrently with field studies, have come some significant generalizations about energy flow which appear to apply fairly well with available field data. For example, from studies based on laboratory populations of algae, microcrustacea, and hydra, Lawrence Slobodkin suggests that in the transfer of energy from one trophic level to the next the *gross ecological efficiency,* as he terms it, is of the order of 10 per cent. Thus if there are 100 calories of net plant production, only about 10 calories net production would be expected at the herbivore level and only 1 calorie at the carnivore level. Various studies to date, however, show a range in gross ecological efficiency from 5 to about 30 per cent, with no consistency within a given ecosystem.

Whether Slobodkin's efficiency "constant" were indeed established, the point it makes and which was made earlier is abundantly clear—namely, that unless an ecosystem is supplied with energy either in the form of sunlight or organic matter from another photosynthesis-dominated ecosystem, the system will collapse. The substantial loss of energy as unutilizable heat via the respiratory process must continually be compensated for. And if the energy stored as detritus is not utilized, it too must be compensated for. This is, then, the elementary principle to be derived from energy flow studies—but not the only one. The corollary was expressed some years ago by the British ecologist Charles Elton, using an old proverb, "One hill cannot shelter two tigers." Although he was alluding directly to territorial behavior, he also established the principle that at the "top" of the energy hill, i.e., at the carnivore level, there is not enough energy to support more than very few carnivores. The trophic or food chain, accompanied by its concomitant energy losses at each step, can be visualized not only as an elegant flowing model (Figure 2-11) but as a static pyramid (Figure 2-12) and thereby readily convey the image of the lone tiger on the hill.

The pyramid shown is based on the energy data from Silver Springs already considered (Table 2-6 and Figure 2-9). As a quick reference, an energy pyramid conveys the general trophic relations in the system and readily reconfirms the major principle of progressive diminution of energy in the higher trophic levels. A less steep-sided pyramid might suggest reduced primary production, more efficient energy transfer, or more efficient utilization of available energy. If a phytoplankton-based system were

ENERGY FLOW IN ECOSYSTEMS

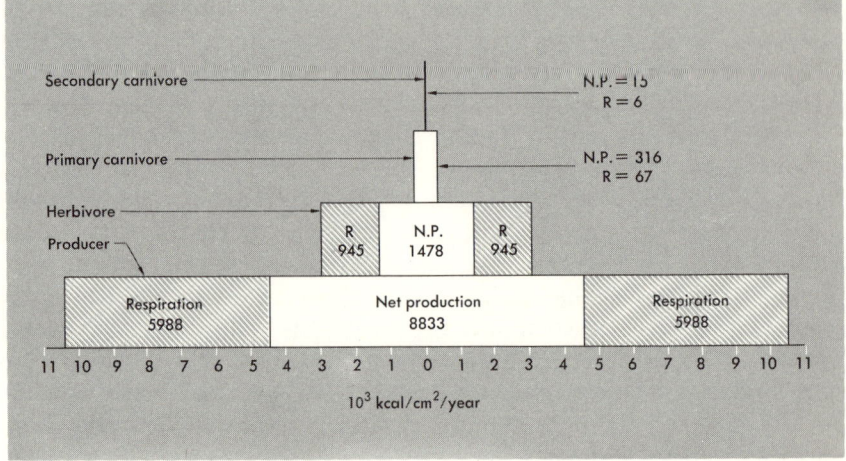

Based on data of H. T. Odum. 1957. Ecological Monographs 27: 55–112.

Fig. 2-12. Energy pyramid of Silver Springs, Florida in kilocalories per square meter per year.

sampled immediately after a period of maximum grazing, which, of course, results in exhaustion of producer populations, an inverted pyramid would be obtained; such patterns must be temporary or if not, their top-heaviness would be an indication of imminent collapse. It is for this reason that there is importance to determining energy flow not on a short run or instantaneous basis but over a relatively long period of time of at least a full year, to adjust for such components as the phytoplankton which turn over energy rather rapidly.

Either by direct measurement, or by appropriate conversion of energy units to biomass, pyramids of biomass may also be constructed. Assuming, as we did earlier, that each gram of dry organic matter was equivalent to 4 kcal, we could express the energy pyramid for Silver Springs as a biomass by changing the scale along the bottom such that each kilocalorie unit would be equivalent to 0.25 gram. Within the limits of this assumption, the shape of the pyramid would be unchanged. The actual biomass data from Silver Springs (in grams per square meter) are: producers, 809; herbivores, 37; primary carnivores, 11; secondary carnivores, 1.5. You may wish to construct a biomass pyramid using these data to compare it with the assumed one and with the energy pyramid shown in Figure 2-9.

It is also possible to move yet another step away from the structure of an ecosystem in energy terms by conducting a census of each of the major categories. An assessment of "who and how many live there" is often of critical significance, as we shall see in Chapter 5. As would be expected, numerous producers are requisite to fewer herbivores and the latter to still fewer carnivores.

Although pyramids of energy, biomass, or number have their value in gaining an assessment of an ecosystem, their limitations are substantial in gaining a comprehensive picture of energy flow. The energy pyramid we have used has no appropriate or easy place for locating the decomposers, and it does not allow for easily representing the loss due to storage. The number pyramid, in addition to these limitations, equates all organisms as identical units—and thus one clump of grass at the producer level would have the same value as the one tiger at the top of the hill. A comparable difficulty inherent in the biomass pyramid is in assuming comparable ecological (energetic) significance to unit weights of widely disparate groups. For example, the British ecologist John Phillipson has noted that 1 g of the mollusc *Ensis* has a caloric equivalent of 3.5 kcal, whereas 1 g of the microcrustacean *Calanus* is equivalent to 7.4 kcal.

To this point we have emphasized the complexity of energy flow and its progressive diminution through ecosystems. The critical reader, however, will have already recognized that ecosystems do not controvert but conform precisely with basic thermodynamic principles. In ecosystems, consistent with the first of the thermodynamic principles, energy is neither created nor destroyed, but it is transformed and the sum total entering can be accounted for on a budget-balance sheet (Table 2-6). And consonant with the second law of thermodynamics, energy is transformed ultimately into a nonusable form—heat. But a system which continually transfers its chemical energy to heat tends towards a state of thermodynamic equilibrium, a state of maximum entropy, of increased randomness and hence of disorganization. We have observed, however, that ecosystems are ordered, and later we shall see that they are relatively stable, but dynamic steady-state systems. Hence, by physical laws of the universe, they must have a continual source of energy to survive. The physicist Erwin Schroedinger stated a resolution of this paradox in a thermodynamic context by indicating that a biological system delays its decay to thermodynamical equilibrium by "feeding on negative entropy" (i.e., on a more ordered, less random system—in this case the sun) and that it maintains its high level of orderliness by "sucking orderliness from its environment."

REFERENCES

Correlated Readings

Kormondy, E. J., 1965. *Readings in Ecology.* Englewood Cliffs, New Jersey: Prentice-Hall, Inc.

  Clarke, G., The utilization of solar energy by aquatic organisms, p. 27.

  Geiger, R., Heat exchange near the ground, p. 24.

Juday, C., The annual energy budget of an inland lake, p. 174.

Lindeman, R., The trophic dynamic aspect of ecology, p. 179.

Odum, H., Trophic structure and productivity of Silver Springs, Florida, p. 188.

Transeau, E., The accumulation of energy by plants, p. 171.

Technical References and Monographs

Crisp, D. J. (ed.), 1964. *Grazing in Terrestrial and Marine Environments.* Oxford: Blackwell Scientific Publications.

Gates, D. M., 1962. *Energy Exchange in the Biosphere.* New York: Harper and Row.

Goldman, C. R. (ed.), 1966. *Primary Productivity in Aquatic Environments.* Berkeley: University of California Press.

Kozlovsky, D. G., 1968. A critical evaluation of the trophic level concept. I. Ecological efficiencies. *Ecology* **49:** 48–60.

Ovington, J. D., 1962. Quantitative ecology and the woodland ecosystem concept. *In* J. B. Cragg, *Advances in Ecological Research,* Vol. I, pp. 103–192. New York: Academic Press.

Phillipson, J., 1966. *Ecological Energetics.* London: Edward Arnold, Ltd.

Strickland, J. D. H., 1960. *Measuring the Production of Marine Phytoplankton.* Bull. 122, Fisheries Research Board of Canada. Ottawa.

Westlake, D. F., 1963. Comparisons of plant productivity. *Biological Reviews* **38:** 385–425.

biogeochemical cycles and ecosystems

CHAPTER 3

The dependency of life on energy is coexistent with a dependency on the availability of some twenty elements required in the dynamics of life processes. Although carbohydrates can be photosynthesized from water and carbon dioxide of the atmosphere, the more complex organic substances require additional components either in considerable abundance, as in the case of nitrogen and phosphorus, or in trace amounts, as in the case of zinc and molybdenum. Further, the very process of photosynthesis occurs in the presence of enzymes which themselves contain an array of elements. It is important then to consider the movement of these nutrients in ecosystems, a movement that has already been described in Chapter 1 as cyclical. We need now more fully to recognize the cyclical patterns of these nutrients, to seek out the general patterns that may exist among them, and subsequently to consider the effects which result from man's inadvertent or purposive interaction with them.

At the outset, three major types of cycles may be recognized. One of these, the hydrologic cycle, involves the movement of a compound, the others the movement of elements. The latter cycles of *chemical* elements involve *bio*logical organisms and their *geo*logical (atmosphere or lithosphere) environment; collectively they are referred to as *biogeochemical* cycles. In one group of biogeochemical cycles, the atmosphere constitutes the major reservoir of the element that exists there in a *gaseous* phase; such cycles show little or no permanent change in the distribution and abundance of the element. Carbon and nitrogen are prime representatives of biogeochemical cycles with a prominent gaseous phase. In the *sedimentary* type of cycle, the major reservoir is the lithosphere from which the elements are released by weathering. The sedimentary types, exemplified by phosphorus, sulfur, and iodine among others, have, as Harvard ecologist George Clarke has put it, a tendency to stagnate; that is, a portion of the supply may get lost, as in the deep ocean sediments, and thereby become inaccessible to organisms and to continual cycling. Actually, sulfur and iodine have gaseous phases, but these are insignificant in that there is no large gaseous reservoir.

THE HYDROLOGIC CYCLE

The major pathway of the hydrologic cycle is an interchange between the Earth's surface and the atmosphere via precipitation and evaporation (Figure 3-1). Ecosystems with their biota constitute an accessory whose presence or absence has no significant effect on this major movement; however, significant amounts of water are incorporated by ecosystems in protoplasmic synthesis and there is a substantial return to the atmosphere which occurs by way of transpiration, the loss factor from living plants. According to ecologist G. Evelyn Hutchinson, world precipitation amounts to about 4.46×10^{20} g annually; of this amount, about 0.99×10^{20} g falls on land surfaces; the remainder, or 3.47×10^{20} g, on ocean surfaces. Although this is an impressive quantity, it is even more significant to note that its source, namely atmospheric water vapor, constitutes an infinitesimal amount relative to the distribution of water on the Earth (Table 3-1). The British meteorologist Sutcliffe has estimated this amount of water vapor as being equivalent to 2.5 cm of rain. Since the south side of the Himalayas

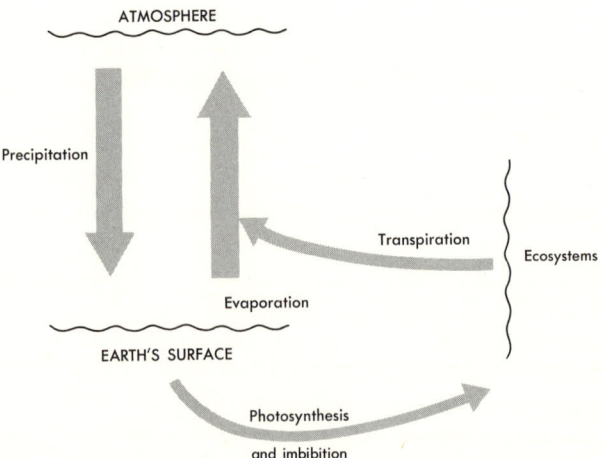

Fig. 3-1. The general pattern of the hydrologic cycle. Note that the significance of ecosystems in the movement of water is largely by way of transpiration; some water is lost from ecosystems as respiration and perspiration and becomes a component of surface evaporation.

BIOGEOCHEMICAL CYCLES AND ECOSYSTEMS

TABLE 3-1. Water Content of the Various Parts of the Earth

	Content (grams)
Primary lithosphere	$250{,}000 \times 10^{20}$
Ocean	$13{,}800 \times 10^{20}$
Sedimentary rocks	2100×10^{20}
Polar caps and other ice	167×10^{20}
Circulating groundwater	2.5×10^{20}
Inland waters	0.25×10^{20}
Atmospheric water vapor	0.13×10^{20}
TOTAL	$266{,}069.88 \times 10^{20}$

By permission, from G. E. Hutchinson, 1957. A Treatise on Limnology. New York: John Wiley and Sons, Inc.

receives some 1200 cm of rain annually, it is evident that there must be a very rapid turnover of atmospheric moisture.

The relative and absolute amounts of precipitation and evaporation dictate a good deal about the structure and function of ecosystems. Although this will be considered in some detail in Chapter 5, it is relevant here to note some of the general patterns of precipitation and the distribution of major types of ecosystems. At the outset, it can be stated that the circulation pattern of the atmosphere is primarily responsible for the peculiar patterns of precipitation distribution (Figure 3-2). The trade winds, for example, move from cooler latitudes toward the equator, taking up moisture as they move and depositing it in the equatorial region; hence, the coast line adjacent to the trade winds north and south of the equator (e.g., southern California, Mexico, Chile) is relatively dry, the equatorial region very wet. By contrast, the westerlies, which are north and south of the trade winds, move from warm to cool latitudes, depositing their water load along the coast (Washington to Alaska, southern Chile).

Of considerable importance to continental rainfall distribution are mountain ranges. As moist air moves over a mountain range it rises and cools to supersaturation, and precipitation results on the windward side of the range (Figure 3-3). As the moisture-depleted air continues to move beyond the divide of the range, it descends, warms, and picks up moisture by evaporation from ground and water surfaces and releases it further to the lee of the mountain. Thus the lee side receives less precipitation than the windward side, an effect that is often referred to as that of a "rain-shadow" in analogy to the shadow made by a tree. Examples of the rain-shadow effect can be seen in Figure 3-3 in western North America (Coast Range, Sierra Nevada, Wasatch, and Rocky Mountains), and in Figure 3-2 in western South America (Andes) and southern Asia (Himalayas). More detailed maps of particular areas make this effect even more striking in appearance.

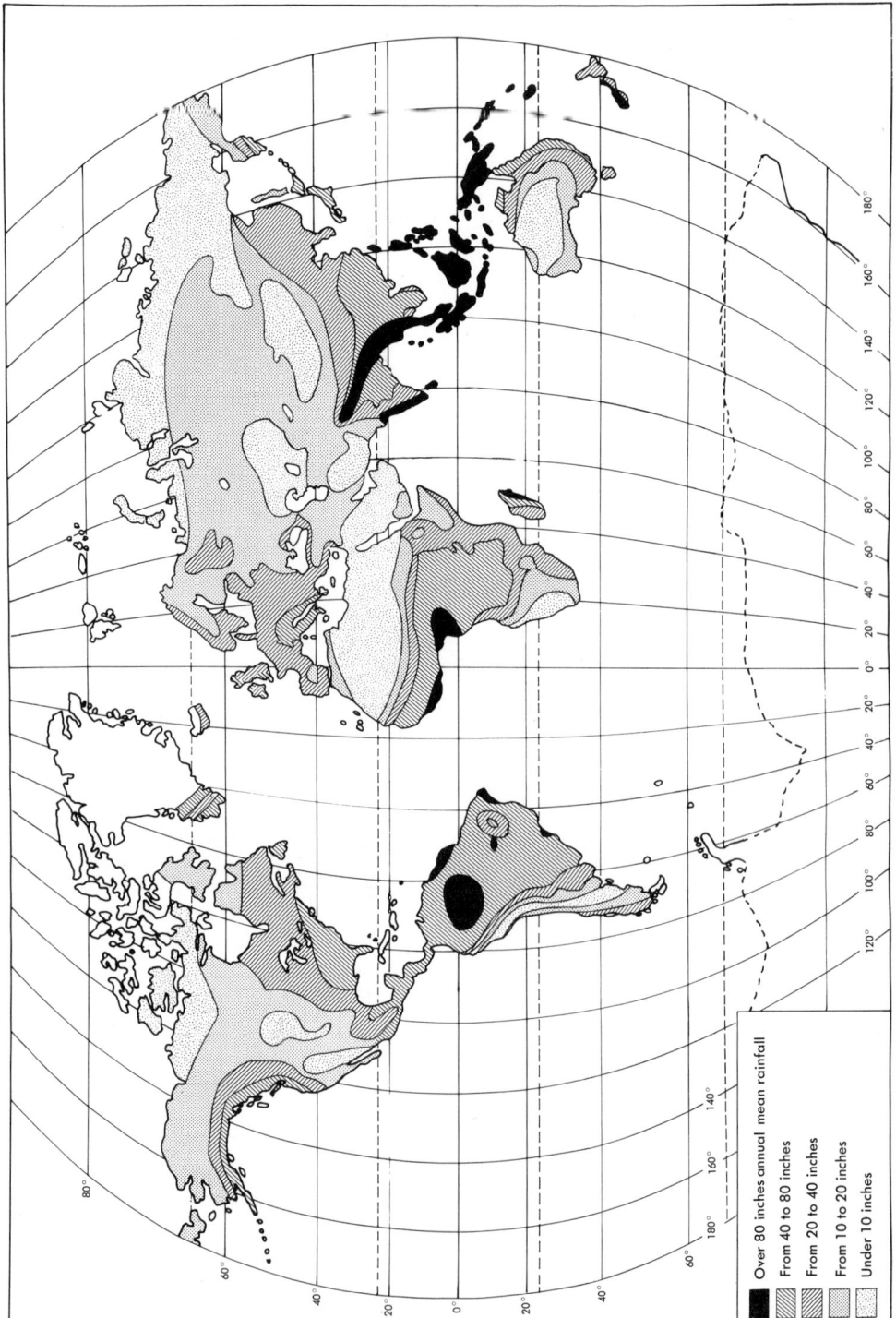

Fig. 3-2. The pattern of world precipitation. Adapted, by permission, from W. G. Kendrew. 1930. Climate. Oxford: Clarendon Press.

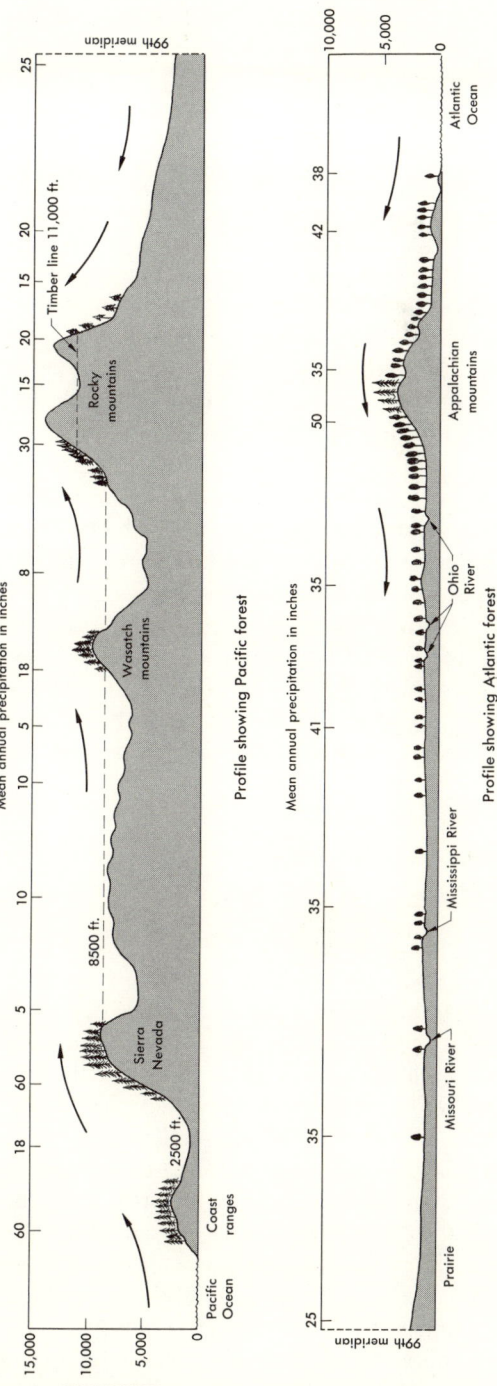

Redrawn from R. Zon. 1941. In, *Climate and Man. U. S. Department of Agriculture Yearbook.*

Fig. 3-3. The influence of topography on precipitation along the thirty-ninth parallel of north latitude.

The general world precipitation pattern, then, is the result of several forces, primary among which is the interaction between atmospheric circulation and continental or island topography. This interaction has much to do with the distribution of major ecosystems (see Figure 5-1). For example, deserts in general receive less than 25 cm of precipitation annually; even a cursory superpositioning of the geography of annual precipitation (Figure 3-2) and the geography of the major desert areas (Figure 5-1) will show considerable coincidence. However, as the basic mechanism of the hydrologic cycle suggests, the rate and amount of evaporation is as critical as is the rate and amount of precipitation. It is the ratio of these two forces which is the crucial factor in determining the distribution of particular types of ecosystems, be they deserts or tropical rain forests. Thus in the western North American desert states (Nevada, eastern Oregon, southern Idaho, western Wyoming, much of Utah and Arizona, and southeastern California) the ratio of precipitation to evaporation is 0.2 or less—that is, potential or actual water loss is greater than water gain. In the relatively arid to moist short grass prairie states (eastern Montana and western North Dakota, south to eastern New Mexico, and northern Texas), the ratio of precipitation to evaporation is between 0.2 and 0.6; in the more moist eastern half of the country, predominated by deciduous forests, the ratio is 0.8 to 1.6.

More refined analyses of interaction of rainfall and evaporation have been conducted to correlate the distribution of major ecosystems; however, discussion of this would go beyond the scope of this chapter. The relevant aspects of moisture and ecosystem distribution will be treated further in Chapter 5.

GASEOUS NUTRIENT CYCLES

The Carbon Cycle

Perhaps the simplest of the nutrient cycles is one whose general components are quite well recognized—the carbon cycle (Figure 3-4). It is essentially a perfect cycle in that carbon is returned to the environment about as fast as it is removed; finally, it is one which involves a gaseous phase, atmospheric carbon dioxide. The basic movement of carbon is from the atmospheric reservoir to producers to consumers and from both these groups to the decomposers, and thence back to the reservoir. In this cycle, the gaseous reservoir is the atmosphere, which has a concentration of about 0.03 to 0.04 per cent carbon dioxide. Inasmuch as from 4 to 9×10^{13} kg of carbon are fixed in photosynthesis annually along with a much smaller amount of direct fixation by marine invertebrates, it is obvious that there is either a great mobility of carbon or an additional reservoir, or both. This

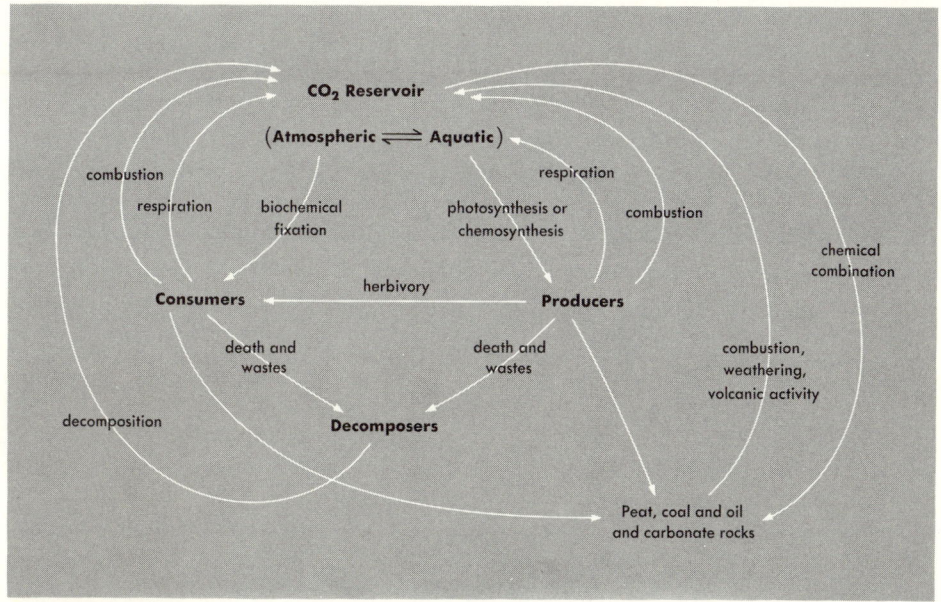

Fig. 3-4. The carbon cycle.

additional and major reservoir is the ocean, which is estimated to contain more than 50 times as much as the air; more significantly, the oceanic reservoir tends to regulate the amount in the atmosphere.

Respiratory activity in the producers and consumers (see Table 2-6) accounts for the return of a considerable amount of the biologically fixed carbon as gaseous CO_2 to the atmosphere; however, the most substantial return is accomplished by the respiratory activity of decomposers in their processing of the waste materials and dead remains of other trophic levels. Additional return from the biota occurs through the nonbiological process of combustion, both through the purposive use of wood in a fireplace and the accidental fire in a forest or building; such combustion can and does involve consumers and decomposers as well as producers.

The geological component of the system involves the deposition of plant material, such as peat, coal, and oil, and of such animal remains as mollusc shells and protozoan tests as carbonate rocks. In addition, a number of aquatic plants occurring in alkaline waters release calcium carbonate as a by-product of photosynthetic assimilation. For example, 100 kg of *Elodea canadensis* can precipitate 2 kg of $CaCO_3$ in 10 hours of sunlight under natural conditions. This pure calcium carbonate precipitate mixes with clay to form marl, which over a long period of time can be compacted as limestone; most of the limestone deposits in the world are presumed to have this kind of biological origin. Upon weathering and dissolution of carbonate rocks, the combustion of the fossil fuels (peat, coal, oil), and volcanic activity involving deposits of both fossil fuel and carbonate rocks, atmospheric carbon is returned to the reservoir.

Because of its significance, the interplay between atmospheric and aquatic carbon dioxide must be considered briefly. Interchange between the two phases occurs through diffusion, the direction of which is dependent on relative concentrations. Passage into the aquatic phase also takes place through precipitation; a liter of rain water, for example, contains about 0.3 cc of CO_2. The dissolved CO_2 combines with water in the soil or in an aquatic ecosystem to form carbonic acid (H_2CO_3) in a reversible reaction. In turn, carbonic acid dissociates in a reversible reaction into hydrogen and bicarbonate ions (HCO_3^-); the latter ion, in turn, dissociates in another reversible reaction into hydrogen and carbonate ions. The various reactions are summarized as follows,

$$\text{Atmospheric } CO_2 \downarrow\uparrow$$
$$\text{Dissolved } CO_2 + H_2O \leftrightarrows H_2CO_3 \leftrightarrows H^+ + HCO_3^- \leftrightarrows H^+ + CO_3^+$$

Since all these reactions are reversible, the direction of the reaction is dependent on the concentration of critical components; thus, a local depletion of atmospheric CO_2 would result in a net movement of CO_2 into the atmosphere from the dissolved phase, triggering a set of compensating reactions. By the same token, the assimilation of the bicarbonate ion (HCO_3^-) in photosynthesis by aquatic plants would tend to shift the equilibrium the other way. Actually the equilibrium system is much more complicated than this. For example, the amount of carbon present as bicarbonate and carbonate is also dependent on the pH of the water; at high pH values (i.e., alkaline conditions) more carbon is present as carbonate; at lower values (i.e., acid conditions) more occurs in the dissolved phase. Thus, manipulation of either pH or CO_2 concentration affects the operation of the system. A further complication to the stability of the system is that, according to Hutchinson, days or weeks may be required to achieve equilibrium with the atmosphere across a water surface.

It is probably now apparent that what initially appeared to be a simple cycle is in fact relatively complicated. Of the many features of the cycle, it is most important to recognize that there are a number of avenues by which carbon is utilized and a much larger number by which it is restored to the atmosphere. Collectively these various pathways constitute self-regulating feedback mechanisms resulting in a relatively homeostatic system. Additions and deletions can be quite readily equilibrated and compensated. To what degree the system will withstand or adapt to long-term disturbance of the existing equilibrium is, of course, uncertain. Most authorities indicate that the past few decades of increased use and incomplete combustion of fossil fuels has resulted in detectable increases of atmospheric carbon; based on careful measurements made in the period 1958-62, the prediction is for a 25 per cent increase in atmospheric CO_2 by the end of the century. What the long-term effects will be of such an increase, or of further increases is a matter of considerable and immediate concern; some aspects of this will be considered in Chapter 6.

Nitrogen Cycle

In terms of its biological significance, nitrogen is in league with carbon, hydrogen, and oxygen. It behooves us then to consider in some detail its biogeochemical cycle, which is quite complex but essentially complete or perfect (Figure 3-5). As with all cycles, it is like the carbon cycle, but there are marked differences. Although organisms live in a nitrogen-rich atmosphere (79 per cent) in contrast to that of carbon (0.03 to 0.04 per cent), the gaseous form of the nitrogen, unlike CO_2, can be used by very few organisms. And whereas organisms dispense both carbon and nitrogen as metabolic waste products, little or none of the nitrogen is lost in gaseous form. Lastly, the biological involvement in the nitrogen cycle is by far more extensive, complicated, and ordered; it is also highly specific in that certain organisms are able to act only in certain phases of the cycle.

Nitrogen Fixation. With an atmospheric concentration of 79 per cent, it would seem that the nitrogen reservoir is the atmosphere, but since most organisms are unable to use atmospheric nitrogen, the crucial reservoir is the store of nitrogen occurring in both inorganic (ammonia, nitrite, and nitrate) and organic (urea, protein, nucleic acids) form. Unlike carbon, which is readily available in reservoir quantities both in the air and water, atmospheric nitrogen must be fixed into an inorganic form, largely nitrate, before it can be tapped for biological processes. Although fixation can occur by both physico-chemical and biological means, the latter is by far the more significant. It has been estimated that electrochemical and photochemical fixation results in an average amount of nitrate in the order of 35 mg/m²/yr; by contrast, biological fixation averages 140 to 700 mg/m²/yr, and in very fertile areas it exceeds 20,000 mg/m²/yr.

The list of bacteria and algae known to be capable of fixing free nitrogen is substantial. However, for convenience, they can be considered in two major groups: symbiotic nitrogen fixers, (largely bacteria, but also including fungi) and free-living nitrogen fixers, including both bacteria and algae and perhaps other microorganisms. Species of the root-nodule bacteria, *Rhizobium,* are both the most important and best understood of the symbiotic nitrogen fixers; this genus is not, however, the only bacterial group

BIOGEOCHEMICAL CYCLES AND ECOSYSTEMS

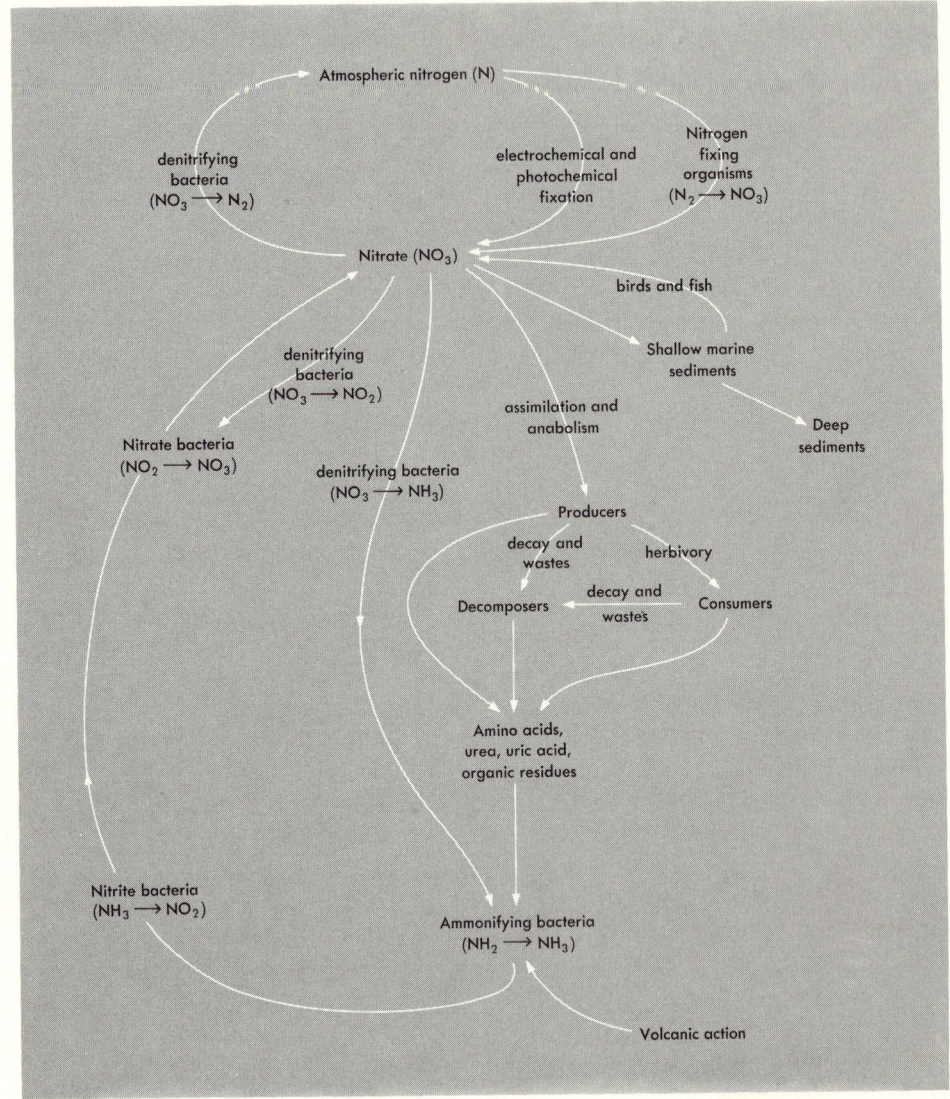

Fig. 3-5. The nitrogen cycle.

known to have this capacity. Interestingly, species of *Rhizobium* are not only absent from aquatic habitats, they are highly host-specific to particular species of leguminous plants (peas, clover, beans, etc.). Hence particular strains are associated only with particular species or strains of legumes. These bacteria penetrate root hairs of the legume, presumably by lysing the cell wall and membrane, and then multiply; the root hair responds to this invasion by a differential growth resulting in an enlargement, the nodule.

Nitrogen fixation occurs within the nodule, fixing annually as much as 500 pounds of nitrogen per acre in clover fields in New Zealand.

Symbiotic nitrogen fixation is apparently exclusively a terrestrial phenomenon; at least, the bulk of fixation in aquatic systems occurs in nonsymbiotic associations. Among the nonsymbiotic nitrogen-fixers are free-living bacteria of both aerobic and anaerobic types and blue-green algae. Aerobic nitrogen-fixing bacteria, such as *Azotobacter,* are widely distributed in soils as well as in fresh and marine waters; the same is true for anaerobic forms such as *Clostridium.* In fact, accumulating evidence indicates that many soil and water bacteria are capable of nitrogen fixation, and since they often occur in abundance, the total amount of nitrogen fixed is likely to be considerable. Because of its significance in soil fertility, data on nitrogen fixation in the soil are extensive. For the most part, however, very few quantitative studies have been made on the contribution these organisms make to the pool of inorganic nitrogen in natural waters. It is important to note that all the symbiotic and nonsymbiotic bacteria require an external supply of carbon compounds as an energy source to effect this endothermic reaction of nitrogen fixation; none of these bacteria is capable of photosynthesis.

Until recently there was also a paucity of information about aquatic nitrogen fixation by blue-green algae; there still is such a gap in terrestrial situations. However, from the work of Richard and Vera Dugdale, John Goering, and John Neess, among others, aquatic nitrogen metabolism is now much better understood. To study aquatic nitrogen fixation, the dissolved atmospheric nitrogen is removed and replaced with a tracer, the stable isotope ^{15}N; the fate of the isotope is then detected by mass spectrometry in methods roughly analogous to those described for using ^{14}C to measure productivity. In a study on Sanctuary Lake in northwest Pennsylvania, the Dugdales showed a positive correlation between high rates of nitrogen fixation and the presence of large populations of three species of the blue-green algae, *Anabaena* (Figure 3-6). Similarly, high fixation rates have been associated with large populations of other blue-green algae including *Gleotrichia echinulata* in Lakes Mendota and Wingra in Wisconsin and *Trichodesmium* in the Sargasso Sea. The energy required for the process is, unlike the nitrogen-fixing bacteria, at the expense of the photosynthetic process of which these algae are capable.

Correlation and causation are, of course, not necessarily equivalent. The absence of nitrogen fixation in October in Sanctuary Lake while large populations of *Anabaena* were still present (Figure 3-6) is a case in point. However, the decline in fixation is likely the result of other factors extrinsic to the algae, factors that regulate expression of the capacity to fix the nitrogen. It has been shown that the presence of nitrogen combined as ammonia affects fixation and that, within limits, there is a direct relationship with temperature and light intensity. Other investigators have shown that

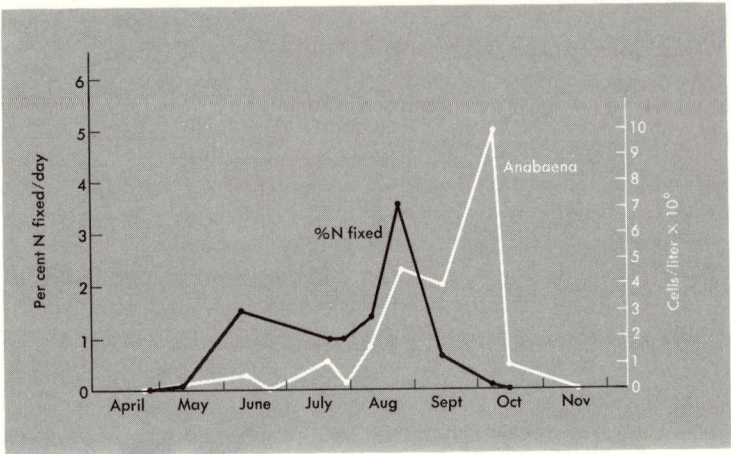

Adapted, by permission, from V. A. and R. C. Dugdale. 1962. Limnology and Oceanography 7: 170–177.

Fig. 3-6. The relationship between rate of nitrogen fixation (%/day) and the abundance of blue-green algae (*Anabaena*) in Sanctuary Lake, Pennsylvania in 1959.

various nutrients such as phosphorus, iron, calcium, molybdenum, and cobalt are important in controlling growth and nitrogen fixation in nitrogen-fixing organisms. Thus, it is apparent that the production of nitrate, the all-important regulative nutrient for nonnitrogen fixers, is in turn regulated by other gradient and nutrient factors. The regulator is itself regulated.

Ammonification. Subsequent to the incorporation of inorganic nitrogen (NO_3) into an organic form in protein and nucleic acid synthesis, it is metabolized and returned to the major part of the cycle as waste products of that metabolism or as organized protoplasm in dead organisms. Many heterotrophic bacteria, actinomycetes, and fungi occurring in both the soil and in water utilize this organic nitrogen-rich substrate; in their metabolism of it, they convert it to and release it in an inorganic form, ammonia. The process is referred to as ammonification or mineralization. Actually, what these microbes are doing is excreting what for them is excess nitrogen. Some of the ammonifying microorganisms are substrate-specific, utilizing only peptone but not simple amino acids, or using urea but not uric acid; by contrast, other species appear to be able to use a wide variety of organic nitrogen sources.

Nitrification. Although some autotrophic and many heterotrophic marine bacteria can use nitrogen occurring as ammonia to synthesize their own protoplasm, it is not generally accessible in this form. The conversion of ammonia, or mostly ammonium salts, to nitrate is termed nitrification, a process which is pH dependent, occurring slowly, if at all, in acid conditions. *Nitrosomonas* can convert ammonia to nitrite (NO_2), a toxic form in even small concentrations, and others, such as *Nitrobacter,* act on nitrite, completing the conversion to nitrate. These nitrifying bacteria are all chemosynthetic autotrophs, obtaining their energy from this oxidation process and then utilizing some of the energy to obtain their needed carbon by reduction from the dioxide or bicarbonate form. In doing so, they produce large quantities of nitrite or nitrate relative to their own growth gain. In their review of nitrogen metabolism in the soil, Richard Jackson and Frank Raw, of the Rothamsted Experimental Station in England, report that for each unit of carbon dioxide assimilated, *Nitrosomonas europaea* oxidizes 35 units of ammonia to nitrite and *Nitrobacter agilis* oxidizes between 76 and 135 units of nitrite to nitrate. Soil nitrate is easily leached out of soil, and unless it is assimilated by plants, it may become "lost" to that ecosystem but become available through ground water circulation to another one elsewhere.

Nitrification in the open ocean and its sediments is poorly understood at present. Nitrifying bacteria occur in the sea and in shore waters but seemingly not to any significant degree in the open ocean. In 1962, Stanley Watson, of the Woods Hole Oceanographic Institution, isolated and described the first nitrifying bacterium ever isolated from open ocean waters, *Nitrosocystis oceanus*. In subsequent studies, Watson has shown that it is an obligate autotroph, using only ammonia as an energy source and carbon dioxide as a carbon source. Using indirect measures, he estimated that they indeed are relatively rare in the open ocean, ranging from 1 bacterium per liter in the North Atlantic to perhaps 1 million per liter in tropical waters— the latter being a small population level for most bacteria. Assuming such populations and estimates of their activity, Watson suggests that nitrification would yield 50×10^3 more nitrate annually in the tropics than in the colder North Atlantic water, but that total production would hardly account for the relatively high nitrate levels in the sea. It is probable, then, that populations of nitrifying bacteria and/or their levels of activity are much higher in the open ocean than studies to date suggest.

Denitrification. The route of nitrate through an assimilatory-anabolism circuit and its return via ammonification and nitrification is but one possible alternative. *Denitrification* to molecular or gaseous nitrogen (N_2) as well as to nitrous and nitric oxide is effected by bacteria, such as *Pseudomonas,* and fungi which use the nitrate as an oxygen source in the presence of glucose and phosphate. However, most denitrifiers reduce nitrate only to nitrite, and still others to ammonia. Denitrification to molecular nitrogen is known to occur under anaerobic or partially anaerobic conditions; thus, it would be expected to occur in soils that are poorly aerated as well as those with considerable organic matter, for the latter have a high oxygen demand and hence are typically essentially anaerobic. By the same token, little denitrification would be expected in the typically oxygen-rich surface waters of lakes and seas, where the process is otherwise theoretically possible. During anoxic periods, however, molecular nitrogen can be formed in aquatic ecosystems, as shown in a recent study by John Goering and Vera Dugdale in an Alaskan lake. Winter water samples taken both at the bottom and one meter below the ice surface were inoculated with nitrogen-labelled nitrate ($K^{15}NO_3$) and then incubated at lake temperature. Analysis by mass spectrometry showed denitrification in the bottom samples to be about six times faster than near the surface, but the only significant end product was molecular nitrogen; there was a small reduction to ammonia, but no nitrous (N_2O) or nitric (NO) oxide was detected. Unless recaptured in nitrogen fixation, this molecular nitrogen can be returned to the atmospheric pool. But whether molecular nitrogen or one of its oxides will result from denitrification is known to be pH dependent. Thus, nitric oxide evolution becomes significant at pH values below 7.0; above a pH value of 7.3, nitrous oxide tends to be reabsorbed and further denitrified to molecular nitrogen.

There are yet other aspects of the cycling of nitrogen which could be assessed, among others the role of volcanic action or sedimentation. By now, however, the point is clear that the movement of nitrogen is by no means unidirectional, unregulated, nor energy-independent. There are numerous routes available at virtually every major way-station, each route is biologically and/or nonbiologically regulated, and energy is consumed or released in each process. These numerous self-regulating, energy dependent, feedback mechanisms result in the steady-state the nitrogen balance seems to have reached. And, most significantly, the major processes of nitrification and denitrification are well attuned to the productivity demands of the ecosystems. For example, these processes are most rapid in winter in temperate zones, resulting in maximal amounts of nitrate in the spring and early summer, the time when nitrate demand for plant growth and reproduction is highest.

SEDIMENTARY NUTRIENT CYCLES

Although some essential nutrients like sulfur may have a gaseous phase (e.g., sulfur dioxide), such phases are insignificant, inasmuch as there is no large reservoir; furthermore, none of them cycles so readily as carbon and nitrogen. In the pathway of each of these there are fewer self-correcting, homeostatic mechanisms and more stages in which short- or long-term stagnation can occur. Most significant of the stagnation stages is sedimentation in the oceans and such deep continental lakes as Lake Superior.

The complexities of the nitrogen cycle having been considered in detail, it will be prudent to but briefly examine the essentials of one sedimentary cycle, that of sulfur, and then to consider that of another (phosphorus) in a given ecosystem in some detail. These two elements have been selected because of their critical significance in growth and metabolism (e.g., sulf-

BIOGEOCHEMICAL CYCLES AND ECOSYSTEMS

hydryl bonding in proteins, phosphate-energy transfer compounds), and because they are relatively well-understood biogeochemical cycles.

Sulfur Cycle

Although a few organisms gain their sulfur requirements in such organic forms as amino acids and cystein (Figure 3-7), inorganic sulfate is the major source of biologically significant sulfur. Most of the biologically incorporated sulfur is mineralized by bacteria and fungi in ordinary decomposition by species of *Aspergillus* and *Neurospora,* among others. Under anaerobic conditions, however, some may be reduced directly to sulfides, including hydrogen sulfide, by bacteria belonging to such genera as *Escherichia* and *Proteus.* And some organic sulfur gains entry into the atmosphere as sulfur dioxide through incomplete combustion of fossil fuels; this is one of the major sources of air pollution today. Inorganic sulfur as sulfate (SO_4) may precipitate out, but since it is relatively soluble, it serves as a source of elemental sulfur in many ecosystems. Sulfate is also reduced under anaerobic conditions to elemental sulfur or to sulfides, including hydrogen sulfide, by such heterotrophic bacteria as species of *Desulfavibrio;* it is also accomplished by species of *Escherichia* and *Aerobacter.* The sulfate-reducing

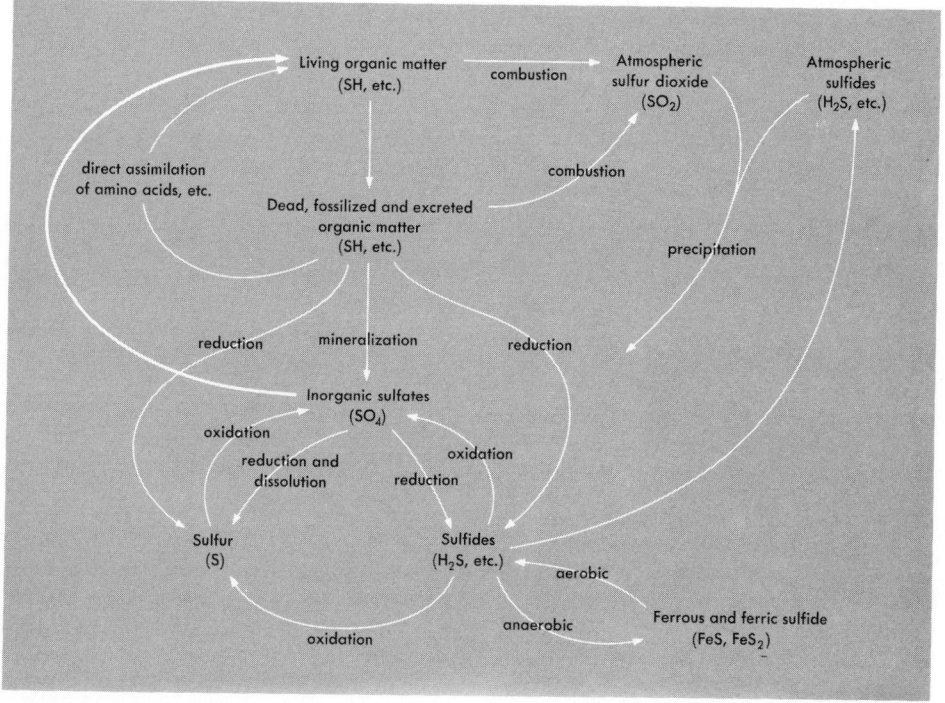

Fig. 3-7. The sulfur cycle.

anaerobic bacteria are heterotrophic, using the sulfate as a hydrogen acceptor in metabolic oxidation in a manner comparable to the use of nitrite and nitrate by denitrifying bacteria. The presence of large quantities of hydrogen sulfide occurring in the anaerobic, and usually deeper, portions of aquatic ecosystems is inimical to most life; its presence probably accounts for the absence of higher animals below 200 m in the Black Sea and has been considered responsible for kills of fish in valley impoundments polluted by pulp-mill effluents, which are rich in sulfates.

As is true of the ecological balance, one organism's poison is another's treat, so to speak. Colorless sulfur bacteria such as species of *Beggiatoa* oxidize hydrogen sulfide to elemental sulfur, and species of *Thiobacillus* oxidize it to sulfate; other species of *Thiobacillus* oxidize sulfide to sulfur, and still others oxidize sulfur to sulfate. For some species, even those of the same genus, the oxidation processes can occur only in the presence of oxygen; for others, oxygen availability is irrelevant. These latter bacteria are chemosynthetic autotrophs, utilizing the energy liberated in the oxidation to obtain their needed carbon by reduction of carbon dioxide; they are comparable to the autotrophic nitrifying bacteria that oxidize ammonia to nitrite and nitrite to nitrate. In addition, these also include the green and purple photosynthetic bacteria that use the hydrogen of hydrogen sulfide as the oxygen acceptor in reducing carbon dioxide; the green bacteria apparently are able to oxidize sulfide only to elemental sulfur, whereas the purple bacteria can carry the oxidation to the sulfate stage.

The sedimentary aspect of the cycle involves the precipitation of sulfur in the presence of iron under anaerobic conditions. Ferrous sulfide is insoluble in neutral or alkaline water, and consequently sulfur has the potential for being bound up under these conditions to the limits of the amount of iron present. Because of the thermodynamics of this ferrous sulfide system, other nutrients important to biological systems can also get trapped for varying periods of time; among these are copper, cadmium, zinc, and cobalt. On the contrary side, however, the very binding of these iron compounds allows the conversion of phosphorus from insoluble to soluble form and thereby makes it accessible. There is little question then but what sulfate and sulfide reduction in the anaerobic sulfur-containing muds controls to a significant degree the biological chemistry of the ecosystem. This sulfur cycle provides an excellent example of the interaction and regulation that exists between different mineral cycles as well as demonstrating again the complex biological and chemical regulation within such cycles.

Phosphorus Movement in Lakes

As a constituent of nucleic acids, phospholipids and numerous phosphorylated compounds, phosphorus is one of the nutrients of major importance to biological systems. Further, as Hutchinson has noted, because the ratio of phosphorus to other elements in organisms tends to be considerably greater than the ratio of phosphorus in the available and primary sources, phosphorus becomes ecologically significant as the most likely limiting or regulating element in productivity.

For their nutrition plants require inorganic phosphate, typically as orthophosphate ions. In typical mineral-cycle fashion, this phosphate is transferred to consumers and decomposers as organic phosphate and subsequently is made available for recycling via mineralizing decomposition. Much phosphate becomes lost to this central cycle by physical processes, such as sedimentation, which take it out of the reach of upwelling and major water circulation; biological processes such as the formation of teeth and bone, both of which are very resistant to weathering, and excretion also account for considerable losses from the major portion of the cycle. In the latter instance, one need consider only the tremendous deposits of guano along the western coast of South America, the result of excretory activity of birds.

The general pattern of the phosphorus cycle is thus similar to that for the other nutrients already discussed; it will be more instructive now to consider the cycling and availability of this critical element in some actual ecosystems rather than in the pattern of a generalized ecosystem. For this purpose, studies by F. H. Rigler, of the University of Toronto, on a group of nine lakes in Ontario are particularly interesting. The lakes were quite varied, including hard-water lakes with pH values between 7.7 and 8.7 and soft-water lakes with pH values between 6.7 and 7.2. Maximum depth in the lakes varied between 6 and 53 m, and surface area varied between 0.5 and 2180 hectares.

Phosphorus in these lakes, as in any aquatic system, occurs in three forms and cycles as follows:

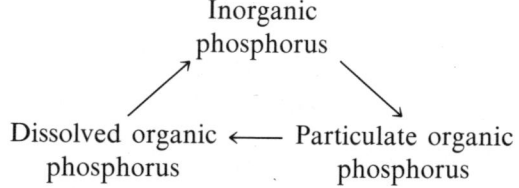

The inorganic phosphorus is typically orthophosphate; particulate organic phosphate is that which occurs in suspension in living and dead protoplasm; dissolved, or soluble, organic phosphorus is derived from the particulate matter by excretion and decomposition. The total phosphorus in a system consists of that in each of the three compartments. Total phosphorus in the nine lakes of Rigler's study ranged between 5 and 133 mg/l.

According to Rigler's findings, two of the lakes can be used to represent

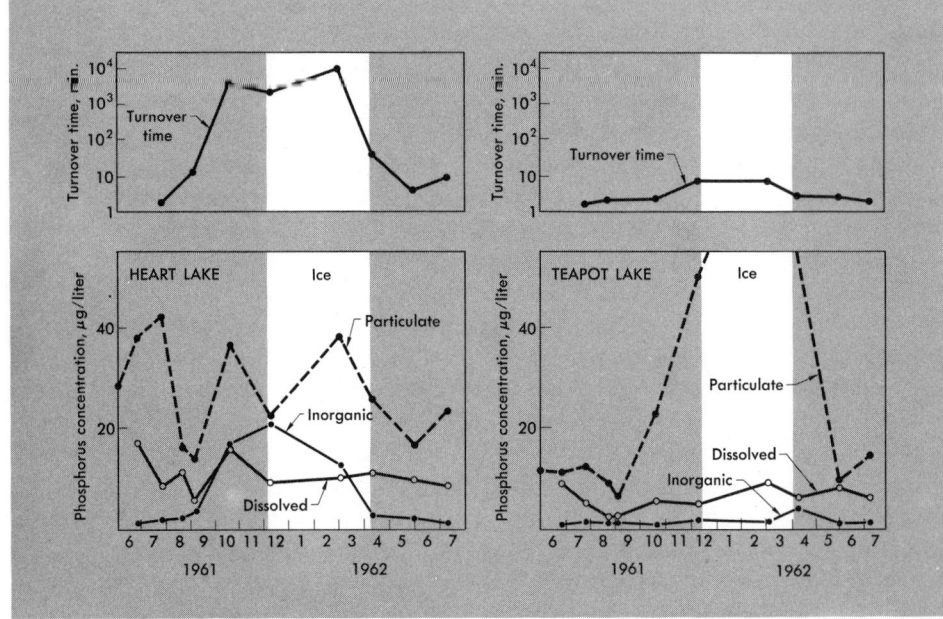

Adapted, by permission, from F. H. Rigler. 1964. *Limnology and Oceanography* 9: 511–518.

Fig. 3-8. Seasonal changes of turnover time of inorganic phosphorus and amounts of the three forms of phosphorus in two lakes in Ontario.

the basic patterns and conditions of the entire series; the annual distribution of the three forms of phosphorus in these two lakes appears in Figure 3-8. Particulate organic phosphorus showed no consistent seasonal pattern, but if there was an increase it tended to be in the winter, as shown for Teapot Lake; the dissolved organic phosphorus showed no seasonal maximum. Inorganic phosphorus was consistently low during most of the year but increased between December and April. This seasonal pattern provides an availability of phosphorus in the only form that can be utilized biologically and at a time of the year when conditions approach optimum for productivity. There is a parallel to nitrification, which is also largely a winter event, and which provides a maximum of nitrate in the spring. Phosphorus tends to become bound in the sediments under oxidized conditions such as occur in the fall and to be released under anoxic conditions, a situation which develops in many temperate lakes during winter stagnation. Thus, the very environment that leads to a binding of sulfur in the presence of iron, namely a reducing environment, is the situation under which phosphorus is released.

In spite of considerable differences in their constitution, the proportion of phosphorus in the three major compartments was strikingly similar during the summer period in eight of the lakes—inorganic phosphorus ranged from

4.8 to 7.8 per cent, dissolved organic phosphorus ranged from 25.0 to 31.7 per cent, and particulate organic phosphorus ranged from 61.8 to 68.2 per cent. The one exceptional lake, Grenadier Pond, had 83.7 per cent of its phosphorus in particulate form and 12.5 per cent in dissolved organic form; the inorganic component was, however, comparable to that of the other lakes, 4.8 per cent. Grenadier Pond is very productive, in part because it is subject to urban drainage known to be rich in particulate phosphorus.

The summer distribution of phosphorus just described for these lakes is a static picture, however. The shifts in distribution shown in Figure 3-8 suggest movement of phosphorus from one compartment to another but give no indication of the rate at which such cycling occurs. By tagging water samples at different times of the year with radioactive phosphorus, ^{32}P, in the form of the inorganic orthophosphate, Rigler was able to get a preliminary estimate of the rate at which phosphorus is utilized or *turned over*. Thus, if 100 units of radioactive phosphorus were introduced as inorganic phosphate and only 90 units were left in the water an hour later, the amount of turnover would be $\frac{10}{100}$ units, or 10 per cent per hour. If this rate of turnover is constant, it would then take ten hours to turn over the phosphorus completely, a period referred to as *turnover time*. The actual computation of turnover time is a bit more complicated, inasmuch as one must account simultaneously for the presence of stable phosphorus and the shift in the ratio of radioactive to stable forms. However, the basic concept of turnover rate is not altered by these adjustments.

The general annual pattern of turnover time in the lakes Rigler studied was much the same: during the summer, average turnover time ranged from 0.9 to 7.5 minutes. As progression through the fall and winter took place, there was a lengthening of turnover time to the maximum, which generally occurred under ice and snow cover. This pattern is shown in the upper part of Figure 3-8 for the two lakes considered earlier; these two lakes also represent the extremes in magnitude. Average winter turnover time was only 7 minutes in Teapot Lake, a 3.5-fold increase from the summer; this winter rate is atypical of the other lakes. In Heart Lake, the average winter turnover time was 10,000 minutes (i.e., 7 days) vs. a summer average of 7.3 minutes.

A number of studies like these of Rigler's has led to the generalization that the turnover time of dissolved and inorganic phosphate is characteristically a matter of minutes in freshwater lakes. Not so in marine water, however. Work by Lawrence Pomeroy, among others, indicates that summer turnover time is a matter of hours (1 to as many as 56) in marine situations (Table 3-2). Interestingly, the winter range of values (30-196 hours) is not especially different from the range observed in most of the lakes Rigler studied (13-166 hours).

Although little of the phosphorus in an ecosystem may be readily available in the inorganic state, the turnover of phosphorus may be, and

TABLE 3-2. Turnover Time of Dissolved Phosphate in Marine Waters at About the Same Latitude and Longitude

Location	Time of Year	Turnover Time (hr)
Estuaries		
Salt-marsh creek, Georgia	July	1
Altamaka River, Georgia	May	1
Altamaka River, Georgia	November	13
Open water		
Continental shelf	July	5
Gulf Stream, surface	July	4
Gulf Stream, 50 m	July	12
Coastal sea water	April	4
Coastal sea water	October and November	46–155
Doboy Sound, Georgia	February	50
Doboy Sound, Georgia	June and July	37–56
Marsh		
Salt marsh, low tide	January and October	40–49
Salt marsh, high tide	November	169

Adapted, by permission, from L. Pomeroy, 1960. Science 161: 1731–1732. Copyright 1960 by the American Association for the Advancement of Science.

usually appears to be, rapid enough to maintain a constant supply, sufficient to turn the ecosystem dynamo. Barring disruption of the system by the introduction of large quantities of inorganic phosphate (via runoff from surrounding fields subject to artificial fertilization, introduction of organic matter, iron-rich or otherwise, etc.) such rapid turnover can in large measure stabilize the system. As a case in point, Dr. Alfred Redfield, of the Woods Hole Oceanographic Institute, maintains that the nitrate in the sea and the oxygen in the atmosphere are controlled by the biogeochemical cycle which is, in turn, ultimately regulated by phosphorus. Although this thesis is supported by considerable evidence, we are far from a complete understanding of the cycle of phosphorus, or, for that matter, that of any other nutrient.

NUTRIENT BUDGETS AND ECOSYSTEMS

For clarity of exposition, the concern in this chapter has been on the movement of individual nutrients with major emphasis on the biological and chemical aspects of their biogeochemistry. Except in passing, no particular attention has been given to such geological processes in ecosystems as the input of nutrients by way of precipitation, dust, and weathering or output by way of runoff and erosion. Further, although a given nutrient may be limiting in a given case, a large number of chemicals are requisite to growth; hence there is need to broaden the scope from individual to aggregate cycles.

Finally, since nutrients may get bound up in the biomass of an ecosystem for long periods of time, as in the trunks of standing trees in a forest, consideration must be given to the availability and source of nutrients in an ecosystem; that is, to the budget of nutrients.

In a sense, there are two nutrient budgets in an ecosystem; one is the *internal,* pertaining to intake and output of the biotic component of the ecosystem, the producer → consumer → decomposer food chain, and the other the *external,* pertaining to the intake and output of the entire ecosystem. Obviously the two are interrelated, and the internal ultimately dependent on limits imposed by the external. Important as this is, well worked out nutrient budgets, either of the internal or external type, are largely wanting.

For internal nutrient budgets, it is a major task to determine the mineral content of the biotic components of an ecosystem, and to assess shifts in this content with time. It is for this reason that most investigators have chosen to work with the cycle of one or two nutrients; even that kind of study is extremely demanding and fraught with technological as well as interpretational difficulties. For example, J. P. Witherspoon used the radioisotope of cesium (^{134}Cs) to study the movement of this nutrient in white oak trees at the Oak Ridge National Laboratory (Figure 3-9). He found

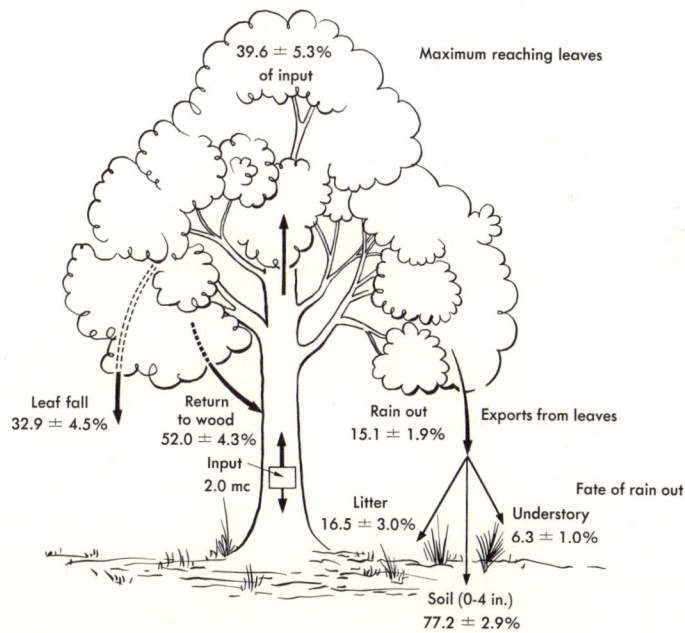

Redrawn, by permission, from J. P. Witherspoon. 1964. *Ecological Monographs* 34: 403–420.

Fig. 3-9. The cycle of cesium-134 in white oak, an average based on twelve trees observed for two growing seasons.

that over two growing seasons, the maximum concentration in the leaves occurred in early June and amounted to about 40 per cent of the total input (2 millicuries), and the remainder spread to the woody tissues in the roots, stem, and branches. Of the total leaf content, 33 per cent was lost through leaf fall, 15 per cent was leached out by rain, and the remainder was incorporated in woody tissues. By November, about 70 per cent of the rain-leached cesium was in the top four inches of the soil, 17 per cent was added to the leaf litter, supplementing that which had come through leaf fall, for a grand total of about 19 per cent of the original input.

For a consideration of the internal nutrient budget of several minerals, Professor Ovington's data on a Scots pine plantation in England are among the very few available (Table 3-3). In each instance, about half or more of the nutrient is taken up by trees rather than ground flora. As can be seen, there is a very substantial amount of nutrient in the litter and unharvested tree roots and crowns; significantly, most of this (95 to 100 per cent) becomes available for recycling through decomposition. (Compare columns on total return to litter and total released by decomposition.)

TABLE 3-3. Budget of Selected Nutrients (in Kilograms per Hectare) for Plantations of *Pinus sylvestris* for the 55 years from the Time of Planting

	Nitrogen	Calcium	Potassium	Magnesium	Phosphorus	Sodium
Trees						
Total uptake	4817	2272	1933	431	413	132
Distribution						
In living trees	453	272	150	64	41	36
Harvested	161	210	98	42	14	5
In crowns and roots of harvested trees	704	386	279	80	75	48
Litter fall (leaves, branches, cones)	3499	1404	1406	245	283	43
Ground flora						
Total uptake	2058	771	876	169	182	72
Distribution						
Present in ground	40	19	22	5	3	4
Litter fall from ground flora	2131	775	877	170	187	70
Total uptake (Trees and ground flora)	6875	3043	2809	600	595	204
Total return to litter and soil	6334	2565	2562	495	545	161
Total released by decomposition	6084	2450	2538	473	526	161
Net uptake from soil	791	593	271	127	73	43

Adapted, by permission, from J. D. Ovington, 1962. *Advances in Ecological Research*, Vol. 1. New York: Academic Press.

Nonetheless, uptake by the plants and release by decomposition are not in balance; more is required for growth and tied up in organized form than is available through decomposition. This growth has occurred by a shift of part of the nutrient capital of the entire ecosystem from the abiotic to the biotic component. (See column on net uptake.) Relative to total uptake, the net uptake from the soil ranges from 9.6 per cent in this case of potassium to 21 per cent in the case of sodium.

Since there is a net movement of nutrients within an ecosystem such as observed in this internal nutrient budget of the Scots pine plantation, the possibility of a net exchange of nutrients in the external budget might also be anticipated. That is, to what degree are nutrients added to and removed from the capital of an ecosystem by such events as precipitation, weathering, and runoff? Data of this sort, as of internal budgets, are in short supply, and for good reason. While it is possible although not especially easy to measure the amount of rainfall and determine the mineral content thereof, it is not so easy or inexpensive to monitor runoff; in most ecosystems the problem is particularly difficult because of loss by way of deep seepage and groundwater circulation. Through the judicious choice and intensive study of small watersheds in New Hampshire, Herbert Bormann and Gene Likens have been able to circumvent the limiting aspects of the study of external nutrient budgets. Each of the six watersheds they selected for study is characterized by watertight bedrock and lateral boundaries that coincide with topographic divides; hence each is discretely isolated from the input or output of adjacent watersheds and none is subject to any deep seepage. Further, the isolation of the forest from sites of active agriculture minimizes the mineral contribution that wind-borne dust brings to many ecosystems, and the homogeneous nature of the bedrock further reduces variability in the system. A further and most propitious aspect of the choice of the watersheds is that they are within the Hubbard Brook Experimental Forest, an established hydrologic laboratory which continuously monitors precipitation and runoff by standard meteorological procedures. Weekly analysis of hydrologic input and output for particular nutrients by atomic absorption spectrophotometry has permitted the establishment of annual budgets for the four significant cations in the forest—calcium, magnesium, potassium, and sodium (Table 3-4).

From 1955 to 1963 average annual precipitation in each of the watersheds was 123 cm; of this, 58 per cent was lost through runoff and 42 per cent by evapotranspiration (i.e., evaporation plus transpiration). During the two years of study reported in Table 3-4, precipitation was below average: 117 cm in 1963–64 and 95 cm in 1964–65. This decreased precipitation in the second year is reflected in the decreased input of calcium and potassium, but not so in the case of magnesium and sodium. The investigators suggest that an intrusion of maritime air during 1964–65 may be responsible for the increases in magnesium and sodium, since these elements are abundant in sea water.

TABLE 3-4. Nutrient Budgets (kilograms per hectare) for Six Watersheds in Hubbard Brook Forest, New Hampshire

	1963–64			1964–65		
	Input	Output	Net Change	Input	Output	Net Change
Ca^{++}	3.0	8.0	−5.0	2.8	3.9	−1.1
Mg^{++}	0.7	2.6	−1.9	1.1	1.8	−0.7
Na^+	1.0	5.9	−4.9	2.1	4.5	−2.4
K^+	2.5	1.8	+0.7	1.8	1.1	+0.7

Data of G. E. Likens, F. H. Bormann, N. M. Johnson, and R. S. Pierce, 1967. Ecology 48: 772–785.

Input is the amount of dissolved cations entering the ecosystems in all forms of precipitation and equals concentration in milligrams per liter times volume of precipitation; output is the amount of dissolved cations leaving the ecosystems in stream water and equals concentration in milligrams per liter times volume of runoff.

Because of differences in precipitation reported for the two years, the amount of runoff would be expected to be different; it was, but what was more striking was that the percentage of runoff in the second year was markedly different from the average—49 per cent vs. the typical 58 per cent. Evapotranspiration accounted for the difference. The amount of water lost by evapotranspiration in the two years was essentially the same, 50 cm in 1963–64 and 48 cm in 1964–65; but, because of reduced precipitation in the second year, the percentage was different. This observation suggests a greater constancy, and hence significance to the ecosystem, of the precipitation-evaporation ratio discussed earlier in this chapter. The decreased amount of runoff in the second year is largely reflected in the smaller cation loss.

Although there are differences in the cation budgets because of changes in rainfall, runoff, and the cation concentration in each, there is a significant amount of calcium, magnesium, and sodium lost from the ecosystem each year. The apparent net gain in potassium, which was indeed very small in relation to the other cations, is not being sustained according to subsequent, and yet unpublished, studies by the investigators. Since some of the cation input becomes part of the resource pool available for biological synthesis, the total "output" is actually greater than that shown. What is being measured here is input and output from the whole system, not input and output within the system, which may or may not be completely balanced on any short-term basis. There is then a net annual loss of cations from Hubbard Brook; this has been shown for a few other ecosystems as well (Table 3-5). All these loss rates are consistent with the known activity for the geochemical cycle of these elements. In themselves, the losses from one ecosystem can constitute an external input to another ecosystem elsewhere and can be compensated for by weathering or chemical decomposition of the underlying substrate. So long as the substrate can supply the ecosystem with its requisite nutrients and also be somewhat profligate in the amount

TABLE 3-5. Cation budgets (kilograms per hectare) for various areas of the world

	Input	Output	Net Change	Location
Calcium	2	12	−10	Finland
	8	26	−18	New Zealand
	6	19	−13	S.E. United States
	3	8	−5	Hubbard Brook
Magnesium	1	4	−3	Finland
	11	13	−2	New Zealand
	2	6	−4	S.E. United States
	0.7	2.6	−1.9	Hubbard Brook
Potassium	2	4	−2	Finland
	8	13	−5	New Zealand
	1	6	−5	S.E. United States
	2.5	1.8	+0.7	Hubbard Brook
Sodium	2	6	−4	Finland
	58	62	−4	New Zealand
	5	26	−21	S.E. United States
	1	5.9	−4.9	Hubbard Brook

Reproduced, by permission, from G. E. Likens, F. H. Bormann, N. M. Johnson, and R. S. Pierce, 1967. Ecology 48: 772–785.

discharged in runoff, the ecosystem can be maintained. If there is a net gain or depletion of one or more of these essential nutrients over a period of time, the system will respond by a change in its composition or function. Although such dynamic changes within ecosystems will be among the topics discussed in Chapter 5, an insight into the effects on nutrient cycles by manipulating ecosystems can be had by considering another aspect of the studies of Bormann and Likens on the Hubbard Brook watersheds.

After the pattern of nutrient cycles had been followed for several years, one of the six watersheds was experimentally subjected to clear cutting of its beech-maple-birch forest during the winter of 1965–66, all the cuttings being left on the ground. In June 1966, a herbicide (Bromacil) was applied to inhibit regrowth of vegetation. Cation and anion gains and losses were monitored for both the cutover watershed and the five intact, forested watershed ecosystems in the manner already described. The findings of the experiment are significant not only in themselves, but also, and importantly, in regard to the effects of lumbering.

One of the expected consequences of clear cutting was an increase in runoff water owing to the loss of a tremendous amount of transpiration surface eliminated by the cutting. However, the order of magnitude of the increase exceeded by 40 per cent that expected for the entire year and the period of peak runoff (June through September) exceeded expectation by 418 per cent. Net losses of cations from the cutover system also increased, the losses of sodium, magnesium, calcium, and potassium being respectively 3, 8, 9, and 20 times greater than in the undisturbed ecosystems. The increased losses result both from the greater quantities of drainage water moving through the system as well as the absence of nutrient uptake by the vegetation. Anion changes were also detected, sulfate loss declining and nitrate loss increasing; in fact, the total loss of nitrate for the year was equivalent to the annual turnover of nitrate, namely about 60 kg/hectare (see earlier discussion of turnover in the section on phosphorous; see also Figure 3-8). The increased nitrate loss is the result of an increase in nitrification in the cutover system, a phenomenon that is ordinarily inhibited in intact forested or otherwise vegetated ecosystems. Since the release from inhibition of nitrification is correlated to the cation losses, it may in fact account to some degree for these losses.

Although this particular study is unique, its results are far from anecdotal, since there is sufficient evidence from small-scale experiments to substantiate the trends of its findings. It is thus without question that removal of timber has effects on both the local hydrologic and nutrient cycles, the magnitude of the effect being directly related to the magnitude of the removal. But importantly, the increased flow of water downstream has potential erosional effects and the increased flow of nutrients enriches and thereby promotes more optimal conditions for primary production downstream. Such enrichment may be beyond the basic capacity of such downstream ecosystems and result in untoward consequences. For example, the Hubbard Brook study has demonstrated nitrate concentrations in the stream from the cutover ecosystem exceeding the established pollution level of ten parts per million. In the final chapter we shall have occasion to refer to this enrichment process and to discuss its effects on ecosystems.

REFERENCES

Correlated Readings

Bormann, F. H. and G. E. Likens, 1967. Nutrient cycling. *Science* **155**: 424–428.

Kormondy, E. J., 1965. *Readings in Ecology.* Englewood Cliffs, New Jersey: Prentice-Hall, Inc.

Arrhenius, O., Hydrogen ion concentration, soil properties and growth of higher plants, p. 193.

Blackman, F. E., Optima and limiting factors, p. 14.

Harvey, H. W., Nitrate in the sea, p. 191.

Henderson, L. J., Water-general considerations, p. 20.

Leopold, A., Lakes in relation to terrestrial life patterns, p. 200.

Liebig, J., Organic chemistry in its application to vegetable physiology and agriculture, p. 12.

Redfield, A. C., The biological control of chemical factors in the environment, p. 196.

Shelford, V. E., Physiological animal geography, p. 17.

Technical References and Monographs

Brock, T., 1966. *Principles of Microbial Ecology.* Englewood Cliffs, New Jersey: Prentice-Hall, Inc.

Goldman, C. R. (ed.), 1966. *Primary Productivity in Aquatic Environments.* Berkeley: University of California Press.

Hutchinson, G. E., 1957. *A Treatise on Limnology,* Vol. I. New York: John Wiley and Sons, Inc.

Jackson, R. M. and F. Raw, 1966. *Life in the Soil.* New York: St. Martin's Press.

Ovington, J. D., 1962. Quantitative ecology and the woodland ecosystem concept. *In* J. B. Cragg, *Advances in Ecological Research,* Vol. 1, pp. 103–192. New York: Academic Press, Inc.

Wood, E. J. F., 1965. *Marine Microbial Ecology.* New York: Reinhold Publishing Co.

ecology of populations

CHAPTER 4

In a study of the common housefly some years ago, the American entomologist L. O. Howard determined that the female produces an average of 120 eggs at a time and that about half of the eggs develop into females; furthermore, he observed that there were seven generations per year. If we assume these data as constants, then of the 120 individuals produced by one female, 60 would be females, each capable of producing 120 eggs, and the number of offspring in the second generation would be 7200. Carrying this further, and assuming that subsequent to reproduction all individuals of the reproducing generation die off, we can see that the first fertile females would be responsible for the ultimate production of over 5 trillion flies in the seventh generation (Table 4-1). If we assume that all individuals survive a full year with the females producing only once, the population at the end of the year would be only slightly greater, namely about 1.7 per cent; but if we assume that all individuals survive and that all the females reproduce in each generation, the population would be increased by about 10 per cent and exceed 6 trillion flies by the seventh generation.

With such potential for reproduction, it is little wonder houseflies are the bane of the housewife's existence. At the other extreme of body size, according to calculations by Charles Darwin, a single pair of elephants would have over 19 million descendents alive after 750 years even with their long gestation period and small number of offspring produced in a lifetime. As a final morsel of such speculations, in 1899, shortly after the English sparrow was introduced into the United States, it was estimated that in ten years a single pair of sparrows could give rise to 275,716,983,698 descendents, and that by 1916–1920 there would be about 575 birds per 100 acres. By the 1916–1920 period, however, there were only 18 to 26 birds per 100

TABLE 4-1. Production of Houseflies (*Musca domestica*) in One Year on the Assumptions That a Female Lays 120 Eggs per Generation, That Half of These Eggs Develop into Females, and That There are Seven Generations per Year

Total Population

Generation	If all Survive but 1 Generation	If all Survive 1 Year but Produce Only Once	If all Survive 1 Year and all Females Produce Each Generation
1	120	120	120
2	7200	7320	7320
3	432,000	439,320	446,520
4	25,920,000	26,359,320	27,237,720
5	1,555,200,000	1,581,559,320	1,661,500,920
6	93,312,000,000	94,893,559,320	101,351,520,120
7	5,598,720,000,000	5,693,613,559,320	6,182,442,727,320

acres, less than 5 per cent of the expected. There were, then, forces acting against this geometric increase of the sparrow; similarly, forces must be operating against the increase potential in houseflies and elephants and other organisms as well. In the case of the sparrow, a number of factors seemed to have been involved, including the development of sparrow-eating habits by hawks and owls, changes in agricultural practices, and, of no small consequence, a decrease in the size of the horse population in cities, and in consequence of the droppings on which the bird feeds. In addition, intraspecific competition for food and nesting sites may also have operated in opposition to the potential for geometric increase in the population.

It is apparent then that there are two opposing forces operating in the growth and development of a population; one of these is inherent in and characteristic of each species population—the ability to reproduce at a given rate. Opposing this is an inherent capacity for death, or, if you are an optimist, for physiological longevity; this opposition to growth comes also from all the forces of the physical and biological environment in which an organism exists. In the late 1920's, the American ecologist, Royal Chapman, referred to these forces respectively as *biotic potential* and *environmental resistance,* terms which still serve as useful handles for considering the complexities of population growth and regulation.

CHARACTERISTICS OF POPULATION GROWTH

The Sigmoid Growth Curve

To gain an understanding of the interaction of biotic potential and environmental resistence, we will turn from the theoretical growth of the housefly to empirical data on yeast presented in 1930 by Raymond Pearl, one of the primary contributors to our understanding of population biology. Pearl used data obtained by a German investigator, T. Carlson, who had determined the growth of yeast by periodically centrifuging the culture and determining its volume and mass. These results were converted to numbers of yeast cells by Pearl; hence the fractional components that appear in Table 4-2. If the data of the first 2 columns (time and number of individuals present) are plotted and the points joined (Figure 4-1), the *growth curve* of the population can be seen to be quite S-shaped, or sigmoidal. In absolute numbers, the initial growth period is slow but is followed by a period of rapid increase and then by a slowing down at the upper level. It is difficult at first glance, however, to determine during what period the increase is greatest and further how the increase and decrease in rate compare. These shifts in rates can be more readily seen by constructing a *curve of growth rate*. The change in the size of the yeast population (symbolized as ΔN, the Greek symbol for delta representing change) in a passage of time (Δt) can be derived directly from the tabulation in the second column of Table 4-2. By the passage of two hours, the population tripled from 9.6 to 29.0 individuals, for an increase of 19.4 individuals; likewise in the next two-hour period, the increase was from 29.0 to 71.1 individuals, a change of 42.1. The data so generated in the third column of Table 4-2 have been

TABLE 4-2. Growth of Yeast Cells in Laboratory Culture

Time (t) (hr)	Number of Individuals (N)	Increase	$\frac{\Delta N}{\Delta t}$
0	9.6	0	
2	29.0	19.4	
4	71.1	42.1	
6	174.6	103.5	
8	350.7	176.1	
10	513.3	162.6	
12	594.4	81.1	
14	640.8	46.4	
16	655.9	15.1	
18	661.8	5.9	

Reprinted by permission of the publisher. The Biology of Population Growth, by Raymond Pearl. Copyright 1925 by Alfred A. Knopf, Inc.

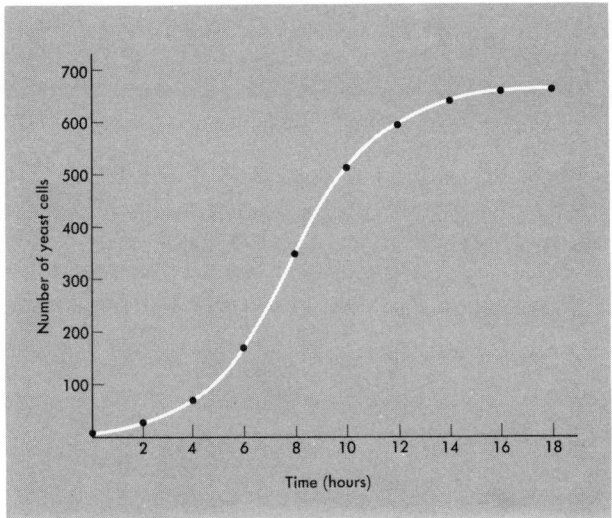

Fig. 4-1. The growth curve of yeast cells in the laboratory. (Based on Table 4-2).

graphed in Figure 4-2, superimposed on the growth curve of the population (Figure 4-1).

Two major components of the growth curve can now be recognized, their interpretation being facilitated by the growth rate curve: the period

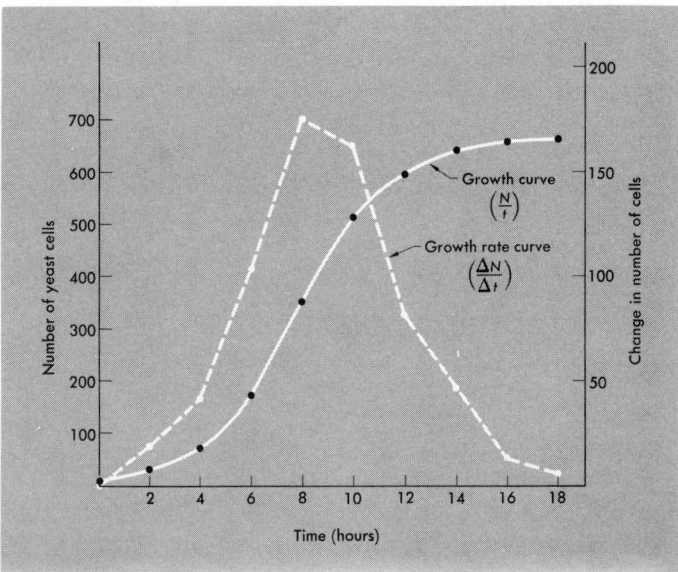

Fig. 4-2. The growth curve and growth rate curve of yeast cells in the laboratory. (Based on Table 4-2.)

of increase and the period of equilibrium. In absolute numbers, during the period of increase (0 to 18 hours) there is a slow acceleration in the first 4 hours followed by a period of rapid growth from 4 to 10 hours. The turning or inflection point of the population is 8 hours; up to that point population increase has been accelerating to its most rapid rate. This rapid growth period of the first eight hours is often referred to as the logarithmic phase, since a straight line would be produced if the data were plotted logarithmically. After this rapid log phase the rate decelerates rapidly at first (10 to 12 hours) and then more gradually and rather uniformly to nearly zero. At the zero point, there is no net change in the population; it is at equilibrium with its environment; that is, it has reached the limit at which the environment can support the population, a limit sometimes referred to as the *carrying capacity* of the environment. If the environment is shifted, a different equilibrium level may result. Environmental shifts may be in the form of a chemical change, such as removing toxic wastes (Figure 4-3), or a physical change, such as an alteration of temperature (Figure 4-4), or still other changes to be discussed subsequently. The major point is that carrying capacity, like most other ecological concepts, is subject to change.

In describing the equilibrium phase of the yeast population just now,

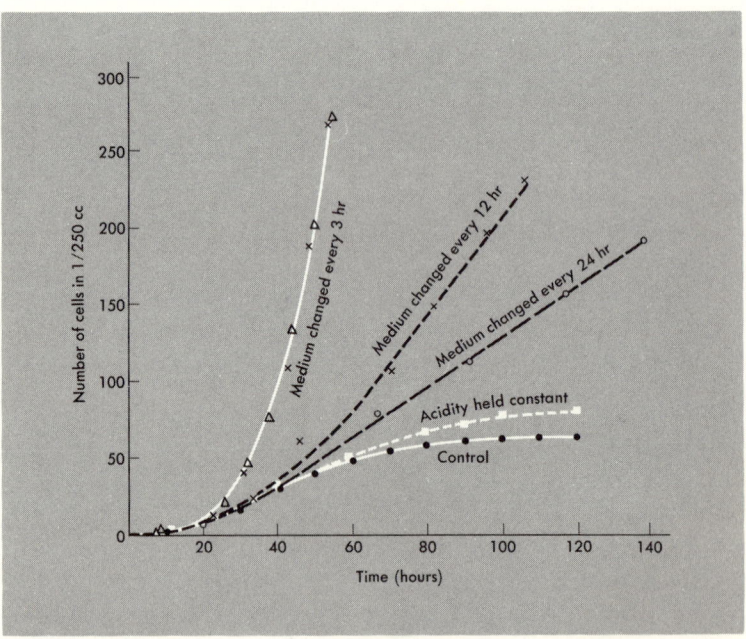

Redrawn, by permission, from O. W. Richards. 1928. Journal of General Physiology 11: 525–538.

Fig. 4-3. Growth curves of the yeast *Saccharomyces cerevisiae* with modifications of the medium.

ECOLOGY OF POPULATIONS

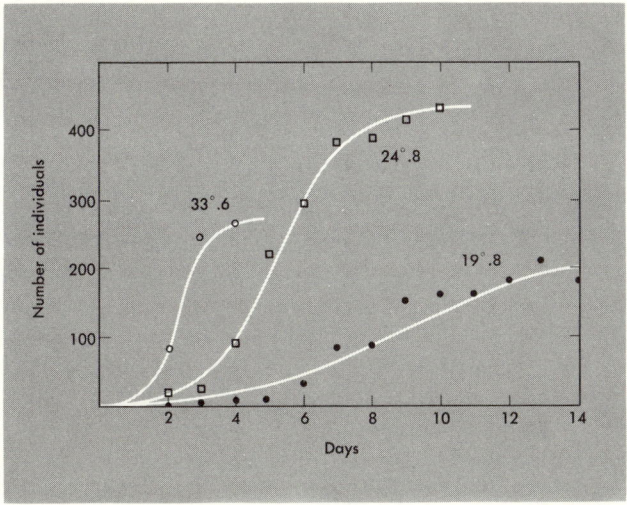

Redrawn, by permission, from A. Terao and T. Tanaka. 1928. *Proceedings of the Imperial Academy of Japan* 4: 550–552.

Fig. 4-4. Growth of the water flea, *Moina macrocopa*, at three different temperatures.

it was stated that there was no net change in population. New individuals are certainly being continually introduced by budding and others are just as certainly being continually lost through death—but these two forces, rate of birth, or *natality,* and rate of death, or *mortality,* are in balance in the equilibrium period. The population increased when they were out of balance, when natality exceeded mortality; it would decrease when mortality exceeded natality. Fundamentally then, natality tends to push the growth curve up and mortality to push it down. Characterization of these two fundamental opposing forces warrants further consideration. But before we do so, it is important to discuss the sigmoid growth curve a bit further. Of particular importance is the question of how generally it is exhibited in nature by populations of different species; after all, the curve presented here was generated by an asexually reproducing organism. Is it typical of populations in general? If it is a typical curve, then we need to see if it can be described in mathematical terms; that is, whether a model or paradigm can be constructed for it.

A good deal of information on population growth has been obtained; however, only relatively few species have been studied, and much of the data has been derived from laboratory study. Although they are difficult to come by, there are enough studies of species populations under natural conditions and enough studies on a spectrum of different kinds of plants and animals to permit the statement that most species show a sigmoidal pattern during the initial stages of their population growth. There is, in such cases, an initial slow rate of growth, in absolute numbers, followed by an increase in rate to a maximum, at which point the curve begins to be deflected downward; it terminates in a rate that gradually lessens to zero, as the population more or less stabilizes itself with respect to its environment.

In some cases, a population continues increasing at any accelerating rate and, instead of leveling off, precipitously decreases its rate to zero by a large die-off of the population; in such instances the growth curve has a J shape (Figure 4-5). J-shaped curves can be observed in the growth of annual plants which die off as the photoperiod changes or as frost arrives, in insect populations which have but one generation a year or which depend on an annual crop (Figure 4-16), and in a number of algae which undergo rapid and tremendous growth seasonally, a phenomenon referred to as a bloom, such as that shown in Figure 4-5 (also see Figure 3-6). In each of these instances there is essentially unrestricted, rapid, exponential growth up to the limits of the environment; as these limits are exhausted (nutrients) or imposed (photoperiod shift, frost, drought, toxic wastes, etc.), the population dies off. In the case of *Dinobryon,* a golden brown alga belonging to the Chrysophyta, Stankovic believes that *D. sociale* outcompetes *D. divergens* for environmental resources (Figure 4-5). In any event, as far as the latter species is concerned, when its environmental resources are exhausted, a rapid

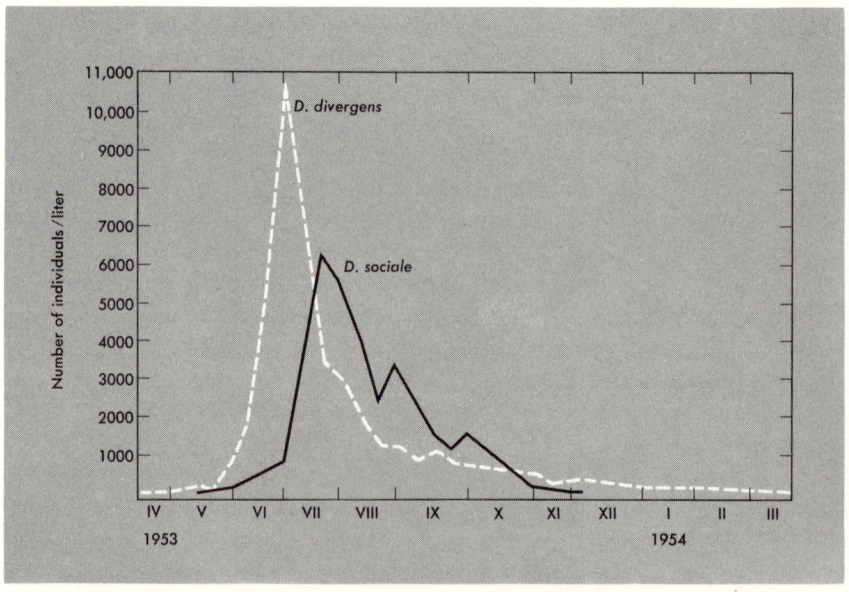

Modified, by permission, from S. Stankovic. 1960. Monographiae Biologicae 9: 1–357.

Fig. 4-5. J-shaped growth curves of two species of golden-brown algae, Dinobryon divergens and D. sociale.

ECOLOGY OF POPULATIONS

die-off occurs, effecting a J-shaped population curve which drops the population to an equilibrium level about one-twentieth of its maximum.

The "Law" of Population Growth

In 1838, the French mathematician P. F. Verhulst wrote:

> I have long tried to determine by analysis what the probable law of population is; but I have abandoned this kind of research because the data provided by observation are too few to permit verification of the formulae in such a way as to leave no doubt as to their exactness. However, since the path I have followed seems to me to lead to the discovery of the true law, once there is sufficient data, and since the results I have obtained may be of interest, at least as a matter for speculation, I felt myself obliged . . . to make them public.

What Verhulst then advanced was a differential equation that takes into account that the instantaneous rate of growth dN/dt in a limited environment is retarded by an increase in the number of inhabitants. A plot of the Verhulst equation yields a sigmoidal curve, which in mathematical lingo is termed a *logistic curve*. Verhulst then applied his mathematical formulation to available but very limited census data and observed a respectably good fit of this empirical data to the theoretical curve. Eighty years later and without knowledge of the Verhulst formulation, Raymond Pearl and Lowell J. Reed, both of The Johns Hopkins University, derived an equation yielding a logistic curve of population growth and applied it to census data of the United States (Figure 6-4). Pearl and Reed saw the function of mathematical representation as "obviously the best general method of estimating population in inter-censal years is that of fitting an appropriate curve to all the available data, and extrapolating for years beyond the last census. . . ." Owing to shifts in factors which were then not foreseeable, the curve generated by the Pearl and Reed logistic equation has missed the mark: the population of the United States reached the 200 million mark in November 1967, some 100 years prior to the date they projected in 1940.

Using the data of the housefly, let us develop the mathematical description of the population curve. In our earlier discussion, it was pointed out that each female housefly was capable of producing 120 eggs. Thus, the potential total number of offspring that could be produced by a population of fertilized female houseflies would be 120 times the number of females present N, or $120N$. The rate of change in the population dN/dt in any one generation would then be given by the equation $dN/dt = 120N$. If $N = 60$, then $dN/dt = 7200$ (see Table 4-1). Hence, the rate of change dN/dt is dependent both on the reproductive capacity or *biotic potential* of each individual, abbreviated *r* and in this case having the value 120, and the number of individuals *N* present at the time. We thus have the general expression for rate of growth at any instant as

$$\frac{dN}{dt} = rN.$$

This is an equation of geometric or exponential increase and would generate the growth pattern of the housefly (Table 4-1) as well as J-shaped population curves, such as that of the alga *Dinobryon* (Figure 4-5). Such populations continue to increase geometrically (1) if *r* remains a constant or changes only slightly, (2) if *N* continues to increase, and (3) if the environment is unlimited or kept nearly so, as in changing the yeast medium every three hours (Figure 4-3).

However, environments are limited to varying degrees and there is thus a maximum population *K* that can exist in a given ecosystem. The difference between the maximum and that already present would be expressed as $K - N$. As the population approaches the maximum, more "resistance" is encountered, since there are fewer unoccupied places in the system. This resistance effect can be expressed quantitatively as $K - N/K$. When *N* is small, the "resistance" value is nearly at unity, but as *N* increases and approximates *K*, the value of the expression comes nearer to zero. For example, if $K = 100$ and $N = 10$, the value of the expression is 0.9; however, if $K = 100$ and $N = 90$, the value of the expression is 0.1.

Since this resistance $(K - N/K)$ acts against the increase potential (rN) of the population, the product of the two would indicate what the rate of change in the population would be at any given time:

$$\frac{dN}{dt} = rN\left(\frac{K-N}{K}\right)$$

When *N* is small, this "resistance" value is, as shown above, nearly at unity and the biotic potential is essentially realized. But, as *N* gets larger and approximates *K*, the value of the expression approaches zero; since the value of *r* is assumed to be a constant, the increase in population size then becomes less and less and finally at carrying capacity, there is no net change.

The equation just presented is the differential or logistic equation that was derived by Verhulst and subsequently and independently by Pearl and Reed; when plotted it yields the logistic curve of sigmoid form. It would be too space-consuming to show that the logistic curve does indeed fit quite well to data on population growth of many species. For example, the data of the control culture of water fleas (Figure 4-4) and of yeast growth (Figure 4-1) fit a logistic curve almost perfectly. However, the ultimate value of the logistic expression is limited—it is not a complete nor the only description of population growth: in many populations it is not a good fit, and there are sigmoid curves other than the logistic which can be applied with as good a fit. In spite of these many limitations, there are a number of values, particularly regarding prediction, in having at least one generally applicable mathematical description of population growth.

Biotic Potential

Having established the two general patterns of initial population growth, the J- and S-shaped curves, we can turn to an analysis of the two major forces in the process, biotic potential, which pushes the curve upward, and environmental resistance, which pushes the curve downward. We have already noted that the increase potential of a population at any moment is dependent on both r, the reproductive potential of each individual, and N, the number of individuals present at the time, and expressed as $dN/dt = rN$. That is, the rate of change of the population is proportional to the number of reproducing units (e.g., females in sexually reproducing species). Under optimal conditions for the housefly, as we already have stated, r has the value 120—that is, each female can produce 120 eggs, and the actual change in the population is then determined by the number of females present (Table 4-1); the magnitude of each succeeding generation in that hypothetical population is based on the assumption that r is a constant. Under the variations of natural environment, however, the reproductive potential shows variation. For example, according to studies by the Australian ecologist L. C. Birch, a single female rice weevil (*Calandra oryzae*) produces 22.4 offspring/yr at 23°C, 30.6 offspring/yr at 29°C, and 6.2 offspring/yr at 33.5°C. A comparable situation is observed in the water flea (Figure 4-4), where the maximum reproductive potential is a temperature intermediate between 20 and 34°. Because of differential tolerance to and optima for the wide variety of physical and chemical factors in the environment, it is reasonable to expect that there will be different reproductive capacities under different environmental conditions. In fact, the value of r for a species has different and unique values for each set of physical conditions. Further, it is also the case that it varies with age of the individual, the age of onset of reproduction, and the length of life. Lastly, it also varies with density (Figure 4-23), generally declining with increased crowding (see discussion of crowding effects, p. 104).

If the reproductive capacity of a population is measured under optimal growth conditions, it is referred to as the *intrinsic rate of natural increase*, the r of the logistic equation. These optimal conditions include not only a physico-chemical environment in which population growth is maximum, but also absence of the effects of increasing density [the $(K - N/K)$ of the logistic curve]; that is, a population having a stable age distribution—where the relative numbers of young to adults is constant. With these limitations, let alone the difficulty of handling the calculations based on mortality statistics, it is little wonder that so little comparative information on this population parameter has been obtained. Francis Evans and Frederick Smith, of the University of Michigan, in a study reporting the value of r for the human louse (*Pediculus humanus*), also included the few available r values as well as the length of a generation for each of several species (Table 4-3). It can be seen that the intrinsic rate of natural increase, r, is almost eight times greater for insects than for rodents, but that among rodents and among insects, there is not much difference. Of considerable interest, however, is the apparent inverse relationships between r and generation time. To remain in the game, as it were, it appears that for a decreased value of r compensations have been achieved by natural selection in increased generation time. In a subsequent study, Smith not only reaffirmed the inverse relationship between r and generation time, but also between body size and r. That is, in general, the larger the animal, the smaller the value of r.

As already noted, there is no increase or decrease in a stabilized population—the rate of change is zero. Since the rate of change has been defined as $dN/dt = rN$ and this has the value of zero in a stable population, the value of r under these conditions must be zero, since N is a positive integer. Since this is the case, Evans and Smith suggest that r measured under natural conditions is a reflection of "the degree to which the natural environment departs from conditions most conducive to growth." That is, the value of

TABLE 4-3. Rates of Increase for Rodents and Insects

	Intrinsic Rate of Natural Increase (r/day)	Generation Time (average in days)	Net Reproduction Rate
Rodents			
English vole (*Microtus agrestis*)	0.0125	141.8	5.9
Norway rat (*Rattus norvegicus*)	0.0147	217.6	25.7
Insects			
Grain beetle (*Tribolium castaneum*)	0.101	55.6	275.0
Rice weevil (*Calandra oryzae*)	0.109	43.4	113.6
Human louse (*Pediculus humanis*)	0.111	30.9	30.9

Adapted, by permission, from F. C. Evans and F. E. Smith, 1952. *American Naturalist* 86: 299–310.

r must be at a level high enough to keep the population in existence. Hence, the larger the value of r, the more rigorous the environment can be assumed to be for the population. For this reason Smith has suggested that the larger value of r, which is typical of small organisms, indicates their environment to be more harsh than is that of large organisms; for example, a protozoan is more subject to diffusion as a factor in its existence than is an elephant.

There is yet one other aspect of reproductive potential that warrants mention—net reproductive rate. This can be defined as the number of female offspring that replace each female offspring of the previous generation. In our example of the housefly, the net reproductive rate would be 60; that is, each female offspring of one generation is expected to produce 120 offspring, of which 60 are female. We are assuming here, of course, that all 60 females survive and are capable of reproducing. It follows, then, that in a stabilized population not only would r be zero, but the net reproductive rate would be 1—each female being replaced by only one female. This should be self-evident, for if the net reproductive rate were 2, each female would be replaced by two, and hence the population would increase. Net reproductive rate then can also give an indication of environmental resistance. For example, according to their net reproductive rates (Table 4-3), rat replacement is five times that of mice; since their r values are so close, it must be the case that about five times as many rats fail to grow to maturity; the life insurance of the Norway rat seems to be by expending life through relatively high mortality. By the same token, the considerably lower net reproductive rate of the human louse as compared to the grain and rice weevils suggests, as Evans and Smith state, "that its natural environment is remarkably secure. . . .[this] is indeed surprising, for a high rate is usually associated with a parasitic mode of life."

Death Rates in Populations

In the preceding paragraph we noted that in view of the difference in their net reproductive rates, there is a difference in amount of death between rats and mice, and between weevils and lice. Since the rate of increase in a population is effectively the difference between birth rate and death rate at any given time, we need now to turn our attention to mortality, or, if you prefer, survival.

The impetus to formulate "laws" of mortality commensurate with those of population growth also came from Raymond Pearl. Analyzing the few existing data that had been collected by others, and accumulating a good many in his own laboratory, Pearl and his students initiated the preparation of life tables for organisms other than man. These were patterned after the actuarial tables used to determine insurance rates for man. Because of the interests of actuaries and other enterprises in the life expectancy and survivorship of man, the development and preparation of life tables had attained considerable sophistication by the 1920's. Although Pearl introduced the life table as a way of assessing another parameter of natural populations in 1921, ecologists were slow to analyze survivorship data in such a fashion as to enable the development of generalizations on mortality. Dr. Edward S. Deevey, Jr. prodded fellow ecologists with a major review of the problem in 1947 with particular emphasis on the life table as a means of conveying survivorship information. Although one cannot complain of a plethora of survivorship data, they have been accumulating. Except for laboratory populations, or natural populations essentially under laboratory-type control, data on survival of natural populations are often indirectly assessed. Survivorship in birds and many other animals is usually done by banding-releasing-recapture methods. Needless to say, such a procedure gives less reliable data than a controlled population in a laboratory culture dish, but statistical reliability is possible by appropriate handling of the data.

To construct a life table, or even to take the space here to introduce it in sufficient detail would be beyond the purpose of the chapter. What we can do, however, is to present graphically one portion of the life table, which is basically a table of probabilities dealing with the rate of death and expectation of life at various time intervals over an organism's life span. The portion with which we shall deal is the expected or probable number of survivors in a population at various age intervals when the initial population is 1000 individuals—data which, when plotted, yield survivorship curves.

Survivorship curves for selected natural and laboratory populations are shown in Figure 4-6. To obviate the confusion that would result from setting the horizontal coordinate to the actual life span of various organisms, which may extend from days to years, life span is expressed as a percentage of the total. The vertical coordinate is logarithmic because of the built-in convenience that a straight line in the graph indicates a constant rate with respect to the horizontal coordinate, in this case, age. The number of survivors, out of an initial population of 1000, at any particular time (percentage) of the life span, can be read directly from the graph. Thus, in the case of the rotifer (Figure 4-6, Group A), about 920 individuals are still alive at the mid-point of the lifespan, but only about 440 individuals are alive at the three-quarter mark.

With the wide variety of life phenomena, one would expect—and, indeed, one observes—a considerable variety of survivorship patterns extending from those with low mortality (high survivorship) throughout most of the life span through to those with high initial mortality (low survivorship). Populations of the rotifer (*Proales*), man, and mountain sheep have a relatively low mortality until well past middle age, after which the death rate increases markedly, and in the case of the rotifer, almost precipitously. In passing, it should be noted that a curve almost identical to that of the

ECOLOGY OF POPULATIONS

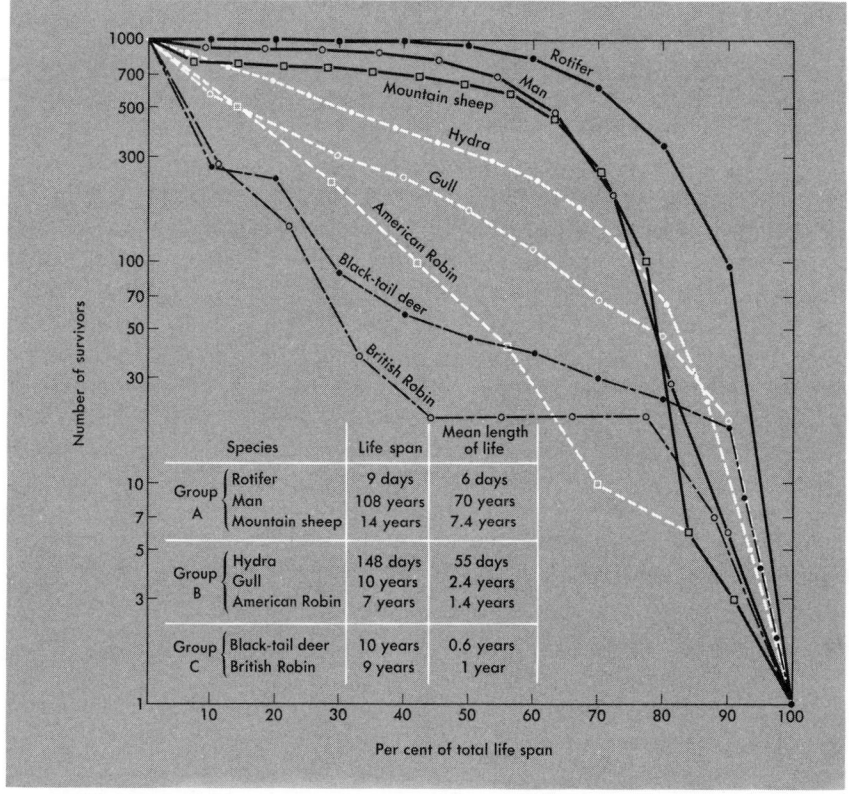

Group A. Rotifer data of B. Noyes. 1922. Journal of Experimental Zoology 35: 225 reinterpreted by R. Pearl and C. R. Doering. 1923. Science 57: 209–212; man data from L. I. Dublin, A. J. Lotka and M. Spiegelman. 1949. Length of Life. New York: Ronald Press; sheep data from E. S. Deevey. 1947. Quarterly Review of Biology 22: 282–314. Group B. Hydra data from R. Pearl and J. N. Miner. 1935. Quarterly Review of Biology 10: 60–79; gull and robin data from E. S. Deevey, op. cit. Group C. Deer data from R. D. Taber and R. F. Dasmann. 1957. Ecology 38: 233–246; robin data from E. S. Deevey, op. cit.

Fig. 4-6. Survivorship curves for laboratory and natural populations; the vertical coordinate is a logarithmic scale. Group A. Laboratory population of the rotifer *Proales decipiens*, and neutral populations of white males, 1939–1941, and of the Dall mountain sheep, *Ovis d. dalli*. Group B. Laboratory population of *Hydra fusca* and natural populations of the gull, *Larus argentatus*, and the American robin, *Turdus m. migratorius*. Group C. Natural population of the Black-tailed deer, *Odocoileus hemionus columbianus* in managed open shrubland at high density of 86 deer/sq mi and natural population of the British robin, *Erithacus rubecula melophilus*.

rotifer can be generated by transferring pupae of the fruit fly (*Drosophila*) to culture bottles lacking food. Under these conditions they survive for only about 70 hours, but most of the population survives for some 70 per cent of those hours. In populations showing the rotifer-man-mountain sheep survivorship pattern, a given individual has a relatively long life expectancy at birth, and even for an individual at about one-third of the life span, the probability of living to a ripe old age is quite good. Another way of considering this type of survivorship is that the mean duration of life, or, as it is often called, mean life expectancy, the point at which one-half the population is still surviving, is much closer to the maximum duration of life (see tabulation in Figure 4-6, Group A). It is of interest to note that what man has been able to achieve through medical and environmental modification, particularly within the last century, is a shift of mean life expectancy closer to the maximum. At the time of the golden age of Greece, for example, life expectancy at birth was only about 30 years; by 1900, it had increased to 45 to 50 years, and at present it is about 70 years. How close to the physiological limit of 100 to 110 years man will be able to push mean life expectancy is intriguing both in the challenge of its possibility and in the concomitant problems of housing, feeding, and attending to the needs of a larger component of older persons.

The next cluster of survivorship curves is represented by the laboratory population of *Hydra* and the natural populations of the gull and American robin. In these populations there is a more or less constant rate of death throughout life (robin) or at all ages until near the end of the life span (*Hydra* and gull). In the case of *Hydra* and the gull, the rate is quite constant from birth through nearly three-fourths of the life span. For a given individual in populations of this sort, there is considerably less chance of survival to old age at, say, the mid-point of the life span, than for individuals in the rotifer-man-mountain sheep type of population. Also characteristic of this cluster of curves is the fact that the mean duration of life is about one-third (*Hydra*, gull) or somewhat less (robin) of the total life span. If those starved fruit flies mentioned above were permitted to feed, their survivorship curve would be intermediate between that of *Hydra* and the mountain sheep.

The third group of curves, represented by the black-tail deer and British robin, is one in which there is a high mortality at the beginning of the life span. Three-fourths of the initial population of the black-tail deer and of the British robin die off within the first 10 per cent of the life span. In both these populations, the death rate does not alter markedly during almost the first half of the life span. Given individuals in populations of this type have a low life expectancy at birth, the mean duration of life being in the order of one-fifteenth of the life span. In 1935, Dr. Pearl suggested that survivorship in India produced this type of curve. Curves with even a more extreme deflection towards the lower left quadrant would be expected in profligate groups like teleost fish and many molluscs, especially the open ocean species, and most annual plants, especially when one considers trees with a long life span and prolific seed production.

These selected examples indicate that more or less distinct patterns of mortality not only exist in nature but that they are species-specific—that is, as characteristic of a species as its birth rate, behavior, anatomy, and physiology. Not only is mortality species-specific, it also appears to be sex-specific within a species (Figure 4-7). And woe to the ego of the male,

ECOLOGY OF POPULATIONS

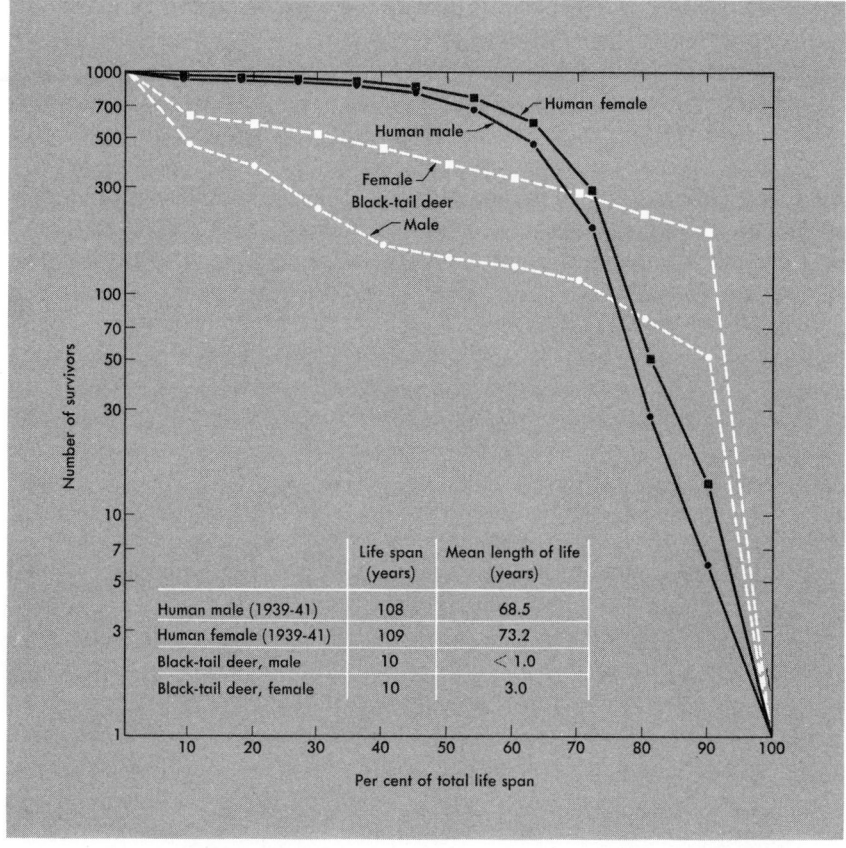

Data on white males and females, 1939–1941, from L. I. Dublin, A. J. Lotka and M. Spiegelman. 1949. Length of Life. New York: Ronald Press; data on deer in unmanaged chapparal at low density of 27 deer/sq. mi. from R. D. Taber and R. F. Dasmann. 1957. Ecology 38: 233–246–cf. Figure 4-6 Group C.

Fig. 4-7. Differences in survivorship based on sex; quite universally, the male of the species has a higher mortality throughout the life span.

for females have the edge in both lessened mortality and a higher mean duration of life, not only in humans but in a number of other species as well. In the case of the black-tail deer of California, Taber and Dasmann, whose study serves as basis for the graph, suggest that the higher mortality of males is related to their higher metabolic rate and nutrient requirement. Especially at two years of age, but also beyond, the male is more subject to predation (hunting) than the female. For the female, the constant rate of death over virtually the entire lifetime is doubtless related to the strains of reproduction. In humans, the evidence on mortality suggests that, in addition to the greater exposure of men to occupational and other environmental hazards, there is an inherent biological difference that favors a higher mortality in men. From birth on, and even during the intrauterine period,

ECOLOGY OF POPULATIONS

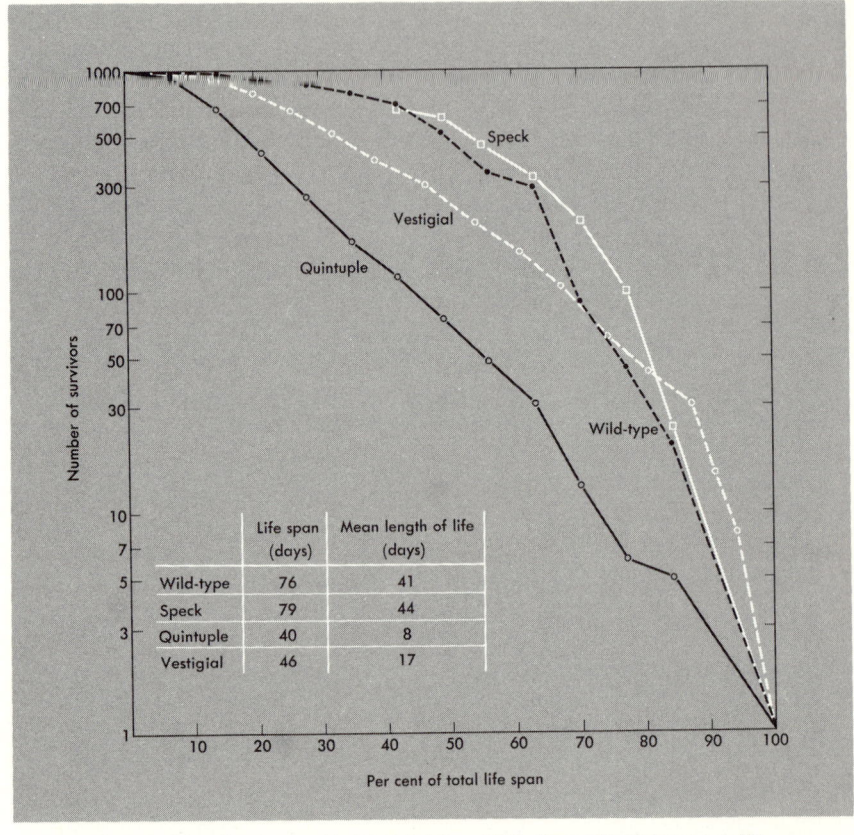

Based on data of Gonzalez reinterpreted by F. S. Bodenheimer. 1958. Monographiae Biologicae 6: 1-276.

Fig. 4-8. Differences in survivorship of genetic mutants of the fruit fly, *Drosophila melanogaster*.

the ratio of male mortality to that of the female is always in excess of 1. According to studies by Dublin, Plotka, and Spiegelman, the ratio peaks twice: at about age 15, it is about 1.49:1; after this it declines to a low of 1.27 at age 30, and then it rises again, reaching its maximum of about 1.54 at about age 55.

That intraspecific differences other than sex also affect species-specific mortality has also been shown. Doctor F. S. Bodenheimer, of the Hebrew University of Jerusalem, who maintained a long, active research interest in problems of animal populations, prepared life table data on mutants of *Drosophila* from raw data collected by Gonzales; these data are presented as survivorship curves in Figure 4-8. The wild, or natural, population (nonstarved) has, as already indicated, a survivorship curve intermediate between the rotifer-man-mountain sheep type and that of hydra-gull-

ECOLOGY OF POPULATIONS

American robin. Survivorship in the vestigial-winged form is of the hydra-gull-American robin type, a constant rate of death at all ages and with a life expectancy about half that of the wild type. Although a natural population is generally assumed to be the best adapted because of the operation of natural selection processes, it is of interest to note that the mutant known as speck conveys a lesser mortality, particularly in the latter half of life. Perhaps in nature, such lessened mortality in the middle of old age in fruit flies is not so critical and hence not particularly advantageous or disadvantageous. Exemplary of the more untoward consequences generally attributed to mutation, the mutant quintuple not only has the highest mortality rate (and one that is constant throughout life—it is virtually identical to that of the American robin, Figure 4-6b), it has the shortest life span and a life expectancy one-fifth that of the wild type.

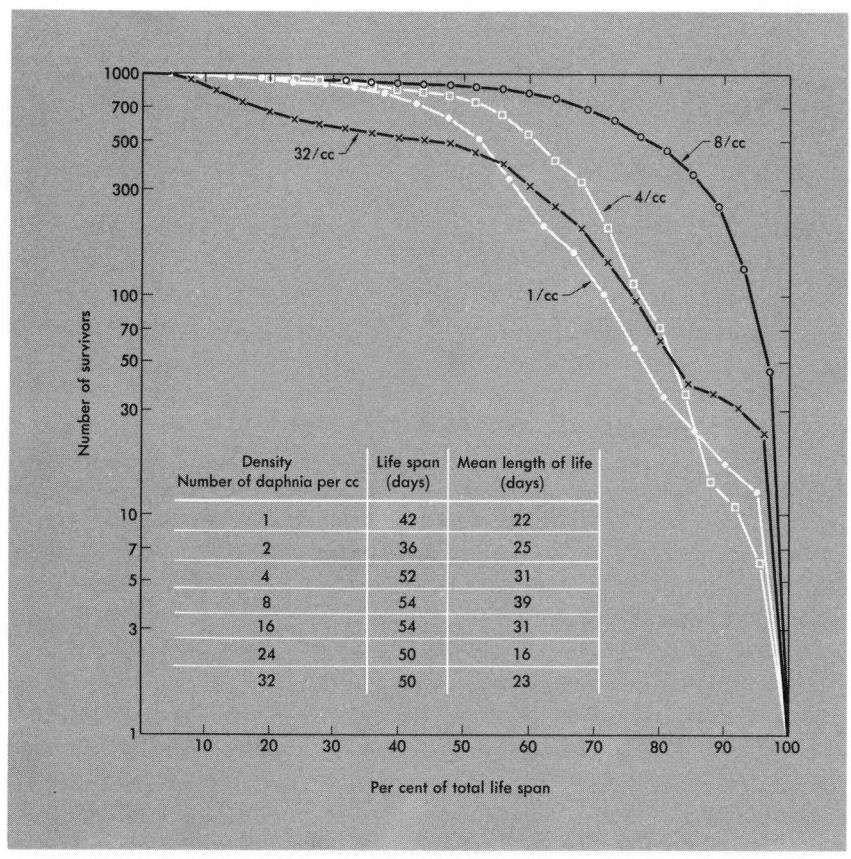

Redrawn, by permission, from P. W. Frank, C. D. Boll and R. W. Kelly. 1957; Physiological Zoology 30: 287–305.

Fig. 4-9. Differences in survivorship as a function of initial density.

Death is, of course, a natural biological event, as natural as birth. As such, its occurrence in any given individual or in a population is subject to the vagaries of the milieu of the individual or population—it can be modified by environmental factors, as we have already observed for birth rate. The survivorship curves of black-tail deer shown in Figures 4-6b and 4-7 is of the same species (*Odocoileus hemionus columbianus*), but the populations represented in each graph are from different habitats and have different densities. The deer population of Figure 4-6b occurred in an open shrubland maintained by fire and that of Figure 4-7 in a well-vegetated chapparal. The shrubland population was more than two and one-half times as dense as the chapparal population, 84 compared to 33 deer per square mile in July. The higher mortality of the shrubland population is partly owing to greater success of predation, since there is less cover for deer; interestingly, this is compensated by a reproductive rate that is more than twice that of the chapparal population. The effect of density on mortality has also been shown for laboratory populations; for example, Peter Frank and his colleagues demonstrated that the optimum density for mortality rate, maximum length of life, and mean life expectancy in the water flea, *Daphnia pulex*, was at an initial density equivalent to eight individuals per cubic centimeter (Figure 4-9). Densities above and below this level were tolerable but not as advantageous in regard to these parameters of population growth.

Age Structure

The preceding analysis of death rate or survivorship may have suggested to you the substantial difference that may exist in the relative proportion of young, middle-aged, and older individuals in a population. A quick look at the various figures on mortality should indicate that if the various populations had continuous input at the left side of the graph, characteristic distributions of different age classes should be one of the results. For example, in those groups in which life expectancy approaches the maximum span of life (rotifer-man-mountain sheep), a greater proportion of the population would be in the older age group than would be true of the hydra-gull-American robin type. However, if the population were modified by shifts in input (natality, immigration) and output (mortality, emigration), the age structure would be expected to shift. These various interrelationships of age structure in populations can indeed become quite complex, but they warrant at least a brief consideration.

From an ecological view, there are three major age groups in a population: prereproductive, reproductive, and postreproductive. These categories, proposed by Bodenheimer, have considerable value in visualizing the status of a population (Figure 4-10). In a rapidly growing population (Figure

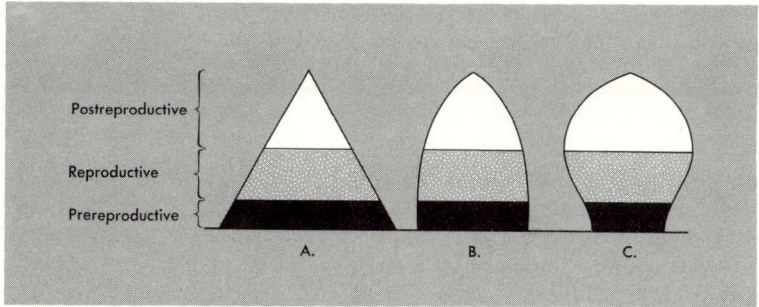

Adapted, by permission, from A. S. Bodenheimer. 1958. *Monographiae Biologicae* 6: 1–276.

Fig. 4-10. Age structure in different types of populations: A. expanding population; B. stable population; C. diminishing population.

4-10a), birth rate is high and population growth may be exponential, as in the case of the housefly, yeast, and paramecium considered previously. Under these conditions each successive generation will be more numerous than the preceding one, and, as a result, a pyramid age structure results. A ready visualization of this effect can be seen by examination of Table 4-1 on the housefly; if the data were plotted as successive layers in bar graph style, a pyramidal structure would result—120 individuals would constitute the oldest group in the population at the top of the pyramid, the base being constituted by some 5.6 trillion very young individuals. As the rate of growth slows and stabilizes (i.e., where r approaches zero and the net reproductive rate approaches unity), the prereproductive and reproductive age groups become more or less equal in size; the postreproductive group remains as the smallest. The graphic representation of this stabilized population is that of a bell (Figure 4-10b). If the birth rate is drastically reduced, the reproductive and postreproductive groups would increase in proportion to the prereproductive, resulting in an urn-shaped age structure (Figure 4-10c) representative of a population that is dying off. In a study of a hive of honey bees, where a seasonal trend in the population takes place, Bodenheimer observed these shifts in age structure (Figure 4-11). There is a change from a rapidly growing population, the triangular shape in January, to a stable population, represented by the bell shape in March, and a progressive dying-off represented by a series of urn shapes from July through November.

The relative proportion of the life cycle that is occupied by each of the "ecological ages" differs from species to species. In man, for example, the prereproductive period (birth to about age 15) occupies about 21 per cent of the mean life expectancy of 70 years, the reproductive, ages 15 to 45, about 42 per cent, and the postreproductive, 37 per cent. In the rat these proportions are about 25, 20, and 55 per cent, respectively. By contrast with these relatively short prereproductive stages many, but by no means all,

ECOLOGY OF POPULATIONS

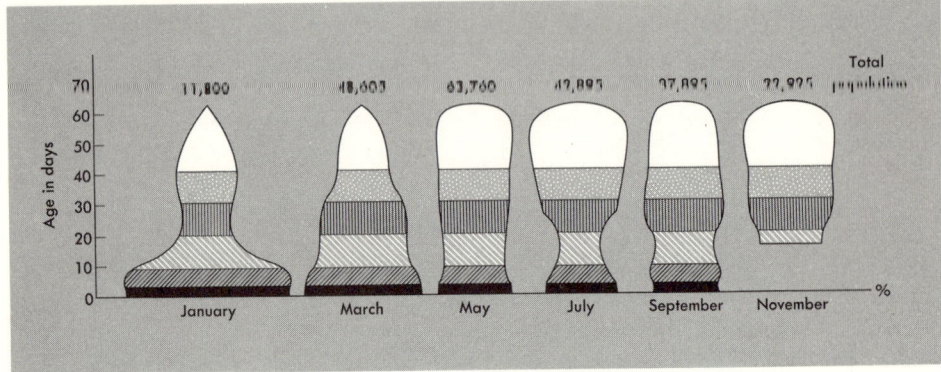

Redrawn, by permission, from F. S. Bodenheimer. 1958. Monographiae Biologicae 6: 1–276.

Fig. 4-11. Changes in age structure in a hive of honey bees over one season.

insects spend well more than half their life cycle in that stage. Some dragonflies spend two years in the egg and larval stages and survive barely four weeks as an adult, being capable of reproduction for as little as only one or two days of that brief span. Many birds and mammals have a very short, if any, postreproductive period. For example, the chapparal black-tail deer is capable of reproduction up until death at an age of 10 years. Since the one-year-olds are not reproductive, the age structure in that population is a diminishing one with a peculiar urn shape: about 42 per cent of the population is in the prereproductive category (age 0–1), and 58 per cent is in the reproductive segment, with about 29 per cent in the age group 1–3 and 29 per cent in age group 3–10. In their study of the human louse, which was discussed above, Evans and Smith determined the stable age distribution to consist of 5.69 per cent adults, 26.43 per cent larvae, and 67.88 per cent eggs. They indicate that similar results were obtained for the grain beetle and rice weevil.

The age structure of a population may differ geographically as a result of differential densities as in the case of the two deer populations (Figures 4-6c and 4-7), or as an effect of a difference in an abiotic regulatory factor. For example, the life history of the dragonfly *Tetragoneuria cynosura* is so regulated by temperature that two years are required to complete development in southern Michigan but only one year in Florida. Peculiarly, however, in North Carolina, 90 to 95 per cent of the population can complete their development in one year; the remaining 5 to 10 per cent of the population requires two years. At any given time of the year, the age structure in each of these populations is presumably stable but is very different. For example, in late April, the Michigan population would consist of a group of two-year-old larvae about to transform to adults and a somewhat larger population of one-year-old larvae. The Florida population would consist only of one-year-old larvae about to transform to adults. The

ECOLOGY OF POPULATIONS

North Carolina population would consist of two chronological but three physiological age groups: about 90 per cent of one-year larvae about to transform to adults, about 10 per cent of one-year larvae that will carry over until the following year, and many fewer two-year larvae, the 10 per cent carried over from the previous year, now about to transform to adulthood.

Age structure of human populations in the major areas of the world, as of 1960, are shown in Figure 4-12. By their bell shape it can be easily

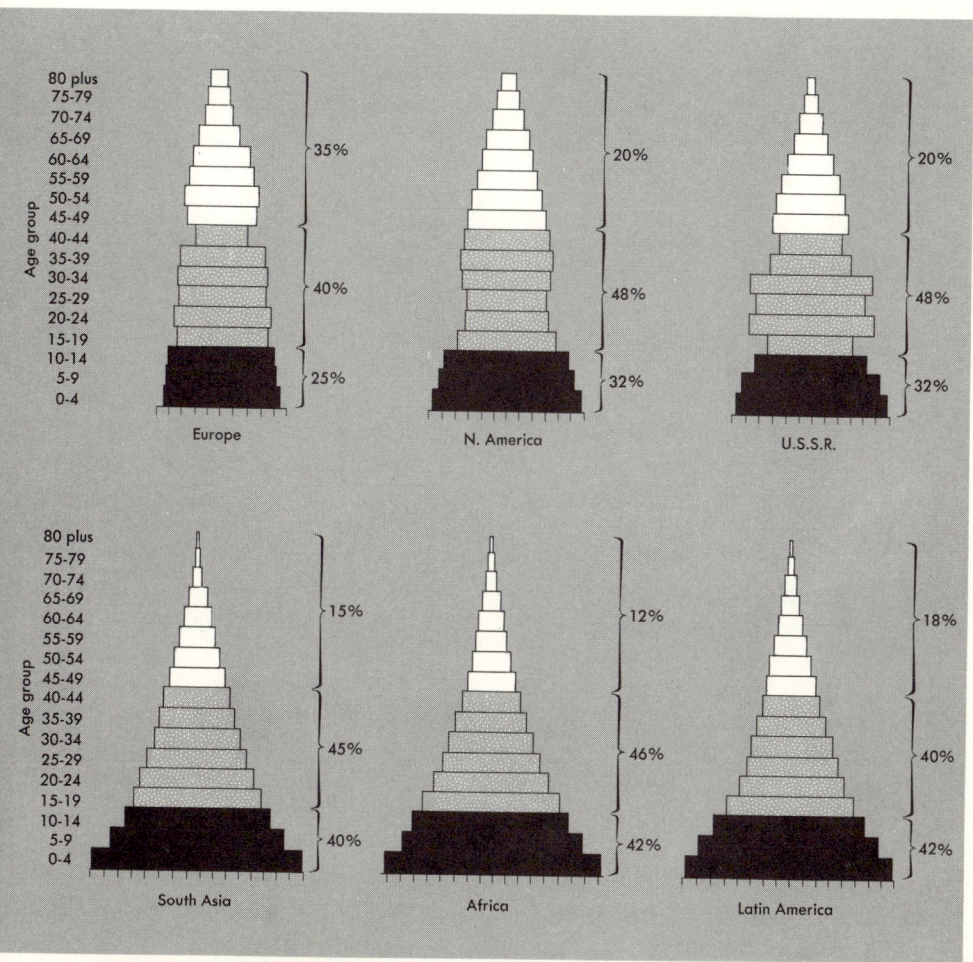

Adapted, by permission, from Population Bulletin Volume 21, Number 4, October, 1965, published by Population Reference Bureau, Inc., Washington, D. C.

Fig. 4-12. Age structure in human populations in the major areas of the world. Each segment in the horizontal scale represents one per cent; black bars are the prereproductive groups, stippled bars the reproductive group, and clear bars the postreproductive groups.

seen that the populations of Europe, North America, and the Union of Soviet Socialist Republics are relatively stabilized by comparison with the wide based triangles of the rapidly growing populations of South Asia, Africa, and Latin America. Among the significant revelations of these age structures is that the proportion of the population in the reproductive age is not strikingly different among the six populations (40 to 48 per cent), but the proportion of prereproductives to postreproductives is; especially noteworthy in this connection is the extremely small proportion of older persons in Africa. In these rapidly developing countries, traditionally high birth rates are now being combined with a quite drastically reduced and rapidly decelerating infant mortality; this results in extremely high proportions of younger persons. As medical advances abate the high mortality in the older age groups and contraception and family planning become more widely practiced, these pyramidal forms should tend toward a bell shape.

Some years ago the biometrician A. J. Lotka advanced mathematical support for his contention that age distribution in any population is variable only within certain limits and that, subsequent to its being disrupted, the population will return to its previous and characteristic type of stable age distribution. The particular age distribution is, of course, not unrelated to the remaining components of the ecosystem. What Lotka has indicated is that only if environmental conditions are restored will a disrupted and peculiar age distribution reinstate itself. Under a more or less permanently altered environment, the stable age structure that develops would likely be different from the previous one. Without exploring the mathematics from which this principle is deduced, it follows from the facts that the stable age distribution is dependent on the value of r (and can be calculated if the value of r is known), and, as we have pointed out, there is a unique value of r for each species for each set of physical conditions. Thus, altering conditions alters r, which, in turn, alters age structure; when conditions are returned to their previous state, r returns to its previous level and so does age structure.

THE "EQUILIBRIUM LEVEL" OF POPULATIONS

Having considered the initial stages of population growth and some aspects and interdependences of natality, mortality, and age structure, we must now give attention to populations as they come to the equilibrium level implicit in the logistic curve. Equilibrium in population considerations, as in perhaps all biological phenomena, does not imply the constancy of the physical scientist but rather a dynamic state of fluctuation around a mean. In some natural populations, the amount of fluctuation is minimal, as in the classic case when sheep were introduced into Tasmania (Figure 4-13). In other populations, the amount of departure from the "equilibrium

ECOLOGY OF POPULATIONS

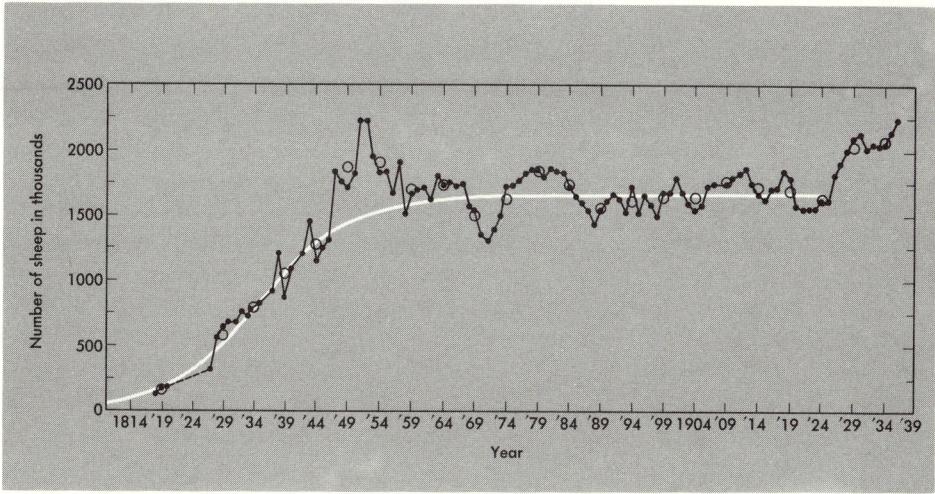

Redrawn, by permission, from J. Davidson. 1938. Transactions of the Royal Society of South Australia 62: 342–346.

Fig. 4-13. The growth curve of sheep subsequent to their introduction in Tasmania showing an initial sigmoidal pattern followed by semi-equilibrium.

level" is greater and either irregular, as in the case of water fleas in the laboratory (Figure 4-14), or rather regular, as in the blow fly in the laboratory (Figure 4-15). In yet other populations, such as the alga *Dinobryon* (Figure 4-5) and the rose thrips (Figure 4-16), the adult population nearly or actually dies out without showing any tendency to equilibrium. Certainly the large

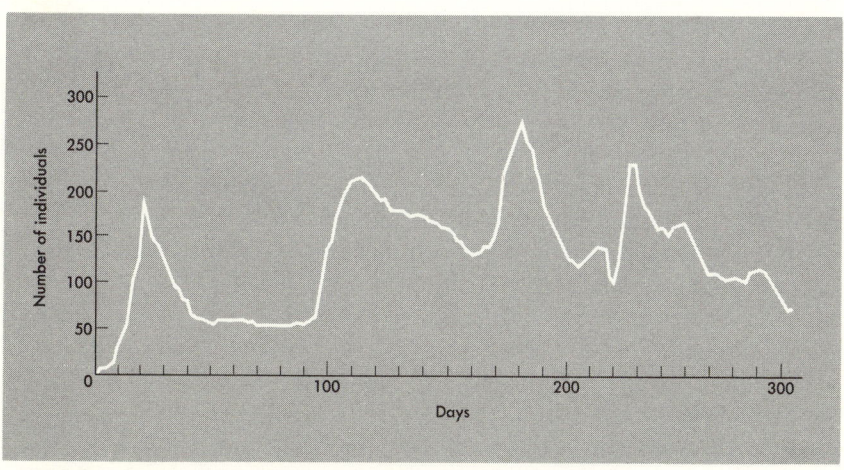

Redrawn, by permission, from L. Slobodkin. 1954. Ecological Monographs 24: 69–88.

Fig. 4-14. The growth curve of the water flea, *Daphnia obtusa*, in the laboratory, showing an initial J-shaped curve followed by irregular fluctuations.

ECOLOGY OF POPULATIONS

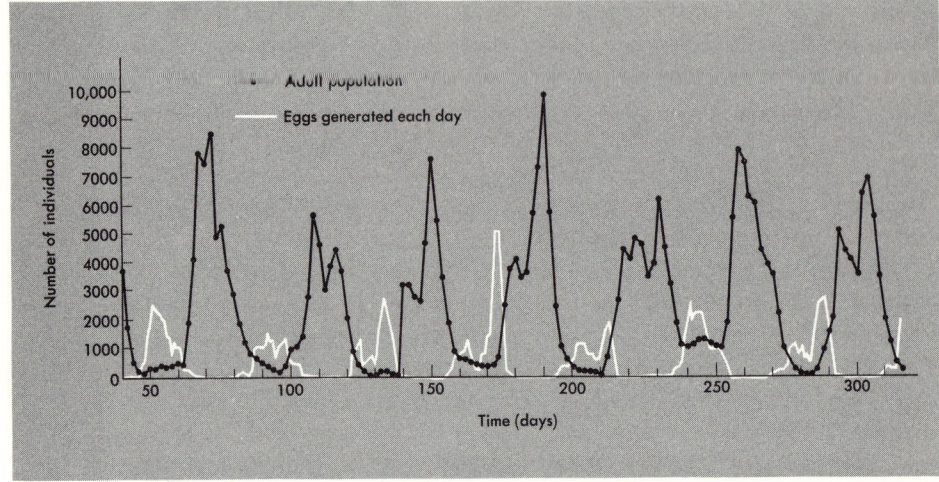

Redrawn, by permission, from A. J. Nicholson. 1955. Australian Journal of Zoology 2: 9–65.

Fig. 4-15. The growth curve of the blowfly, *Lucilia cuprina*, in the laboratory, showing an initial J-shaped curve followed by rather regular fluctuations.

fluctuations in the blow fly (Figure 4-15) come close to extinction, but there are a sufficient number of young introduced to maintain the population. In still other populations, there is a quite regular oscillation around the mean with or without the near extinction exemplified by the blow flies; certain predator-prey interactions (Figures 4-17c and 4-18) show such oscillations; lemmings, meadow voles, and snowy owls show a 3- to 5-year oscillation, and ruffed grouse, ptarmigan, muskrat, snowshoe rabbit, and lynx a 9- to 10-year oscillation.

In spite of the sharp differences in growth patterns typified by the post-initial growth phase or "equilibrium levels" of sheep, water fleas, blow flies, and lemmings, there seems to be an inherent ability of populations to maintain themselves or to be so regulated as to be maintained. It has already been shown that two major factors of a population's growth pattern, natality and mortality, are subject to both abiotic (Figure 4-4) and biotic (Figure 4-9) environmental influences. A more systematic consideration of the role played by these components of ecosystems in effecting population size and distribution is now in order.

The Influence of Abiotic Factors on
Population Size and Distribution

In the earlier discussion of mineral cycling, it was noted in a general way that the supply and/or availability of particular nutrients can be a major limiting factor in an ecosystem. As particular examples of this phenomenon at the population level, we will consider the regulatory effect of sodium on the density and distribution of meadow voles and of phosphorus on the density and distribution of woodland herbs.

An analysis of published records of the meadow vole (*Microtus pennsylvanicus*) (Table 4-4) by G. D. Aumann and J. T. Emlen showed a substantial correlation between the level of sodium in the soil and population density. This relationship prompted a set of experiments to test the effect of restricted and unrestricted sodium chloride diets on reproduction and population growth of a laboratory colony of voles established from a natural population. Experimental animals were offered distilled water and either unrestricted or restricted amounts of a 0.5 per cent sodium chloride solution, both in standard water bottles; control animals had access only to distilled water. Among the major findings of the study were the following: (1) experimental animals on an unrestricted sodium diet and in ratios of either 2♂:2♀ or 1♂:3♀ produced, respectively, 48 and 63 per cent more young than the controls and maintained a significantly higher net population during the test period of 15 to 19 weeks; (2) high-density populations selected more salt solution than populations at one-fourth the density, the salt preference being higher in females than in males; (3) as density was increased sixfold and then decreased to the original density, the ratio of selection of salt solution to water correspondingly rose from 2:1 to 10:1 and dropped back to 4:1.

The investigators suggest that the higher selection of sodium solution under crowding conditions was caused by a sodium deficiency in the animals perhaps resulting from inadequate adrenocortical regulation of sodium metabolism under the stress conditions of high density. Later in this chapter we will consider some further evidence on adrenal interaction in population regulation. From their experimental work and with consideration of the field data, Aumann and Emlen conclude that sodium is the critical factor limiting the population of meadow voles in many areas. Low soil-sodium

TABLE 4-4. Relationship of Sodium Level in Soil and Population Density in Meadow Voles (*Microtus pennsylvanicus*)

Sodium Level	Highest Density Reported (Number/acre)	Number and Percentage of Reports of More Than 30 Individuals Per Acre
Low	230	$\frac{12}{63}$ or 19%
Medium	400	$\frac{16}{22}$ or 72%
High	1000+	$\frac{30}{33}$ or 91%

Data from G. D. Aumann and J. T. Emlen, 1965. Nature 208: 198–199.

levels would tend to restrict population growth by physiological (adrenocortical) responses associated with crowding; high soil-sodium levels would tend to unleash population growth to the limits imposed by some other factor.

Until quite recently it was generally believed that the distribution of nettle, *Urtica dioica,* was controlled primarily by the supply of nitrogen. By the use of incubation techniques, it had been shown that nettle occurred in soils with a high intensity of nitrification as well as with high concentrations of other plant nutrients. Recently, two British ecologists, C. D. Pigott and K. Taylor, showed that midsummer nitrogen and phosphorus levels in the aerial shoots of *Urtica* are about three times greater than in another broad-leaved, herbaceous perennial (*Mercurialis perennis*) that is commonly associated with it. Pigott and Taylor found little difference in the amount of either total or inorganic nitrogen in soils directly associated with each of these two perennials, but, as a reminder of a major principle developed in Chapter 3, the amount available says little if anything about the rate of turnover of a nutrient. Under greenhouse conditions, additions of nitrogen as nitrate to various soils resulted in no greater growth of nettle, and in a few instances produced a reduction; addition of phosphate, with or without nitrogen, resulted in a 15- to 42-fold increase in growth on all soils. No significant growth response was obtained when other essential nutrients were used in the absence of phosphate.

Investigations on other herbs associated with nettle indicated that it was the most sensitive to phosphate deficiency, and, as might be anticipated, field experiments showed that there was a highly significant interaction between phosphate concentration and light intensity (Table 4-5). From these results, Pigott and Taylor concluded that, except in deep shade: (1) the failure of nettle to become established, and hence, a direct agent in its distribution, is attributable to a low supply of available phosphorus, and (2) the growth of the population is regulated by the amount of phosphorus available.

Chemical interaction in regulating population growth and distribution

TABLE 4-5. Interaction of Light Intensity and Phosphate Supplement on the Growth of Nettle, *Urtica dioica*, in the Field Between April 8 and September 1. (Data in Milligrams of Dry Weight, mean ± Standard Error.)

	No Phosphate Added	5 g/m^2 Phosphate Added
Low light intensity	2.0 ± 0.2	10.5 ± 1.1
High light intensity	15.2 ± 2.5	177.7 ± 24.0

Modified, by permission, from C. D. Pigott and K. Taylor, 1964. Journal of Ecology 52 (Suppl.): 175–185.

is certainly evident in meadow voles and nettle. Of the physical parameters of the abiotic environment, the incidence and quality of light has obvious effects, particularly on autotrophs; the quantitative effect on nettle, for example, was shown in Table 4-5, and the seasonal effects were discussed in Chapter 2. Catastrophic weather events, such as hurricanes, tornados, and those precipitation deluges that result in flooding, likewise can severely decimate or entirely eliminate populations within the area affected; this seems scarcely to be regulatory in an equilibrium-oriented sense, however. Less drastically, periodic weather events associated with seasonal progression and involving changes in temperature and moisture may effectively regulate some populations. This would be particularly true for populations that are dependent on yet other populations attuned to those periodicities—for example, an insect population that feeds on a plant whose growth is subject to seasonal changes. A well-analyzed instance of this sort, observed by J. Davidson and H. G. Andrewartha, involves thrips (*Thrips imaginis*) and roses in South Australia (Figure 4-16).

The number of adult thrips on roses is low at the beginning of spring (September in the Southern Hemisphere); the period of increase to maximum size, about December 1, occurs over several months, but the decline is rather precipitous, producing essentially a J-shaped growth curve. There has been annual variation in the maximum size of the population, but the pattern was virtually identical over a seven-year study period. This population pattern of the thrips parallels the pattern of flowering in the roses on which the thrips feed: during the dry summer, few flowers are available, but in spring they are abundant. The few available but scattered rose flowers in the summer provide food and moisture for those thrips which then become the progenitors of the spring population. Breeding and development of this tiny insect is continuous throughout the year, but birth rate and survival rate are very low during both midsummer and midwinter. Eggs imbedded in the tissues of the flower are relatively safe from desiccation during the summer, as are those nymphs and adults fortunate enough to be resident on living plants. The immobile pupa, however, is subject to desiccation and is the group showing highest mortality during the dry summer. In contrast, the nymphal stages are more subject to mortality during the cold winter months, when flowers do not last long enough for them to complete their development.

Thus, during the spring there is not only an abundance of food, it is also readily accessible—the population increases; during summer, there are fewer flowers, which tend to be more widely scattered, and the thrips have more difficulty finding food—the population diminishes. But those thrips which do find flowers have a high survival potential; there is no absolute shortage of food for them. From these and other studies, Davidson and Andrewartha and their colleague L. C. Birch contend that abundance and distribution of thrips is related to the seasonal change in availability as well

ECOLOGY OF POPULATIONS

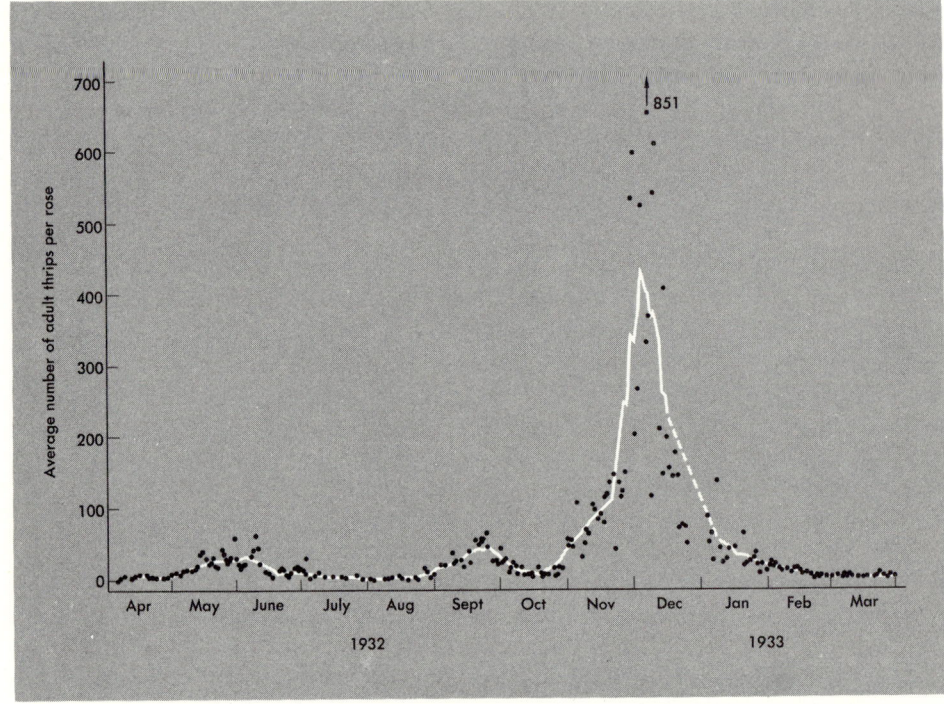

Redrawn, by permission, from J. Davidson and H. G. Andrewartha. 1948. Journal of Animal Ecology 17: 193–199.

Fig. 4-16. The population pattern of the thysanopteran insect, Thrips imaginis, on roses in South Australia. Each point represents a daily record; the curve is a 15-day moving average computed for a given sample by averaging the data of that day with the 15 previous days.

as accessibility of food and that the latter is dependent on the influence of weather, particularly the effective degree-days between the first fall rain and the end of winter, and the total inches of rain during September and October. Their evidence that food is not limiting and that density levels of the thrips correlate with flower density is convincing and leads to their view that this is an animal population whose numbers are regulated by weather. These investigators extend this principle of weather regulation to a number of other natural populations as well.

There is, however, considerable debate about the degree to which weather directly regulates population growth independent of biotic factors, particularly those related to the density of the population itself. Frederick Smith, among others, has subjected the thrip-rose data, the example par excellence of weather regulation, to extensive analysis and concludes not only that the analytical models used by the Australian ecologists were inappropriate to their interpretation, but that direct analysis demonstrates, among other findings, an inverse correlation between population change and population size, the relationship expected when change depends on size; that is, when a density-dependence exists. There seems little question but what the actual regulation of the thrip populations is yet to be found and may well be in some interaction with other populations such as will be discussed subsequently.

In spite of this reservation, it is certainly the case that, in those environments in which physical or even physico-chemical factors show considerable seasonal fluctuation, weather may play a critical role in determining the distribution and abundance of some organisms. Muskrats, for example, are continually subject to the vagaries of water-level fluctuations interacting with temperature. Low water levels in the fall followed by extremely cold weather result in unplugged burrow entrances, owing to a lack of available unfrozen mud, and in turn result in many animals freezing to death both in the burrows and as they search for unfrozen food; low water levels also make their normally well-isolated houses more subject to predation by fox and mink. Conversely, high water levels in the spring flood the burrows, drown the young, and force the adults closer to shore, where they are again more subject to predation. In less drastic environments, physico-chemical factors still have some effect, to be sure, but population patterns appear to be more subject to biological regulation through myriad intra- and interspecific interactions. A few examples of the effects of parasitism, predation, and competition will suffice to suggest the role that these kinds of biotic relationships may play in regulating populations.

Interspecific Relationships in Population Size and Distribution

Parasitism. In 1904, the sac fungus *Endothia parasitica* was accidentally introduced into the United States. In its native China, *Endothia* is parasitic on the bark of the oriental chestnut and is kept in check by a variety of natural mechanisms; in the United States, however, the majestic, towering American chestnut proved to be no match for the tiny fungus. By the late 1940's, the chestnut, which had been predominant in the forests of the Appalachian region of eastern North America, was virtually extinct. Unless effective population control is found for the sac fungus *Ceratostomella ulmi* or its transfer agent, the elm bark beetle, the fate of the Dutch elm may well be the same as the American chestnut—reduction of population size to a low level, if not extinction.

The effect of these kinds of parasitic relationships, which are numerous in recorded and even in fossil history, are comparable to that of the effect of a high flood; a population may be eliminated but not regulated in such a way as to establish some kind of equilibrium. Adjustment of both parasite and host by way of adaptation and selection, on the other hand, has enabled a tremendous number of parasite-host relationships to exist well below an extinction level. Impatient man has sidestepped the longer time generally required for such adjustments to occur and by chemotherapy has largely precluded the opportunity for adaptation in the case of pathogenic parasites. But even man shows a classic situation of adaptation to a parasite in the instance of the sickle-cell trait and malaria. Abnormal hemoglobin and the resultant sickle-shaped red blood cells, being less efficient and having less capacity for oxygen, are generally less advantageous to survival; however, the presence of some of these abnormal, sickle-shaped, red blood cells in the blood of African Negroes living in malarial areas confers a higher degree of resistance to the disease than the nonsickled condition. The history of malarial death and debilitation in nonadapted man is a dramatic tale, indeed. Outside of malarial areas, the sickle condition is less advantageous and tends to be selected against; hence it is not so frequent in later generations of African Negro populations in the United States, for example. Chemotherapy has conveyed a nonheritable or somatic adaptation of nongenetically adapted man to the protozoan parasites causing malaria.

Implicit in the case of the Chinese chestnut and its fungus and of man (sickle-cell variety) and malaria is regulation; both host and parasite populations continue to exist, although the parasite has, or had at one time, the potential for completely exterminating its host. By contrast, the parasite in a new association tends to devastate and debilitate rather than regulate in the equilibrium sense; yet if the balance of the adapted host-parasite relationship is shifted, the consequences can be devastating. In an experiment on game destruction in Africa, W. H. Potts and C. H. N. Jackson, of the East African Tsetse and Trypanosomiasis Research and Reclamation Organization in Tanzania, followed the effects on three species of tsetse fly (*Glossina*), alternate hosts for African sleeping sickness. In the area of the study, the tsetse fly feeds by sucking blood mainly from hoofed game animals, including zebra, rhinoceros, antelope, giraffe, reedbuck, impala, and gazelle. As the number of animals was purposely reduced (some 8500 animals killed in an area of 600 square miles over a period of five years), the population of the flies correspondingly dropped off in size. Comparable in a way to the thrips that were successful in finding a rose flower for food, those tsetse flies that happened to find one of the now scarce game animals had an abundance of food. But most individuals would not be so successful, with a consequent rise in population mortality. Furthermore, fewer individual flies meant fewer opportunities for encountering the opposite sex and thus a lowering of birth rate. Continual analysis verified that indeed the proportion of virgin females in the population increased as the population size decreased. The combined effects of decreased natality occasioned by too few potential mates and increased mortality occasioned by relative scarcity of food resulted in complete extinction of the parasite in the region of study. Barring their reintroduction from adjacent populations, which proved to be unlikely and uncontrollable, the area would remain free from the parasite. To put the study in proper perspective, the investigators considered the game reduction approach to regulating the tsetse fly as both unnecessarily expensive and untoward relative to game animals, but also ineffective because of continued immigration of game animals into the area.

By reducing populations of mosquitoes with various insecticide sprays, it has been possible to control and virtually eliminate such populations, the key being to bring the population below the critical density where encounter of male and female is an almost unlikely event. Alternately, effective reduction of populations of the screw-worm fly, a devastating parasite on cattle in the southern United States, was achieved by releasing males which had been sterilized by X-irradiation. Again, such measures are not equilibrium-oriented—and some of their consequences, as well as the control techniques, may be less desirable than the original problem. We shall consider some further aspects of man's tinkering with these intra-ecosystem balances in the final chapter.

Predation. In many of their manifestations, host-parasite and predator-prey relationships are quite similar. Fundamentally different, however, is the source of their energy income. Some years ago, the British ecologist Charles Elton put the difference well, in economic terms, in noting that predators live on capital, whereas parasites live on interest. Brief reflection on the analogy will demonstrate its worth. Predators do generally consume all or enough of their prey that they do or can potentially eliminate them; both laboratory and field studies as well as theoretical ones demonstrate that this is an unlikely consequence, however.

Among a number of now classic studies by the Russian biologist G. F. Gause are those involving the interaction of two ciliated protozoans, *Paramecium caudatum,* which thrives well on yeast and bacteria, and *Didinium nasutum,* which thrives well on a diet of fresh Paramecia. In the first of these experiments (Figure 4-17a), five Paramecia were introduced into a small test tube containing an oat medium conducive to bacterial growth; two days later, three Didinia were introduced. Three and four days later respectively, both the Paramecium and Didinium populations were entirely extinct. Variations in the time of introducing the predator and even in the size of container always produced the same result—the increase and decrease of prey was a phase ahead of the successive increase and decrease of the predator, and both prey and predator were eliminated. Gause then modified the uniform or homogeneous oat medium environment by introducing some sediment which, in effect, created what he called "refuges" where paramecia could hide. The effect of this hiding is evident in the second graph (Figure 4-17b): the simultaneous introduction of predator and prey is followed by continued increase of prey and extinction of the predator. From replicates of this study Gause concluded that as the microcosm

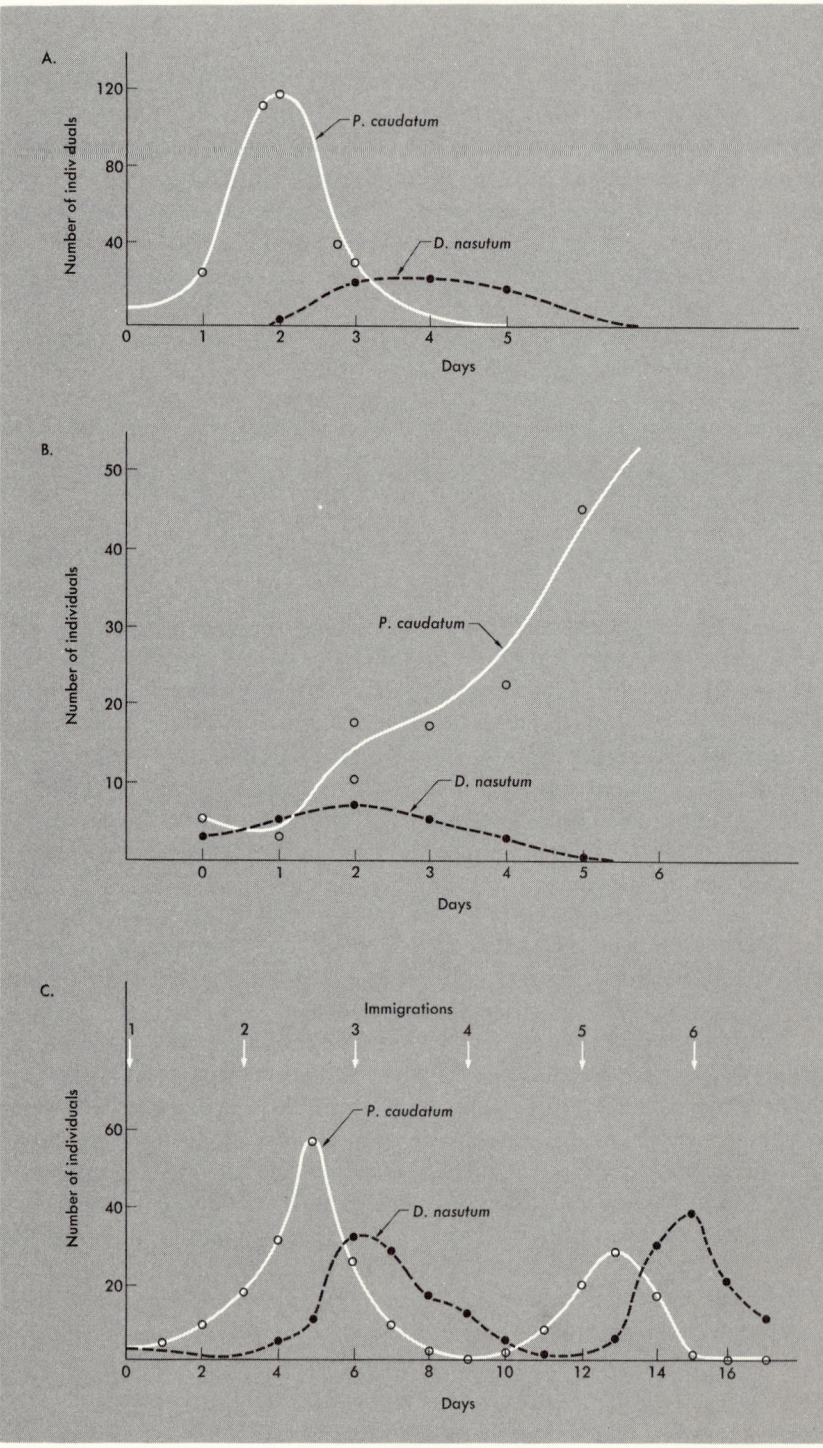

Redrawn, by permission, from G. F. Gause. 1934. The Struggle for Existence. Baltimore: Williams and Wilkins Co.

ECOLOGY OF POPULATIONS

approaches the natural heterogeneous conditions found in nature, population control is subject to a multiplicity of causes. In this particular instance, the simple predator-prey relationship (as in Figure 4-17a) becomes complicated by the accident of a heterogeneous environment in which paramecia are not so readily caught.

The extinction effect of the prey-predator relationship in a homogeneous environment can be mitigated to an oscillatory pattern by repeated immigration (Figure 4-17c). In this third series of experiments, one Paramecium and one Didinium were introduced on the first day and every three days thereafter. At the outset, the predator died out, probably from failure to find the too-few available prey; by the second immigration, the prey concentration was sufficiently high to permit successful predation, with a consequent growth of the predator population; by the fourth immigration, all the prey had been consumed, and in the absence of food shortly afterward the predator population itself became extinguished. The fourth immigration of prey and fifth immigration of predator (like the first and second immigrations) initiated this cycle of oscillation again.

Among other important things, Gause's experiments point to the significance of heterogeneity in the environment as a significant factor in population interaction. They also give laboratory evidence to out-of-phase oscillations of interacting predator-prey populations. Such an oscillation pattern is obvious in the case of the snowshoe hare and the lynx (Figure 4-18), where the period of oscillation averages about 9.6 years. Since the hare is the major food item of the lynx, the two cycles are certainly related; to what extent a direct and exclusively causal relationship exists is, however, more difficult to determine. In at least one classic instance, that of the Kaibab Plateau deer, however, the effects of disruption of prey-predator relationship can be readily seen (Figure 4-19), a disruption that is parallel to the tsetse fly-game animal situation in that it involved removal of one type of the interacting populations.

Prior to 1907, the deer herd on the Kaibab Plateau, which consists of some 727,000 acres and is on the north side of the Grand Canyon in Arizona, numbered about 4000. In 1907, a bounty was placed on cougars, wolves, and coyotes—all natural predators of deer. Within 15 to 20 years, there was a substantial extirpation of these predators (over 8000) and a consequent and immediate irruption of the deer population. By 1918, the deer population had increased more than tenfold; the evident overbrowsing of the area brought the first of a series of warnings by competent investigators, none of which produced a much needed quick change in either the bounty policy

◀Fig. 4-17. Prey-predator relationships in two ciliated protozoans, *Paramecium caudatum* and *Didinium nasutum*: A. in a homogeneous environment; B. in a heterogeneous environment; C. in a homogeneous environment with repeated immigrations of both predator and prey.

96
ECOLOGY OF POPULATIONS

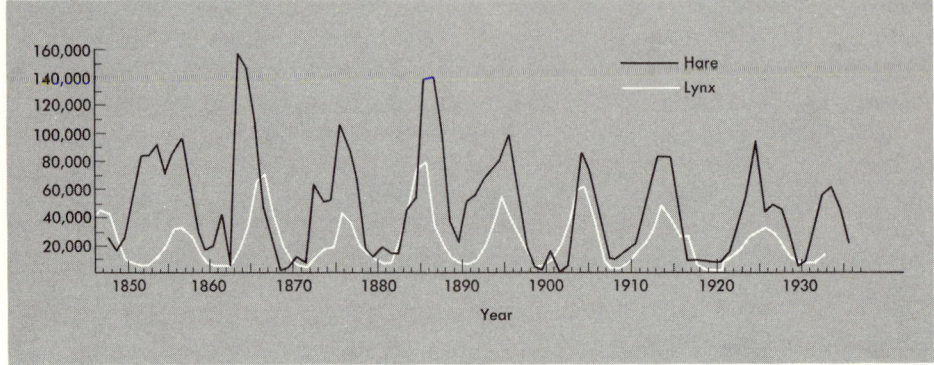

Redrawn, by permission, from D. A. MacLulich. 1937. University of Toronto Studies, Biological Series No. 43.

Fig. 4-18. Oscillations in populations of the snowshoe hare and lynx based on pelts received by the Hudson Bay Company.

or that dealing with deer removal. In the absence of predation by its natural predators (cougars, wolves, coyotes) or by man as a hunter, the herd reached 100,000 in 1924; in the absence of sufficient food, 60 per cent of the herd died off in two successive winters. By then, the girdling of so much of the

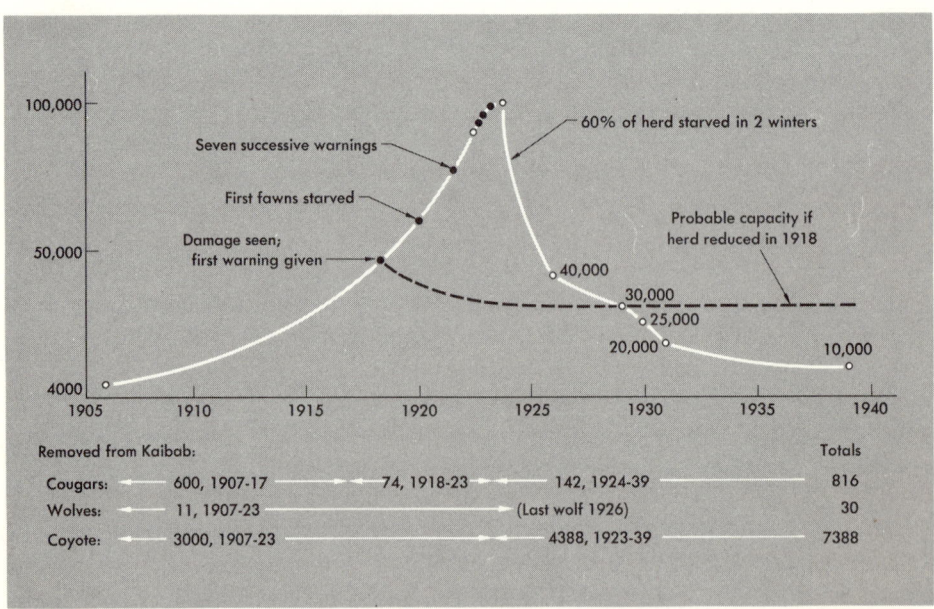

Redrawn, by permission, from A. S. Leopold. 1943. Wisconsin Conservation Bulletin No. 321.

Fig. 4-19. The effect of removal of natural predators on the deer population on the 727,000 acres of the Kaibab Plateau on the north rim of the Grand Canyon, Arizona.

vegetation through browsing precluded recovery of the food reserve to such an extent that subsequent die-off and reduced natality yielded a population about half that which could theoretically have been previously maintained. Perhaps the most pertinent statement relative to the matter of the inter-regulatory effect of predator and prey is the following by Aldo Leopold, one of the most significant of recent figures on the conservation scene:

> We have found no record of a deer irruption in North America antedating the removal of deer predators. Those parts of the continent which still retain the native predators have reported no irruptions. This circumstantial evidence supports the surmise that removal of predators predisposes a deer herd to irruptive behavior.
>
> (Wisconsin Conservation Bulletin No. 321. 1943)

It is beyond the scope of this treatment to present the argument mathematically, but during the 1920's, the biometricians A. J. Lotka and V. Volterra showed that prey-predator interaction would result in oscillatory patterns. From the experiments of Gause, it can be seen that in a heterogeneous environment or one with repeated immigrations such patterns are possible. One would also expect that natural selection would operate to increase the efficiency of the predator in capturing food on the one hand and simultaneously to increase the efficiency of the prey to avoid being captured. Thus population patterns are also dependent on adaptive behavior; a "good" predator, in the sense of being well adapted, would be like a "good" parasite, living off the interest or at least the expendable capital of a population. The long-range trend of such prey-predator interaction would be a system of built-in checks and balances between the two populations as well as between each of them and their myriad other relationships within the ecosystem they occupy.

Yet another intriguing, and for this discussion final, aspect of the theoretical-mathematical principles of prey-predator relations deduced by Volterra is that any factor that is moderately destructive to both predator and prey will increase the average prey population and decrease that of the predator. Thus, as MacArthur and Connell recently pointed out, the application of the general insecticide DDT to control scale insects (*Icerya purchasi*) that had already been brought under control by a natural predator, the lady-bird beetle (*Novius cardinalis*), actually resulted in an increase of the scale insect, a parasite of citrus trees. It is indeed the case that such complex interrelationships need much greater understanding before they should be tinkered with—a point we shall explore further in the final chapter.

Competition. If two different species populations require a common resource such as a nutrient, space, light, etc. that is potentially limited and actually becomes so, they are said to be in competition for it. Under such conditions, can they exist together, or will one displace the other? If they exist together, can or do they maintain the same population size as when separate? Independent of each other, in the 1920's Lotka and Volterra, both of whom were mentioned in the previous section, developed mathematical formulas relating to competing populations: these formulations indicate that only one species will survive, that there will be an exclusion of one of the populations by competition. Because of his empirical studies on competing populations that showed this effect, this principle of competitive exclusion is sometimes referred to as Gause's principle.

Using a culture medium conducive to the growth of two species of *Paramecium*, *P. aurelia* and *P. caudatum,* Gause determined the growth pattern of each when cultured separately and together (Figure 4-20). Each population has a quite typical sigmoidal growth pattern when grown separately, as well as during the first 6 to 8 days when grown together; in the latter situation, however, there is a gradual diminishing of *caudatum* and

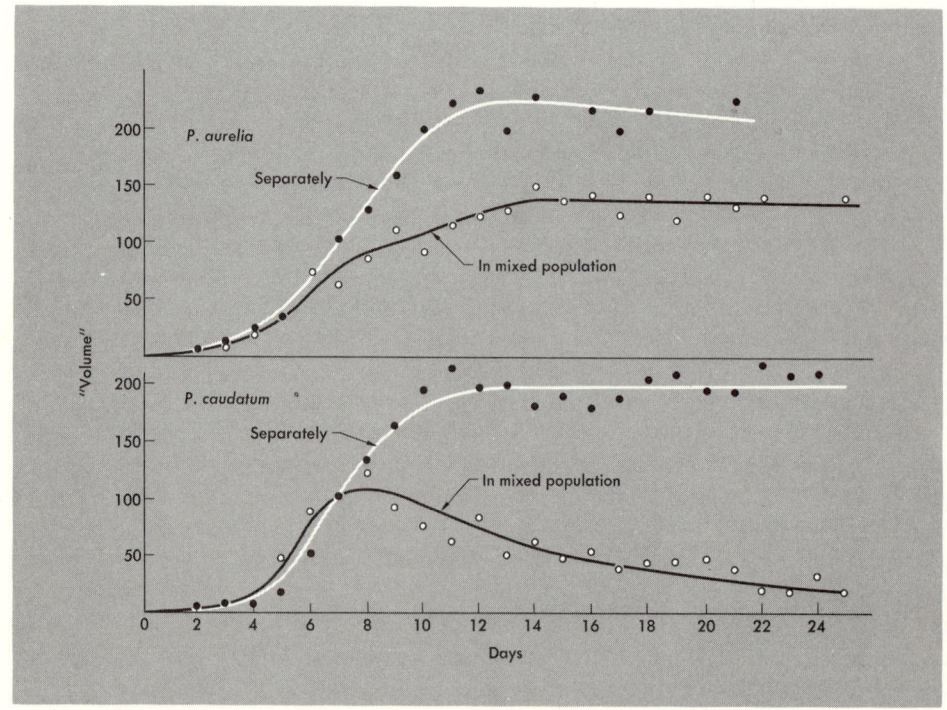

Redrawn, by permission, from G. F. Gause. 1934. The Struggle for Existence. Baltimore: Williams and Wilkins Co.

Fig. 4-20. The growth of two closely related ciliated protozoans, *Paramecium aurelia* and *P. caudatum*, when grown separately and in mixed culture demonstrating competitive exclusion of *P. caudatum*.

ECOLOGY OF POPULATIONS

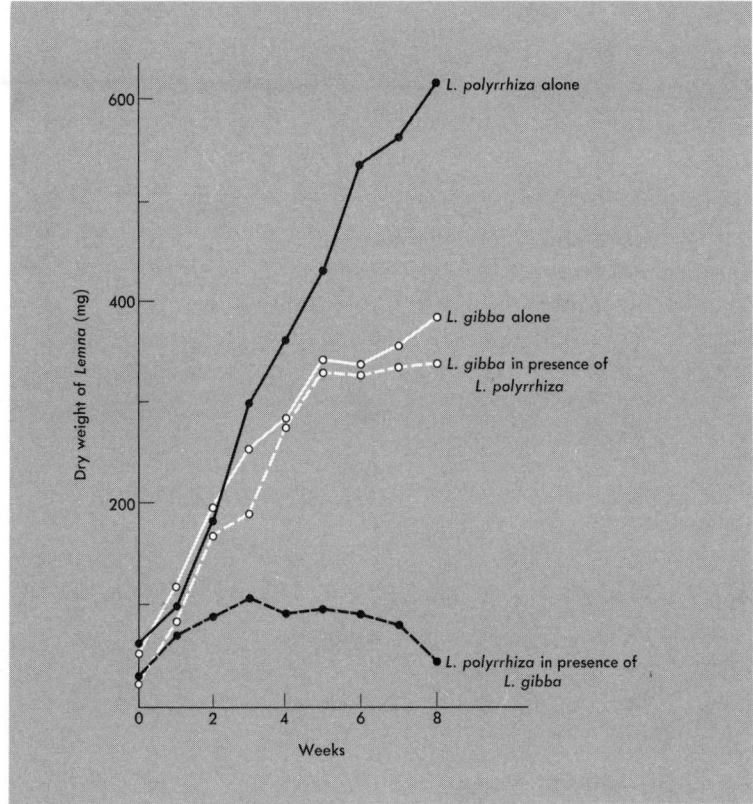

Redrawn, by permission, from J. L. Harper. 1961. *Symposium of the Society for Experimental Biology* 15: 1–39.

Fig. 4-21. The growth of two species of duckweed, *Lemna polyrrhiza* and *L. gibba*, separately and in mixed culture demonstrating competitive exclusion of *L. polyrrhiza*.

a gradual increase in *aurelia*, but not to the level attained when cultured separately. These results are consistent with the competitive exclusion principle predicted by mathematical theory; comparable results have also been obtained in the laboratory with some considerable variety of competing populations including other protozoa, *Daphnia*, grain beetles, and more recently, the small floating aquatic plant *Lemna*, commonly known as duckweed.

In his studies on duckweed (see Figure 4-21), the British ecologist John Harper noted that in an uncrowded condition, the sequence of intrinsic growth rates, in descending order, of the four species of *Lemna* cultured separately is *minor* > *natans* > *gibba* > *polyrrhiza*. Under crowded conditions, however, *minor* is least productive, the sequence of diminishing intrinsic growth rates being *natans* > *polyrrhiza* > *gibba* > *minor*. Since an addition of nutrients to the various cultures had no effect, Harper concluded that the shifts in growth rates were not caused by nutrient exhaustion but to competition for light; in *Lemna minor,* this interspecific competition has a greater toll on growth rate than on the other species. Stunting of growth with increasing population density has also been recognized in other species. It is of interest to note that in his study Harper noted that "no single parameter of growth of two species in pure cultures was a reliable indicator of their fate in mixtures." This statement is also derivable from other findings in various population studies to date.

Other studies by Gause indicate that if the conditions of the experimental environment are modified, the competitive advantage may come to rest with the previously "disadvantaged" population. For example, in a nonbacterial culture medium, *P. caudatum* has a higher coefficient of increase than *P. aurelia* and would supplant it as the surviving population in joint culture; in the experiment described above (Figure 4-19), however, bacteria were present, giving a competitive advantage to *P. aurelia,* which is less sensitive to bacterial waste products. Thus, as Gause himself noted,

> There is in nature a great diversity of "niches" with different conditions, and in one niche the first competitor possessing advantages over the second will displace him, but in another niche with different conditions the advantages will belong to the second species which will completely displace the first. Therefore side by side in one community, but occupying somewhat different niches, two or more nearly related species will continue to live in a certain state of equilibrium.

A superb example of this niche specialization is to be seen in the 14 distinct species of finches (*Geospizidae*) on the Galapagos Islands, which were first studied by Charles Darwin. Derived initially from a small number of generalized finch-like birds, the types now include 6 species of ground feeders, several of which have heavy beaks used in crushing heavy-coated seeds. The remaining 8 species are adapted to perching on trees and feeding on insects, largely by removing the bark with their beaks. Among the most specialized is the so-called cactus finch, which plucks a long spine from the cactus, holds it in its beak, and uses it both to probe crevices of the cactus stem for insects and to remove them. Thus, these finches continue to live side by side in one community, avoiding competition by niche diversification. Conversely, among plants, the British ecologist A. G. Tansley, in 1917, showed that in the case of the herb known commonly as sticktight or bedstraw, *Galium saxatile* is outcompeted by a closely related species, *G. sylvestre,* when grown in mixed stands on calcareous soil, but that the competitive position is reversed on acid peat. More recently, G. A. Harris has not only shown the existence of competition in two grasses but also the probable explanation of the competitive advantage of one of them.

The perennial bluebunch wheatgrass (*Agropyron spicatum*) was the dominant plant species on the semiarid, intermontane region of the northwest United States prior to man's introduction of European agricultural practices (plowing, use of domestic livestock, fire control, etc.). Subsequent to those changes, annual grasses from Europe and Asia, and particularly cheatgrass (*Bromus tectorum*) invaded and dominated land previously held by wheatgrass. Subsequent and more recent efforts to restore the land to the more valuable perennial grasses have been singularly unsuccessful; hence, an understanding of the competitive relationships between the major annual cheatgrass and perennial wheatgrass becomes crucial.

Harris observed direct competitive effects in experimental seeding of wheatgrass in the presence of different densities of cheatgrass; for example, average survival of wheatgrass was 39, 69, and 86 per cent in dense, moderate, and sparse populations, respectively, of cheatgrass. Further, the wheatgrass seedlings weighed 9 times more when grown under a sparse as against a dense competing population of cheatgrass.

Among the competitive advantages of cheatgrass which Harris found are a greater seed production, 65 to 200 times, and a more rapid seed germination in moist fall weather. Wheatgrass also germinates in the fall but to a lesser extent. But the most significant advantage of cheatgrass is its 50 per cent faster rate of root elongation. Under field conditions, cheatgrass roots grew throughout the winter, reaching average depths of 87 cm by March 9; by contrast, wheatgrass roots grew only slightly, reaching only 14 cm by the same date. Thus, in spring upper soil moisture is robbed by cheatgrass, which capitalizes on its winter root growth before the principal season of wheatgrass growth begins. In a parallel study of root growth under different competition densities, Harris found that increasing densities of cheatgrass decreased the average root length of wheatgrass (Table 4-6). Conversely, cheatgrass roots grew deeper with increasing densities of wheatgrass; this suggests that there may be *intraspecific* competition in cheatgrass when it is grown alone.

TABLE 4-6. Average Root Lengths of Wheatgrass (*Agropyron spicatus*) and Cheatgrass (*Bromus tectorum*) Grown Together Under Different Densities of Each Plant

	Wheatgrass (cm)	Cheatgrass (cm)
Grown separately	64.4	82.8
4 wheatgrass : 1 cheatgrass	56.9	85.4
1 wheatgrass : 1 cheatgrass	47.2	91.1
1 wheatgrass : 4 cheatgrass	41.0	82.1

Reproduced, by permission, from G. A. Harris, 1967. *Ecological Monographs* 87: 89–111.

In summary, given a moist fall and spring with normal temperatures, cheatgrass has the competitive advantage by extending its roots more rapidly and thereby being able to outcompete wheatgrass for available soil moisture, especially during the dry summer. But given a weather shift of delayed fall rains, a dry cool spring, or one of the infrequent moist summers, wheatgrass may become established; if so, mature wheatgrass has competitive advantage over cheatgrass for factors other than soil moisture.

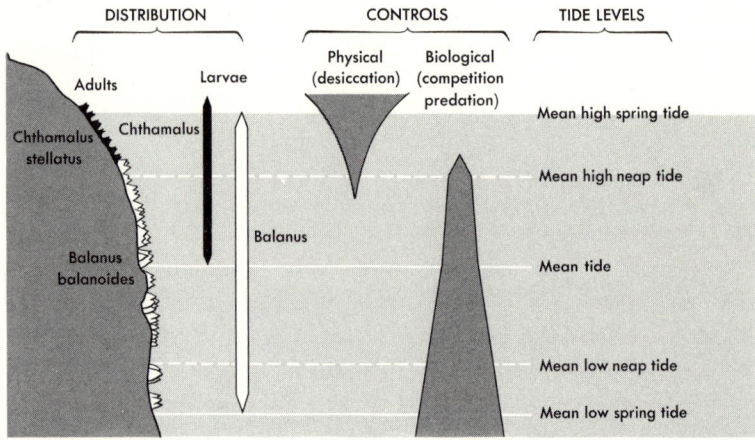

Redrawn, by permission, from E. P. Odum. 1963. Ecology. New York: Holt, Rinehart and Winston, and based on J. Connell. 1961. Ecology 42: 710–723.

Fig. 4-22. The potential and actual distribution of two species of barnacles, *Chthamalus stellatus* and *Balanus balanoides*, in the intertidal zone. Desiccation is the primary controlling factor in the upper part of the zone for *Balanus*; competition with *Balanus* is the primary controlling factor in the lower part of the upper half of the zone for *Chthamalus*; predation by the whelk, *Thais lapillus*, and intraspecific competition are the primary controlling factors in the lower part of the zone for *Balanus*.

As an example of a more aggressive type of competition, the kind most people seem to associate with the term, a study that Joseph Connell conducted in Scotland on two species of barnacles will be most instructive. Although larvae of *Chthamalus stellatus* can attach to rocks down to the mean tide level (Figure 4-22), in the presence of another barnacle, *Balanus balanoides*, they are successful in doing so only to about the level of the mean high neap tide. (The neap tides are the lowest monthly tides; spring tides the highest.) Using a mapping technique, Connell showed that *Balanus*, which has a higher growth rate, actually pried *Chthamalus* larvae off the rocks or simply grew over them—competitive exclusion by direct, aggressive behavior for available space. When *Balanus* was removed from the area, *Chthamalus* populated the intertidal zone to the mean tide level. In the absence of a *Chthamalus* population, *Balanus* was found to be unsuccessful in maintaining populations above the mean high neap tide. Here control is effected by adverse weather especially during the first year of life; it should be noted that for this barnacle, adverse weather is warm and calm weather. Below the mean high neap tide level, the size of the *Balanus* population is regulated by itself and by predation. As young *Balanus* grow, they compete for space, undercutting, displacing, growing over, and thereby smothering their own kind. This *intraspecific* competition, about which more will be said later, is one of the most significant factors in survival of the species during the first year. Individuals older than six months are preyed upon by the whelk, *Thais lapillus,* accounting for virtually all of the summer mortality. Thus, as Connell's illustration (Figure 4-22) indicates, physical factors (weather) regulate zonation of barnacles at the upper part of the intertidal zone and have a greater effect on *Balanus* than on *Chthamalus.* Biological factors are significant in the lower part of the intertidal zone: interspecific competition results in the exclusion of *Chthamalus* by *Balanus;* intraspecific competition in *Balanus* results in elimination of less successful individuals, and predation on *Balanus* by the whelk imposes a regulation on those survivors of the intraspecific competition.

Gause's principle of competitive exclusion is sometimes stated in the form that no two species with identical niche requirements can continue to coexist. Perhaps the key term in this statement is niche, an inclusive concept which means the sum total of all the ecological requisites and activities of a species, or what Eugene Odum has called its profession. It would follow that the likelihood of two species having identical niches is the likelihood of their being phylogenetically related—the closer the relationship, the more likely the identity of the niche. Thus Herbert Ross, of the Illinois Natural History Survey, noted that six species of the same genus of leafhoppers (*Erythroneura*) were all found feeding on the same part of sycamore trees at the same time and in the same way; further, they appeared to have identical species of predators. Doubtless the niche of each of these leafhoppers is extremely similar, if not identical in most parameters. However, it is doubtful that they are absolutely identical in all aspects; otherwise they would not be separable as species. Because of his observations, Ross concluded that no interspecific competition occurred during the period of study. However, one cannot but speculate that in the period of study there was an abundance and ready accessibility of food and a total environment conducive to or within the tolerance of each of the species. Interestingly, Ross noted that trees with small leafhopper populations harbored only two species, *E. lawsoni* and *E. acta,* whereas trees with large populations almost always supported all six species. It would be especially instructive to follow up these observations with experimental determinations of the effects of limiting the environment on the operation of the competitive exclusion principle.

Intraspecific Relationships in Population Size and Distribution

From the concept of the niche it follows that competition would be expected to be most keen among individuals of the same species, for here the niche requirements are indeed identical, although they would vary with age, sex, etc. We have already noted that individual *Balanus* undercut or overgrow their own kind. The effect of increased crowding, and/or the resulting increased competition, on mortality and life expectancy was also previously shown for the black-tail deer (Figures 4-6 and 4-7) and water fleas (Figure 4-9). In this same study on water fleas, Dr. Frank also showed the effects of crowding on birth rate (Figure 4-23). In contrast to a better

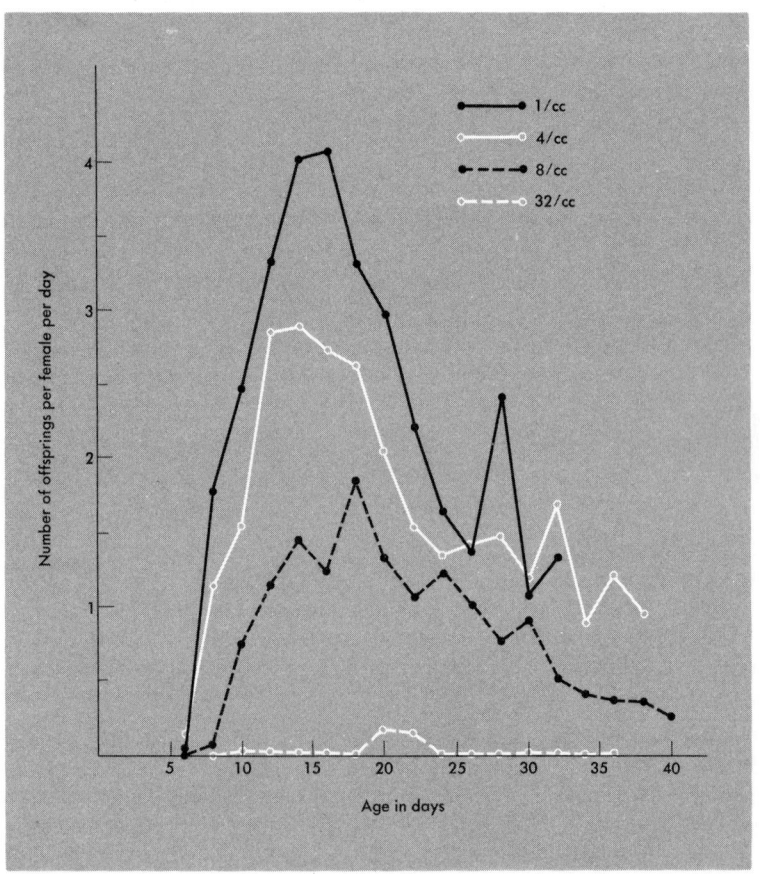

Redrawn, by permission, from P. Frank, C. D. Boll and R. W. Kelly. 1957. *Physiological Zoology* 30: 287–305.

Fig. 4-23. Average number of births per female per day in the water flea, *Daphnia pulex*, at different densities.

TABLE 4-7. The Influence of Density on Fecundity in the House-mouse, *Mus musculus*

	Sparse	Medium	Dense	Very dense
Average number/m^3	34	118	350	1600
Average percentage pregnant	58.3	49.4	51.0	43.4
Average number young per litter	6.2	5.7	5.6	5.1

Adapted, by permission, from C. Southwick, 1958. *Proceedings of the Zoological Society of London* 131: 163–175.

survivorship at moderate densities, birth rates show a consistent decline with increased crowding. Such effects have been observed with other well-studied laboratory populations. In the flour beetle, for example, Thomas Park, of the University of Chicago, showed that as the density of pairs increased along the gradient 1, 8, 40, and 80, there was a corresponding decrease in number of eggs per female per day of 10, 6, 2, and 1. This reduction in fecundity is apparently related to several factors: inimical excretory products in the culture, interference with copulation as well as feeding, and even an actual reduction in egg laying owing to a reduced opportunity for doing so.

Among many studies of mammals, one by Charles Southwick on house mice living in corn stocks in England may be cited. Even in the absence of predators and any deprivation or limitation in the environment, there is reduced fecundity with increasing density (Table 4-7); the effect is evident both on the percentage of females pregnant and the average litter size. To be sure, a simple computation of the number of pregnant females and the average litter size gives ample assurance of an abundance of house mice in the succeeding generation in any event.

It is suggestive, if not evident, from these few examples that increasing density tends adversely to affect mortality, natality, and thereby population growth. This being so, the "pressure" on a population will vary with population size—as the population increases, the factors promoting a decrease tend to become increasingly effective, and the result would be some kind of fluctuation, great or small. In the case of the blowfly (Figure 4-15), the fluctuations are considerable, in number, magnitude, and regularity. Interestingly, however, the population maintains itself without immigration, the mechanism which enables survival in thrips (Figure 4-16). Instead it does so by what Australian ecologist A. J. Nicholson refers to as self-adjustment to change, in this case a change in the availability of food. Doctor Nicholson, along with others, maintains that the ability to adjust to changes in the environment is inherent in all populations; he has put the position as follows:

> Populations are self-governing systems. They regulate their densities in relation to their own properties and those of their environments. This they

do by depleting or impairing essential things to the threshold of favourability, or by maintaining reactive inimical factors, such as the attack of natural enemies, at the limit of tolerance.

The mechanism of density governance is almost always intraspecific competition, either amongst the animals for a specific requisite, or amongst natural enemies for which the animals concerned are requisites.

In the particular experiment of Nicholson's illustrated in Figure 4-15, the adjustment of population size is tied directly to egg production. At high densities, competition among adults for food is so severe that no individuals are secure enough to enable the development of eggs. Mortality reduces the population of adults to the point that some individuals are able to obtain enough food to permit the development and laying of eggs. From that point until new adults hatch requires 16 days, 2 for development of the egg in the female and 14 for development from the egg-larva-pupa stage to the adult. During this time, the initial adult population continues to decline and is replaced by a new generation that increases in size, with the built-in time lag involved in growing up, to a point where competition again precludes egg production; thus, by compensatory reactions, the cycle continues. In other experiments, Nicholson showed that other kinds of compensatory reactions may be involved. One of the more intriguing of these follows: with an ample food supply supporting a large adult population, normal egg production resulted in overcrowding of larvae; the ensuing larval competition for food in turn resulted in stunting, with pupal size eventually diminishing to a critical point at which metamorphosis no longer could occur. No new adults were then produced to replace those depleted by natural mortality; the adult population declined, thus producing fewer eggs, which, in turn, eventually resulted in the larval competition being sufficiently reduced to permit some of them to surpass the critical size for metamorphosis. These new adults then started the cycle all over again.

In mammals, self-adjustment of populations to environmental changes may be regulated to a considerable extent by the endocrine system responding to socio-psychological factors in intraspecific competition. In laboratory experiments with house mice and voles, John Christian used the weights of the adrenal, thymus, testes, and other sex accessory glands as measures of their function. Increases in population size in the same space resulted in increased adrenal weight and decreased thymus weight, an indication of increased adrenocortical activity; concurrently, reproductive glands decreased in weight, an indication of inhibition of reproductive function. In a parallel set of experiments, other populations of males, of the same density as in the foregoing experiments, were placed in cages providing 42 times more area; interestingly, the adrenocortical responses were comparable to the first findings. This strongly suggested to Christian that the response was not to density itself but rather to the presence of other mice; that is, a

ECOLOGY OF POPULATIONS

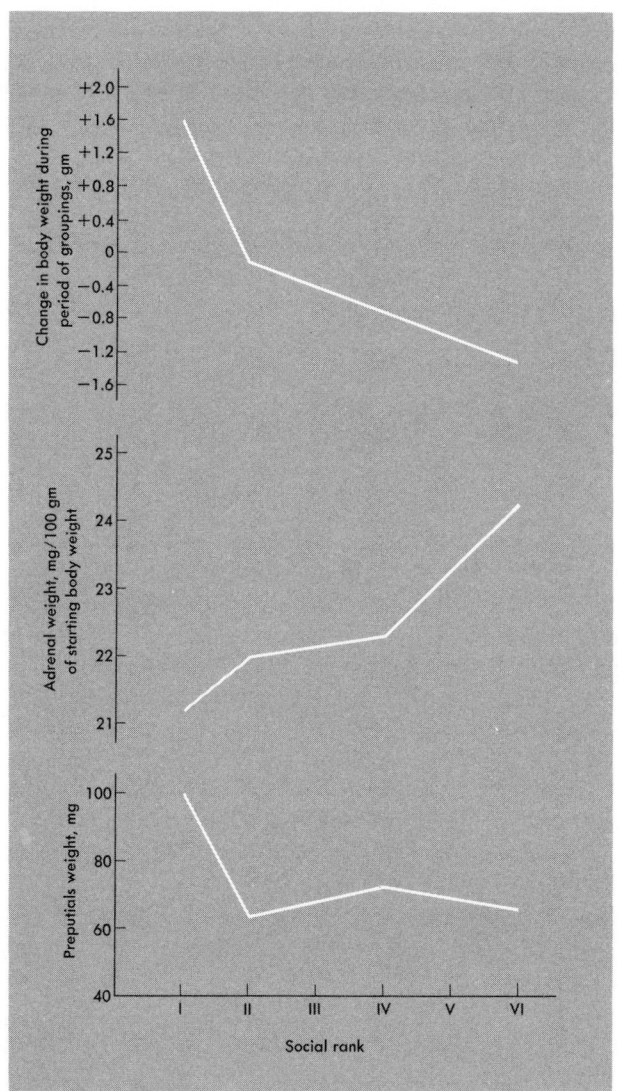

Modified, by permission, from J. J. Christian. 1961. Proceedings of the National Academy of Sciences 47: 428–449.

Fig. 4-24. Changes in adrenal, body, and preputial weights with social rank (I being most dominant, VI the least) for male wild-stock house mice; based on 14 populations of 6 mice each.

socio-psychological response. To provide further verification of this relationship, advantage was taken of the dominant-subordinate relationship in which male mice rank themselves, the so-called "peck-order" phenomenon. As shown in Figure 4-24, adrenal weights were least in the dominant animals, greatest in the most subordinate, and more or less spread out in linear fashion in the intermediate social ranks. Importantly, Christian showed that these adrenal changes are not associated with fighting nor with competition for food, but with the social hierarchy. Comparable findings were obtained in studies on female mice; with increasing population size, reproduction declines, lactation is deficient, and maturation and growth are inhibited, many of the females never bearing young. Since the output of adrenal glucocorticoids is decreased, and these are a major source of resistance to disease by inhibiting antibody formation and phagocytosis among other things, increased population density tends to reduce the population's major line of defense against infectious disease. This, coupled with inhibition of growth, maturation, and reproductive function, would collectively act as a damper against further population increases.

Whether the socio-psychological stress manifested in the "shock disease" of the laboratory house mice studied by Christian operated in the field study of the same species by Southwick (Table 4-7) is not known, since adrenal weights and other aspects of the stress syndrome were not measured. However, field studies on snowshoe hares, voles in Wales and in Germany, and Sika deer in Maryland, as well as a number of other laboratory and field studies, lend support to the "shock disease" hypothesis. Contrariwise, studies on population irruptions of the brown lemming in northern Canada and Alaska and on the vole in Wisconsin do not show associated changes in adrenal weight as suggestive of deficiency or shock disease. Proponents of the social interaction-endocrine response mechanism espoused by Christian argue, however, that detection of the tissue changes involved requires consideration of factors (microscopic examination, age, and maturation of tissues) that were not examined in these nonconfirming studies.

Some investigators, notably Frank Pitelka, tie these oscillations of herbivore populations not to an endocrine response but to periodic changes in the quantity and quality of forage and the rate of its decomposition. As the lemming population increases, grazing increases and more of the nutrients that are also required for plant growth are incorporated in the herbivores; although excrement is then added to the soil at increasing rates with the increasing population size, overgrazing decreases the insulating quality of the vegetation cover and thereby adversely alters decomposition-mineralization rates. With die-off of the lemmings, the vegetation cover increases, restoring and improving soil insulation, and decomposition can then proceed at an accelerated pace, restoring nutrients to the soil. The cycle begins again with the next season's plant growth.

Although the interaction of soil-vegetation-lemming changes may play the major regulatory role in lemming "cycles," the behavioral-physiological aspect may also be functional but either less readily recognized or not recognized as yet. There is little question that behavior has a population regulatory function; the effect of social hierarchy on mice has already been noted. In many social insects, the removal of the queen liberates her previously subordinate associates from inhibition of egg-laying, and one or more begin to do so within a matter of hours. Not atypically, one of these subordinate egg-layers, by some means, gains queenly status and establishes a new regulatory-inhibitory role on the other potential queens in the population.

Among the more obvious kinds of social behavior that have regulatory effects on a population are the family and other social groupings, territoriality, and migration. The seasonal movement to and from given areas has a very significant regulatory role, both in the decimating effects of the migration movement itself and in avoiding an otherwise limiting environment during particular seasons. Migratory behavior and the intriguing navigational processes involved are considerations that would take us beyond the purposes of this chapter. As an example of but one type of social behavior in regulating population, let us consider territoriality.

Territoriality is space-oriented behavior and is evident in many invertebrates and vertebrates, with its greatest expression in birds and mammals. An individual, or a group, stakes out a geographic area, which it then defends in some manner; the extent of the territory is itself determined by a number of factors—vigor of the holder, amount of competition by would-be intruders, etc. If the size of the territory is consistent with a sufficient food supply, the holder of the territory has greater assurance of survival and reproduction than those excluded from the territory. Holding of the territory may, and often does, involve intense agonistic behavior; sometimes, however, it is achieved by a conspicuous visual or acoustical display. As one example of the many that might be cited of the regulation of population size by territorial behavior, the study of the Australian black-backed magpie, *Gymnorhina tibicen*, by Robert Carrick is particularly telling.

Observations over three years on 1345 banded birds in a study area of five square miles of savannah woodland in Canberra revealed that there are two discrete but interacting subpopulations: (1) territorial groups of 2 to 8 birds, consisting of a pair or up to three adults along with immature birds of each sex. This group occurs in the woodland areas, fights as a team, and never leaves the home territory; (2) loose flocks of up to several hundred birds. The flock occurs in the open treeless areas, and is characterized by both sedentary birds and others showing limited movement of a few miles.

Breeding occurs only in the territorial groups; immature birds remain as part of the group for one or two years before moving out into the flock. New groups, formed in the flock, continually attempt to take over an occupied territory but are not often successful in doing so. The nonbreeding flocks contain a large proportion of immature individuals and also females known to have bred when they were members of a territorial group. During the season when breeding occurred in the territorial groups, the ovaries of these former territorial birds were found to be less well developed than their territorial counterparts. The end effect of this restriction of breeding to the territorial birds is a more or less steady equilibrium level in that subpopulation, a level that is unaffected by the density of the flock. This latter subpopulation may and indeed does fluctuate markedly, especially owing to its greater susceptibility to the spread of disease. Carrick reported two instances of heavy mortality in flock birds, one involving a contact-spread disease, the other a fungus associated with their food source; strikingly, in neither instance were the territorial birds affected. Thus, the territorial birds not only have the capacity for breeding but a buffering against disease—two major selective advantages over the flock birds.

From these several instances, social organization does appear to be a significant population regulator in some species. Professor V. C. Wynne-Edwards contends that the real test of sociality in a species is whether or not it has the potential of regulating its density by automatic and self-contained processes inherent in the population. According to this view, social populations are those which provide both for the exclusion of individuals from the group or habitat and for the recruiting or producing of new individuals into the population. Territorial species, typified here by the magpie, certainly demonstrate these criteria. In other territorial forms, other social regulators, such as antibiosis, migration, and peck order may be effective. Among other mechanisms, Wynne-Edwards suggests that the intensity and volume of the dawn chorus of a territorial species might serve as an index of population density and appropriately stimulate or inhibit breeding behavior, thereby effectively regulating population size. Whether such behavioral communication is indeed operational and whether it involves interaction at the hormonal level remain to be established.

****

The foregoing discussion of the nature of population growth and regulation has barely scratched the surface of an exceedingly exciting and active area of ecology. More empirical and theoretical studies are needed to provide a welding of great diversity of population expression into a cohesive framework. To be sure, much progress has been made; much remains to be done.

In spite of these limitations of the as yet unexplored and of those imposed by the scope and audience for this book, much has been suggested about the operation of different sorts of factors that may function at given times in populations. At a critical time in the life history of a given population, a physical factor such as light or a nutrient may be significant as a regulatory agent; at another time, parasitism, predation, or competition, or even some other physical factor may become the operative factor. As complex and as variable as the niche of any species is, it is unlikely that this regulation comes about by any single agency. However, there does appear to be considerable and mounting evidence, both empirical and theoretical, to suggest that populations are self-regulating through automatic feedback mechanisms. Various mechanisms and interactions appear to operate both in providing the information and in the manner of responding to it, and with the exceptional case of a catastrophe, the stimulus to do so appears to depend directly on the density of the population. The end effect is one of avoiding destruction of a population's own environment and thereby avoiding its own extinction.

There are numerous additional aspects of the population to which attention might still be given—the relationship of population ecology to natural selection, the role of nonsocial and social behavior, including such fascinating topics as navigation and communication, among others. However, these topics are deserving of much more treatment than the intent of this volume permits; moreover, they are topics that have had recent elaboration in "small" books like this one. What we need to do now is to integrate the preceding treatments of energetics, mineral cycling, and populations back into an ecosystem. As these last pages have suggested, populations are not isolated; they interact with their physico-chemical environment and with other populations. They do so as associations of different populations, a *community,* interacting with each other and with their abiotic environment. Thus, we should now turn to a consideration of the community and some aspects of its structure and function.

REFERENCES

Correlated Readings

Christian, J. J. and D. E. Davis, 1964. Endocrines, behavior and populations. *Science* **146:** 1550–1560.

Comfort, A., 1961. The life span of animals. *Scientific American* **205** (August): 108–119.

Deevey, E. S., 1960. The hare and the haruspex. *American Scientist* **48:** 415–430.

Errington, P. L., 1963. The phenomenon of predation. *American Scientist* **51:** 180–192.

Kormondy, E. J., 1965. *Readings in Ecology.* Englewood Cliffs, New Jersey: Prentice-Hall, Inc.

> Birch, L. C., The role of weather in determining the distribution and abundance of animals, p. 106.
>
> Chapman, R. N., The quantitative analysis of environmental factors, p. 69.
>
> Connell, J. H., The influence of interspecific competition and other factors on the distribution of the barnacle *Chthamalus stelletus,* p. 86.

Elton, C. S., Periodic fluctuations in the numbers of animals: their causes and effects, p. 73.

Gause, G. F., Competition for common food in protozoa, p. 82.

Hairston, N. G., F. E. Smith, and L. B. Slobodkin, Community structure, population control and competition, p. 113.

Lack, D., Natural selection and family size in the starling, p. 102.

Nicholson, A. J., The self-adjustment of populations to change, p. 109.

Pearl, R. and L. Reed, On the rate of growth of the population of the United States since 1790 and its mathematical representation, p. 66.

Verhulst, P. F., Notice sur la loi que la population suit dans son accroisement, p. 64.

Wynne-Edwards, V. C., 1964. Population control in animals. *Scientific American* **211** (June): 68–74.

Technical References and Monographs

Allee, W. C., A. E. Emerson, O. Park, T. Park, and K. P. Schmidt, 1949. *Principles of Animal Ecology.* Philadelphia: W. B. Saunders and Company. Chapters 18–22.

Andrewartha, H. G. and L. C. Birch, 1954. *The Distribution and Abundance of Animals.* Chicago: University of Chicago Press.

Browning, T. O., 1963. *Animal Populations.* New York: Harper and Row.

MacArthur, R. and J. Connell, 1966. *The Biology of Populations.* New York: John Wiley and Sons.

Mechanisms in Biological Competition, 1961. Symposium of the Society for Experimental Biology, Number 15.

Miller, R. S., 1967. Pattern and process in competition. *In* J. B. Cragg, *Advances in Ecological Research,* Vol. 4, pp. 1–74. New York: Academic Press.

Population Studies: Animal Ecology and Demography, 1957. Cold Spring Harbor Symposia on Quantitative Biology, Vol. 22.

Slobodkin, L. B., 1961. *Growth and Regulation of Animal Populations.* New York: Holt, Rinehart and Winston.

Energy flow, nutrient cycling, population self-regulation—these are the significant properties of ecosystems discussed in the preceding chapters. The sharp focus on each of these broad concepts has permitted some initial understanding of their operation, but this has been achieved at the expense of abstracting and extracting from given ecosystems without particular relevance to the total set of particularities and peculiarities of any given system. It has been made apparent, however, that none of these ecological processes occurs in isolation; each is manifested by particular assemblages of different species populations in particular physico-chemical environments. Thus, the flow of energy, the cycling of nutrients, and the regulation of populations occur in an assemblage that may consist of broomsedge, field mice, and weasel populations while a few feet distant the assemblage may consist of populations of herbs, rabbits, and fox. Attention thus must be turned to a consideration of the characteristics and properties of these assemblages of species populations, of ecological communities.

In moving towards the open water of a lake or pond starting some distance from the shoreline, there is a progressive change in vegetation (Figures 5-12, 5-27b, 5-28). Although you may never have taken time or had the curiosity to notice the particular plants or their sequence, almost everyone has been aware of change. Such a sequence might take the form of passing from terrestrial plants such as maples and elms to semi-terrestrial, or, if you prefer, semi-aquatic plants such as the willows and buttonbush, and finally to various aquatic plants. In the latter group, the sequence is typically from emergent reeds and sedges to progressively more submerged plants and to floating water lilies, and finally to completely submerged forms like the stonewort alga. Zonation of this sort is also encountered in moving from a plowed field

the organization and dynamics of ecological communities

CHAPTER 5

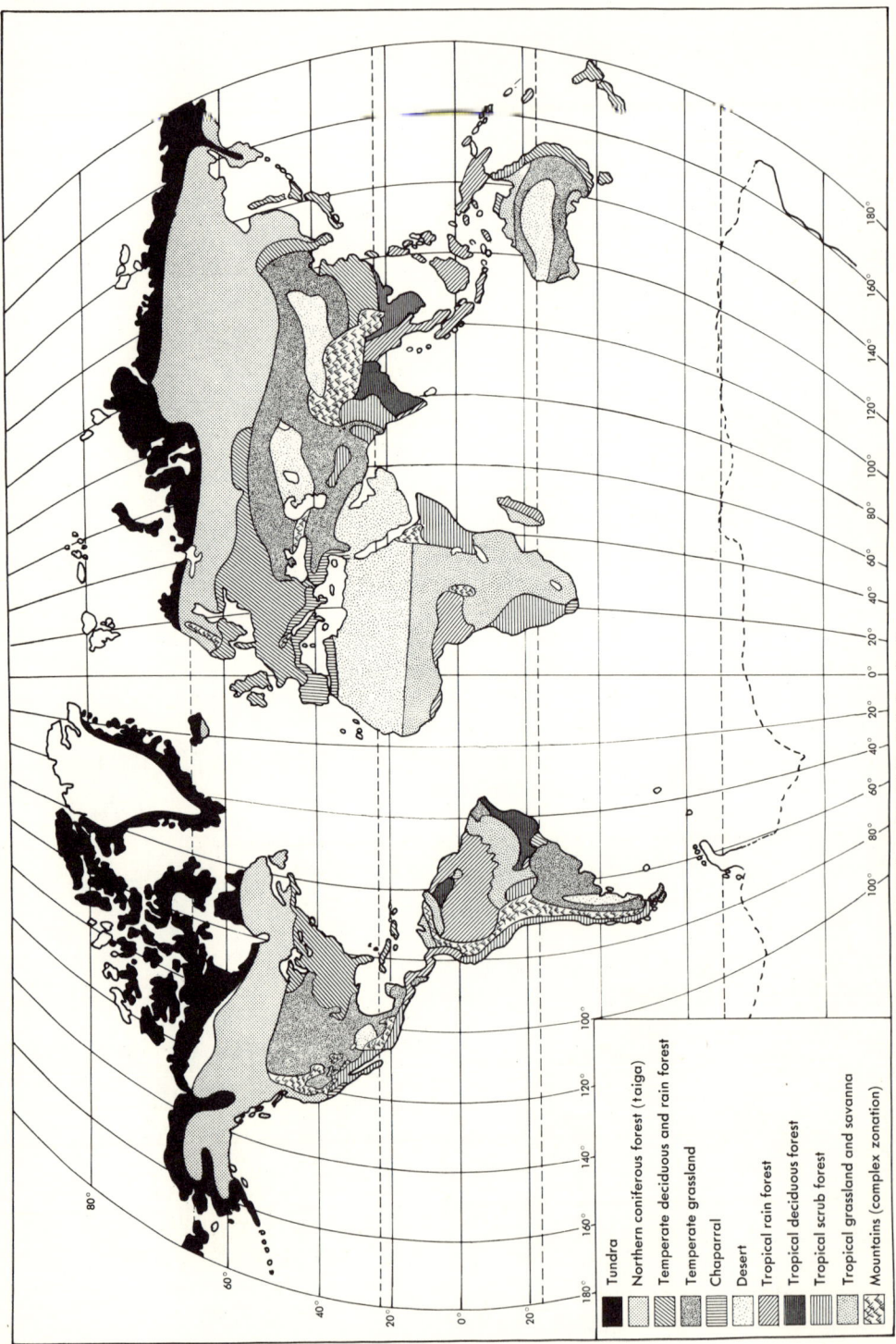

Redrawn, by permission, from E. P. Odum. 1959. Fundamentals of Ecology. Philadelphia: W. B. Saunders Co.

into a neighboring woodlot, including passing through an intermediate zone, which may be composed of various proportions of herbs, briers, shrubs, and saplings. On a much broader scale, in traveling from the southwest United States diagonally northeast the change is from desert to prairie to deciduous forest to coniferous forest and finally to tundra (Figure 5-1). The climber or motorist ascending tall mountains like Mt. Washington in the east or Mt. Rainier in the west likewise passes through a series of vegetative changes, and if the mountain is high enough the changes may not be unlike those witnessed in traveling north through the continental United States (Figures 5-2, 5-17). Each of these minor and major belts or zones are recognized because they appear to be characterized by particular assemblages of organisms (sagebrush or ponderosa pine or Engelman spruce, etc.) or by a particular physiognomy (deciduous or coniferous trees, short or tall grass, etc.). The recognition of an apparent pattern requires more critical investigation to establish its actuality and to determine controlling and causal factors as well as characteristic functional attributes.

THE MAJOR TERRESTRIAL ECOSYSTEMS

In the broadest sense, there are two major types of ecosystems—terrestrial and aquatic. In turn, each of these major types can be recognized as consisting of subdivisions; thus one can distinguish freshwater and marine aquatic ecosystems, and several major types of terrestrial ecosystems such as prairies, forests, tundra, etc. The former are separated on the basis of a major chemical difference (i.e., salt content), the latter generally on the basis of the dominant type of vegetation (grasses, trees, etc.). These major terrestrial ecosystems are most often referred to as *biomes,* although such other terms as provinces, biochores, regions, and formations are used by some ecologists. The major biomes of North America and the world distribution of similar biomes are shown in Figure 5-1.

One of the striking aspects of distribution of types is that many of the division lines tend to parallel the lines of latitude. This is especially evident in the Old World. In the Americas, the latitudinal divisions are evident in eastern North and South America, but not in the high mountain regions that form the western "backbone" of the two continents. Not only are demarcations of biome-types more or less latitudinal, but, more strikingly, the same type of biome is found within the same general latitudes; this is particularly evident in the case of the tundra and boreal forest in the Old and New Worlds. Finally, in tall mountains, such as the Rockies, Andes, and Himalayas, the division lines between biomes is altitudinal rather than latitudinal (Figure 5-2). However, the particular biomes to be found at a given altitude also vary with latitudes, a given zone occurring at progressively lower altitudes at progressively more northerly latitudes (Table 5-1).

ECOLOGICAL COMMUNITIES

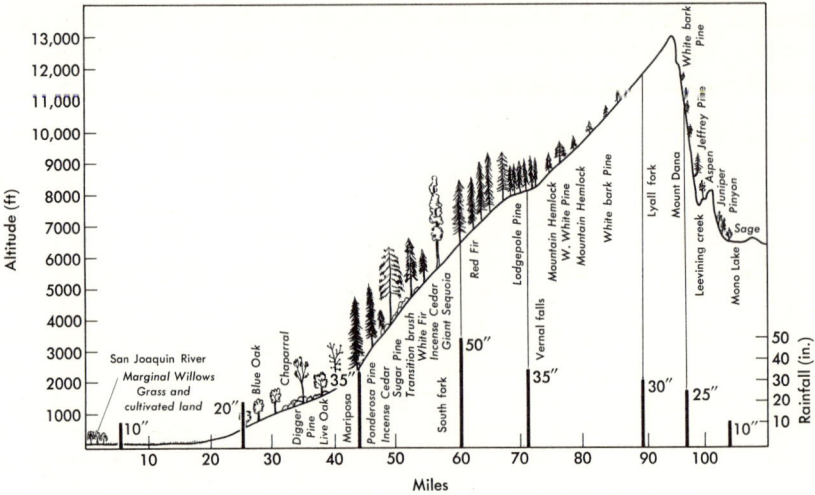

Redrawn, from B. O. Hughes and D. Dunning. 1949. Pine Forests of California. U. S. Department of Agriculture Yearbook.

Fig. 5-2. Profile of central Sierra Nevada showing altitudinal distribution of principal forest types.

The zone of Douglas fir-ponderosa pine, for example, lies between 2000–6000 feet in the Cascade Mountains of the northwest, 4000–7000 feet in the central, and 5000–8000 feet in the southern Sierra Nevadas.

Since temperature is largely dependent on the incidence of solar radiation, which is, in turn, directly associated with latitude (Figure 2-1), and since precipitation patterns are strongly influenced by major wind patterns, which are also associated with latitude (Figure 3-3), the suggestion is virtually self-evident that climate plays a most significant role in the distribution of biomes. Inferences of this kind appear in the earliest of ecological writing.

Table 5-1. The Change in Vegetation with Altitude at Different Latitudes

Latitudinal Zonation	Altitudinal Zonation			
	0–3000 ft	3000–6000 ft	6000–12,000 ft	12,000–18,000 ft
Tropical (0°–20°)	tropical	subtropical	temperate	arctic–alpine
Subtropical (20°–40°)	subtropical	temperate	arctic–alpine	–
Temperate (40°–60°)	temperate	arctic–alpine	–	–
Arctic and Antarctic (60°–80°)	arctic–alpine	–	–	–

Adapted, by permission, from R. Good, 1953. The Geography of Flowering Plants, 2nd ed. London: Longmans, Green and Company, Inc.

However, were a map of the major soil groups of the world superimposed on one of biome-type distribution, a striking coincidence would be evident. Since the biome is recognized by the type of vegetation and all but a few exceptional species root in the soil, there would seem to be substantial reason to suggest that soil type might also be a major regulatory factor in biome distribution. At this juncture, it would be advantageous to put these questions of causality to laboratory investigations, but obviously this is out of the question. Can you imagine the size of a growth chamber or modern phytotron that would be required to handle such an investigation? The ecologist is thus beset again with a natural phenomenon about which the best that can be done is to make inferences from abundant but noncontrolled as well as noncontrollable observations. Cause and effect in biome distribution is confounded because of the complexity of interaction among the components—vegetation, climate, and soil. Soil and vegetation are parts of the same ecosystem; they develop in parallel, influencing each other and influencing and being influenced by climate. From the experiment on forested watersheds described in Chapter 3 one can see evidence of the influence of vegetation on rates of weathering of primary materials, with the presence of vegetation inhibiting nitrification and the absence of vegetation resulting in significant mineral as well as soil water loss from the ecosystem; and in the phosphate enrichment experiments on nettle, also described in Chapter 3, one sees a simple example of the influence of soil on vegetation. Influence in another direction occurs between soil and climate, and then on vegetation, in that high evaporation rates with or without high precipitation tend to keep nutrients near the surface—a situation that is evident in the rich soils of the prairies, enabling the high rates of production characteristic of the central grasslands of North America. And the rather rapid decomposition made possible by suitable climate facilitates the release of nutrients to sustain these high yields. By contrast, under conditions of high rainfall with reduced evaporation, and particularly where vegetation is either sparse of shallowly rooted, nutrients may be leached from the soil and make their way out of the ecosystem through circulating groundwater; this is the situation in the highly mineral deficient podzol soils of the northern part of the boreal forest or taiga. Although these well-recognized soil-climate-vegetation interactions do obviate precise causal analysis, the prevailing opinion is that the distribution of biomes is primarily controlled by climate. In addition to the quite excellent correlations that can be derived from our present knowledge of distribution of biome-types and patterns of temperature, precipitation, and evaporation, there is supporting evidence from studies of biome distribution and climatic patterns in the past, recorded as it is in the growth of tree rings and in fossilized pollen.

To characterize adequately each of the major biomes of North America would be beyond the scope and purpose of this book; not to treat them at all would leave a major ecological concept like a skeleton, having no real character until it is fleshed out. As a compromise between these extremes, the vegetation and climate of each of the major biomes in North America will be very briefly characterized and illustrated and then one of them, the deciduous forest, will be treated in some detail. The serious student is referred to the extensive treatment of this topic in advanced texts such as those by Ayre, Oosting, and Shelford cited at the end of the chapter.

Tundra, which means "marshy plain," lies largely north of latitude 57°N and is characterized by the absence of trees and an upper ground surface that is spongy and uneven, or hummocky, as a result of freezing and thawing of this poorly drained land (Figure 5-3). Also characteristic is the presence of a permanently frozen soil (permafrost) at a depth of a few inches to several feet; the permafrost line is the ultimate limit of plant root growth, but the immediate control is the depth to which soil is thawed in summer. Although there is variation from place to place within the biome, temperature, precipitation, and evaporation are characteristically low, the warmest months averaging below 10°C and the wettest with about an inch of precipitation (Figure 5-4e). The vegetation consists of relatively few species: grasses and sedges are characteristic of the numerous marshes and poorly drained areas, but large areas consist of ericaceous heath plants (bilberries and dwarf

Photo courtesy of W. C. Steere.

Fig. 5-3. Tundra biome: patterned ground near Point Barrow, Alaska. The polygons, 15 to 25 feet across, result from winter freezing; the cracks are filled with ice, which thaws at the surface in summer. Note where a tracked vehicle, a "weasel," has passed, lower left; the tracks of a "weasel" are nearly 5 feet at the outer edges and hence make an excellent scale in the photograph.

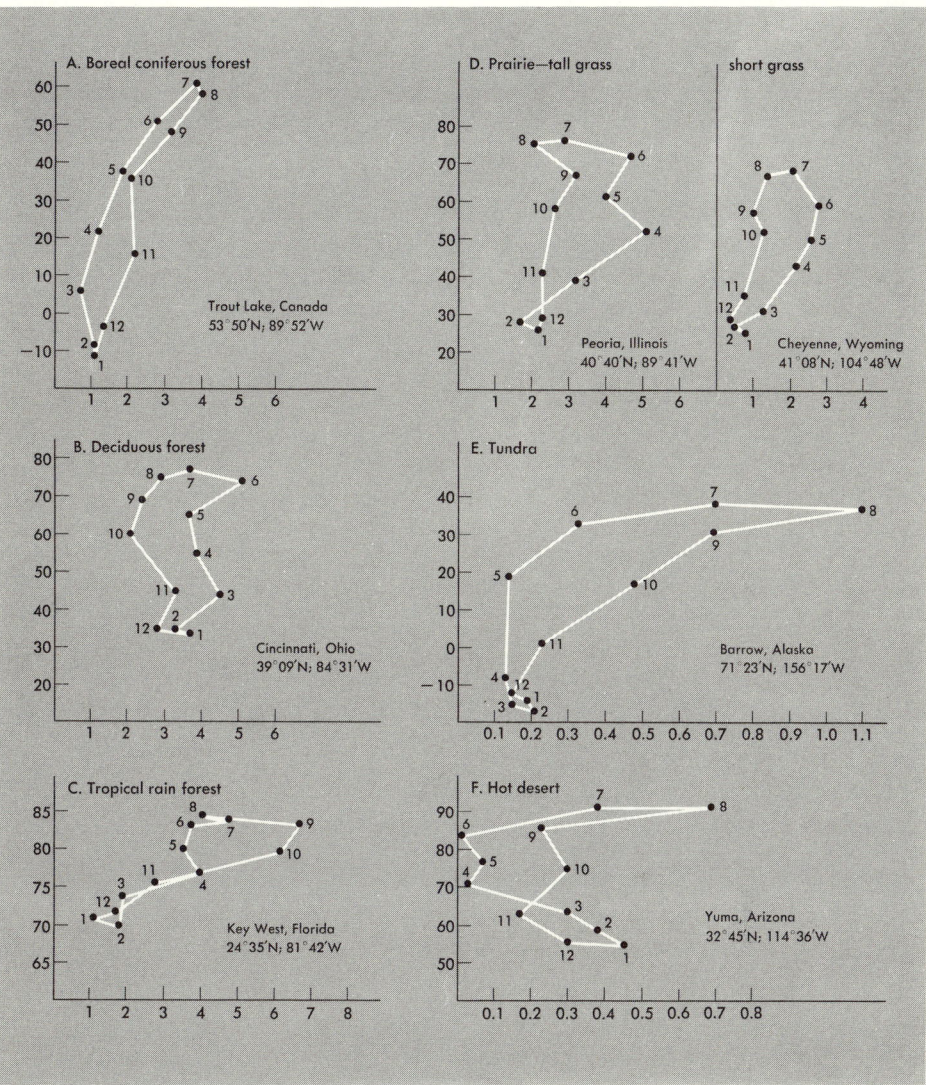

Fig. 5-4. Climographs of representative locations in the major biomes of North America. The vertical axis is temperature (°F); the horizontal axis is precipitation (inches); numbers refer to months (1 = January, 2 = February, etc.). Data are monthly averages for the period 1941–1950 from *World Weather Records 1941–50*, Department of Commerce, 1959.

huckleberries), low flowering herbs, and lichens. Perhaps the most characteristic arctic tundra plant is the lichen known as "reindeer moss" (*Cladonia*). Alpine tundra is quite similar to arctic tundra, but in the absence of permafrost and the presence of better drainage and generally a longer growing season, mosses and lichens are less prominent, flowering plants more so. Also, whereas the transition between alpine tundra and boreal forest is characteristically rather abrupt, in the arctic it is gradual and of wide dimension, up to a hundred miles or so.

Boreal Coniferous Forest. This moist-cool, transcontinental coniferous forest biome, sometimes referred to in literary parlance as "the great north woods" and lying largely between the 45th and 57th north latitudes, has counterparts in mountain regions as far south as Costa Rica (Figure 5-5). The climate is cool to cold with precipitation greater than the tundra and occurring mostly in the summer (Figure 5-4a). The predominant vegetation is of the needle-leaf, evergreen variety, notably white spruce (*Picea glauca*) and balsam fir (*Abies balsamea*) east of the Rocky Mountains and red pine, white pine, and hemlock in the Great Lakes region. Other conifers, such as tamarack (*Larix laricina*) and black spruce (*Picea mariana*), are common in moister situations, and jack pine (*Pinus Banksiana*) in drier and fire-

U. S. Forest Service.

Fig. 5-5. Boreal forest biome: western red cedar and Alaska cedar on Skowl Arm, near Old Kasaan, Prince of Wales Island, South Tongass National Forest, Alaska.

burned areas. Dominance of jack pine in the latter situation results from the nature of the cone, which remains unopened until subjected to burning; thus, following a fire that may wipe out mature trees as well as seedlings and seeds of other conifers, the seeds newly released from fire-scorched jack pine cones can establish a new community. Quaking aspen (*Populus tremuloides*), balsam poplar (*Populus balsamifera*), and paper birch (*Betula papyrifera*)—all nonconiferous—are also characteristic of burned areas in this biome, but generally on more moist soils such as along streams and in wet valleys. The understory is relatively limited as a result of the continual low light penetration; however, among common understory associates are orchids and ericaceous shrubs like the blueberry.

Boreal forest soils are characteristically acidic and mineral deficient, the result of the movement of a large amount of water through the soil; in the absence of a significant counter upward movement of evaporation, this leaches soluble essential nutrients like calcium, nitrogen, potassium, etc., sometimes beyond the reach of roots and leaves no alkaline-oriented cations to counter the organic acids of the accumulating litter (see Tables 3-4, 3-5 and accompanying discussion).

Temperate Deciduous Forest Biome. As its name indicates, this region is characterized by a moderate climate (Figure 5-4b) and deciduous trees

U. S. Forest Service.

Fig. 5-6. Deciduous forest biome: 120-year-old stand of sugar maple, beech, and hemlock in Pennsylvania.

(Figure 5-6). It occupies most of the eastern half of the United States and has been very extensively affected by human activity. Among the predominant genera in upland areas are maples (*Acer*) and beech (*Fagus*) on moist soils, and oak (*Quercus*) and hickory (*Carya*) on drier soils; basswood (*Tilia*) and, prior to the 1920's, chestnut (*Castanea*) are also common. Along stream bottoms, cottonwood (*Populus deltoides*), sycamore (*Platanus*), elm (*Ulmus*), and willow (*Salix*) are common. In some locations, coniferous vegetation may be quite predominant, and among such elements one may find white pine, hemlock, and cedar. The understory of shrubs and herbs in the deciduous forest is typically well-developed and richly diversified, with a considerable portion of the flowering attuned to the short days of the spring season, prior to the leafing out of and consequent shading by the tree canopy. Climate in this region, although varying considerably from north to south, is moderate with a definite winter period, characterized by snow and frozen soil and lakes in the northern portions, rain and coolness in the southern portions; precipitation is quite evenly distributed throughout the year.

Grassland. In central North America are the grasslands, the tall grass prairie toward the east and the short grass prairie, or plains, westward. Prior to its conversion to agriculture and urban development, the tall grass prairie was dominated by species of bluestem (*Andropogon*) forming dense covers four to six feet tall. Westward, Buffalo grass (*Buchloe dactyloides*) and other grasses but a few inches high dominated the landscape. Flowering herbs, including many kinds of composites, are common, but are relatively insignificant; trees are largely limited to stream valleys, where cottonwood is dominant (Figure 5-7), and to low mountains, such as the Black Hills of South Dakota. The transition westward from tall to short grass is correlated with increasing aridity, a result of reduced rainfall (Figure 3-3) coupled with increased evaporation. The tall grass prairie is characterized by irregular rainfall, which is reduced towards the end of summer; in the eastern portion, the pattern of temperature and rainfall (Figure 5-4d) is quite comparable to that of the deciduous forest (Figure 5-4b), but precipitation drops progressively westward. Since the precipitation-evaporation ratio is below 1 in the grassland, leaching is considerably less than in the eastern soils; the chernozem soils, or black-earths, of the tall grass prairie are among the richest in nutrients and consequently the most fertile in the world. Organic matter accumulates in the upper portion of the soil, rendering it dark; this upper portion remains neutral to slightly alkaline because of the continued replenishment of cations like calcium and potassium through the upward movement associated with evaporation. Westward, the conditions in the direction of shorter grass are not so much a limitation of nutrients, whose rather complete cycling parallels that of the chernozem soils, but rather increasing aridity.

Photo by author.

Fig. 5-7. Grassland biome: short grass on the sand hills of north central Nebraska, near Valentine; note the presence of trees only in the valley.

Desert. In its most typical form, the desert consists of bush-covered land in which plants are quite dispersed with much bare ground between; for example, creosote bush (*Larrea divaricata*), the dominant plant of the hot deserts (Mojave, Sonoran, Chihuahua) of the southwest United States (southeast California, southern Nevada, south and west Arizona, and southern New Mexico and Texas), is quite regularly spaced at intervals of 15 to 30 feet (Figure 5-8). In the cold Great Basin Desert of the northwest between the Cascade-Sierra chain and the Rocky mountains (see Figure 3-3), and including Nevada, western Utah, and the bordering parts of California, Oregon, Idaho, and Wyoming, the predominant sagebrush (*Artemisia tridentata*) is similarly dispersed, although the spacing is not so great. Although the vegetation of the Great Basin Desert and the Mojave is simple, the Sonoran (Figure 5-8) has well-developed, complex communities, especially along streambeds. Low erratic precipitation (Figure 5-4f) coupled with soil and air temperatures that are extremely high by day and drop abruptly by night (Figure 5-22), low humidity, and high insolation are the major desiccating environmental factors to which desert vegetation has adapted. There are drought-resistant species adapted to a reduction of tissue water content by the development of considerable sclerophyll tissue, which strengthens tissues otherwise held turgid in many species by water or by undergoing dormancy during low-water periods. In addition to drought-resistant species, there are short-lived annuals that complete their life cycle

U. S. Forest Service.

Fig. 5-8. Desert biome: Saguaro cactus and creosote bush in the Sonoran Desert in Saguaro National Monument, near Tucson, Arizona.

during the short moist period. Finally, particularly in the warm southern deserts, water-storing succulents, such as Joshua tree, Saguaro cactus, and the century plant, are adapted by their protoplasmic colloids, which enable the accumulation of substantial water reserves, as well as by a reduced leaf surface, which obviates water loss via evapotranspiration.

Lesser Biomes. In addition to the major biomes, there are several others in the United States which deserve brief mention. One of these, the *eastern pine-oak,* occupies the coastal plain from Long Island and New Jersey to the border of Texas; it is dominated in upland, well-drained sites by extensive pine forests—pitch pine (*Pinus rigida*) to the north and loblolly (*P. taeda*), slash (*P. caribaea*), and longleaf (*P. australis*) farther south (Figure 5-9). The soil is sandy and consequently low both in nutrients and water-

U. S. Forest Service.

Fig. 5-9. Eastern pine-oak biome: the pine barrens with a young stand of pitch pine with an understory of oak and sassafras, Ocean County, New Jersey.

retention properties. Considerable evidence indicates that these coastal pines are dependent on recurrent fires for their maintenance; under conditions in which fire has been curtailed, hardwood forest invariably develops. As in the case of jack pine noted above, fire hastens the opening of cones, releasing seeds that are able to germinate on soil laid bare by the burning off of organic matter.

At the very southern tip of Florida and westward on the Keys is the *subtropical biome,* which is subject to a quite uniformly warm annual temperature and abundant precipitation (Figure 5-4c). In driving through the Everglades, for example, one first observes the freshwater marshes dominated by tall sawgrass (*Cladium jamaicensis*), but as salinity increases coastward in the tidal and subtidal areas, there is a gradual transition to virtually pure dense swamps of red mangrove (*Rhizopora Mangle*). Scattered islands of trees, or hammocks, occur in the freshwater marshes, and they constitute, in miniature, tropical forests such as would be encountered farther south. These hammocks are characterized by both evergreen and deciduous trees, notably mahogany, gumbo limbo, bays, and palms laden with epiphytes (largely members of the pineapple and orchid families), ferns, and vines, or lianas, including the well-known strangler fig (*Ficus aureus*).

To the west, and best developed on the coastal ranges of southern

California, is a region characterized by species with thick, hard evergreen leaves, the *broad-sclerophyll biome* (Figure 5-10). North-facing and moister slopes are characteristically dominated by trees, including several species of evergreen oaks. South-facing and drier slopes are dominated by low dense thickets of evergreen shrubs such as chamise (*Adenostoma*) and manzanita (*Arctostaphylos*); such formations are referred to as chapparal. The climate is temperate to subtropical, rainfall occurring largely during the winter months; the long dry summer coupled with the nature of the vegetation make the region subject to frequent fire, an event that generally favors the extension of chapparal at the expense of the sclerophyll forest.

It is possible, of course, to recognize finer subdivisions of each of these major ecosystems—for example, the wetter hemlock-fir and drier redwood-sequoia regions of the west; such finer discrimination would be in order in a more extended monograph. As it is, our discussion has been limited to a brief description of vegetation, soil, and climate and has been subject to considerable generalization. It must be recognized that these "typical" situations are abstractions, yet not without basis in fact. What has been described is the predominant vegetational life-form obtaining in given areas, and although the biome-type map (Figure 5-1) suggests sharp, discrete separations of the various vegetation zones, anyone who has traveled even

U. S. Forest Service.

Fig. 5-10. Broad-sclerophyll biome: chaparral predominated by red shank, ceanothus, and sage, with Mt. Palomar in background, Cleveland National Forest, California.

moderately has recognized that this is not so and that the transition zones are sometimes of considerable magnitude. Occasionally the transitions may be quite abrupt, as between the deciduous forest and coastal pine; here the boundary is largely related to a sharp discontinuity in the type of soil.

It is also true that within any given biome one may find areas that do not seem to belong. For example, in certain parts of northern Indiana and Ohio one finds prairie vegetation and chernozem soil, although this area lies within deciduous forest biome and should be characterized by a different soil type. In this particular instance, the presence of this prairie peninsula, as it is called, is an historical accident, a remnant of a different climatic regime. In other cases, as will be seen later, the "misfit" is the result of local topographic and/or microclimatological influences. In spite of their internal variability and lack of discrete boundaries, coupled with the hazards of broad generalization, the concept of the biome as a major ecological system has its worth. A more thorough consideration of some aspects of one biome will enable further understanding of the organization and regulation of these major terrestrial ecosystems. However, before we do so, it will be helpful to take a brief overview of the comparative productivity and mineral cycling of the major biomes, bringing back into focus two of the major ecological principles discussed earlier.

The accumulation, productivity, and distribution of biomass in the major biomes is illustrated in Figure 5-11. In the earlier discussion (Chapter 2), it was noted that tropical ecosystems are considerably more productive than their temperate counterparts (Table 2-5). The greatest accumulation of organic matter is not only in forest systems, but is progressively greater toward the equator. Within the boreal forest, for instance, total accumulation increases from 100,000 kg/ha in northern taiga spruce forests to 330,000 kg/ha in southern taiga spruce forests. The more northerly deciduous forests of beech have accumulations around 370,000 kg/ha in comparison with 400,000 kg/ha in more southerly deciduous forests of oak. Comparable trends can also be noted in the rate at which the organic matter accumulates.

Especially striking is the difference in biomass distribution in the major biomes (Figure 5-11). It is of particular significance that the three major forest biomes (boreal coniferous, deciduous, tropical) all show very much the same pattern—less than one-fourth of their biomass in roots and nearly three-fourths in their perennial stems and branches. The substantial root biomass of the desert biome has already been implied in the preceding discussion of extensive root systems as a major adaptation to aridity, but what is especially noteworthy is the large proportion of desert biome biomass that occurs as litter. Finally, a parallel to the desert is seen in the very large proportion of tundra biome biomass that exists as roots, probably more an adaptation to cold than to relative aridity.

Inferences about mineral cycling in each of these biomes can be made

ECOLOGICAL COMMUNITIES

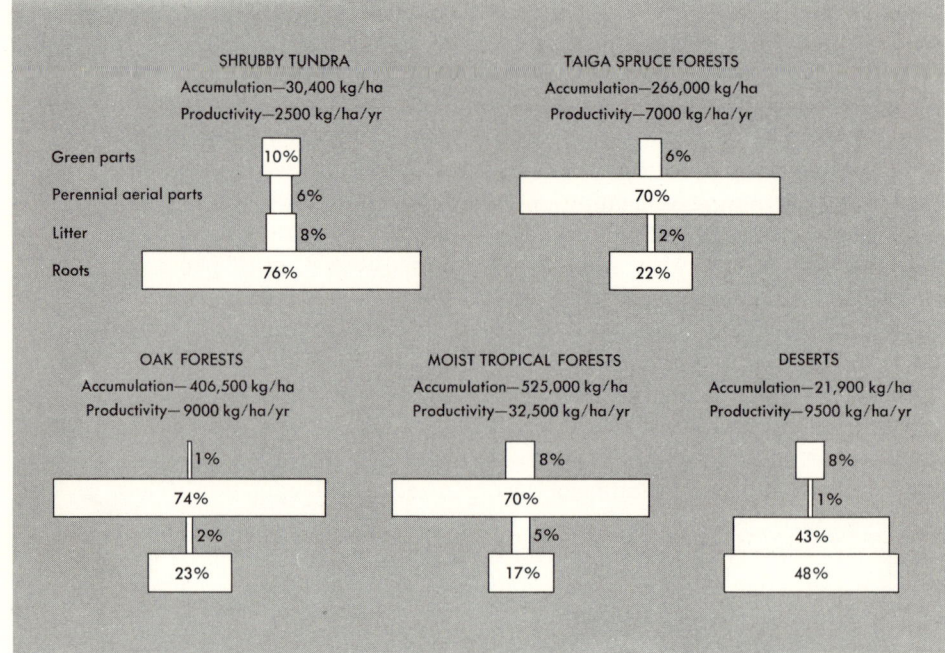

Based on data from L. E. Rodin and N. I. Bazilevič. 1964. Doklady Akademii Nauk SSSR 157: 215–218.

Fig. 5-11. The accumulation, productivity, and distribution of biomass in selected major biomes.

TABLE 5-2. The Accumulation and Annual Changes in the Litter and Humus of the Major Biomes, in Kilograms per Hectare

	Shrubby Tundra	Boreal Spruce Forests	Oak Forests	Moist Tropical Forests	Deserts
Litter	2400	5000	6500	25,000	9400
Annual net increment in litter	10	2000	2500	7500	10
Per cent of productivity	4	29	28	23	11
Dead organic residues (humus)	83,500	45,000	15,000	2000	–
Organic residues: green litter	92:1	15:1	4:1	0.1:1	–

Data from L. E. Rodin and N. I. Bazilevič, 1964. Doklady Akademii Nauk SSSR 157: 215–218.

from considerations of the annual increment in the litter, the amount of humus, or dead organic residues, and the ratio of the latter to fresh, or green, litter (Table 5-2). Although the trend is toward an increase in the annual net increment in litter toward the equator, this seems to be more a reflection of total productivity, inasmuch as the percentage of annual productivity that it represents is about the same for each of the major forest biomes. However, the retention of this organic matter and its bound minerals is considerably less toward the equator, as can be seen both by the diminution of humus and the ratio of humus to green litter. The accumulation of litter and retention of humus is indicative of low rates of decomposition—the tundra situation illustrates this condition; by contrast the absence of humus (deserts) or its low accumulation (tropical forests) is indicative of high rates of decomposition and of rapid mineral cycling.

STRUCTURAL ASPECTS OF THE DECIDUOUS FOREST

Description of Structure

In the preceding brief treatment, the deciduous forest biome was characterized in two fashions. In the first instance, it was described as experiencing an annual leaf fall, thereby suggesting a quite different appearance in summer and in winter. Second, it was described with reference to some of the predominant genera of trees encountered. These major terrestrial ecosystems as well as the myriad minor ones that comprise them can thus be described by their structural appearance, or physiognomy, as well as by their floristic composition. Each approach assesses somewhat different aspects of a community; each has certain advantages and limitations, and, as might be expected, each has its proponents in ecological circles.

One of the earlier attempts toward community description that has had wide application was the recognition of *life forms* based on the position of regenerating parts. A scheme developed by the Danish botanist Christen Raunkiaer in 1903 recognized a number of categories into which plants were grouped, regardless of their taxonomic status, based on the "amount and kind of protection afforded to the buds and shoot apices." These categories, illustrated in Figure 5-12, are described as follows:

Therophytes – plants of the summer or of the favorable season; annuals.

Cryptophytes – surviving buds or shoot-apices are buried in the ground at a distance from the surface that varies in different species; tuberous and bulbous herbs.

130
ECOLOGICAL COMMUNITIES

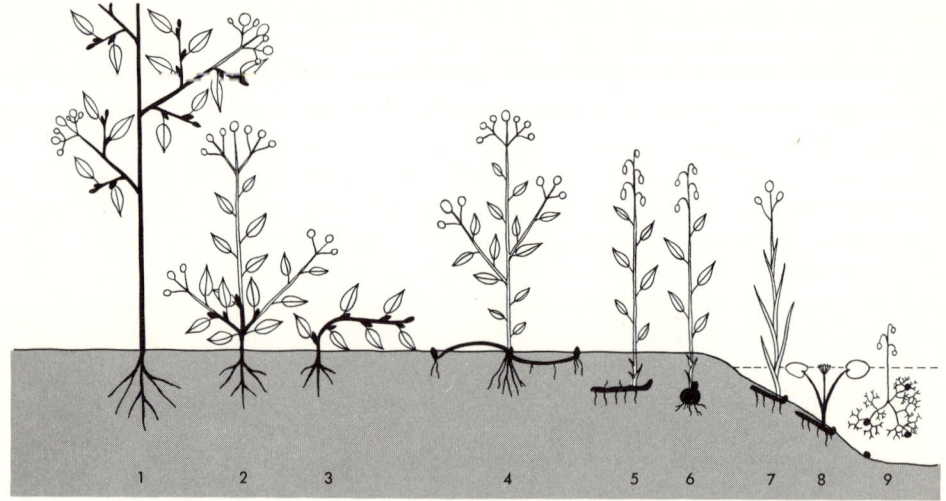

Redrawn, by permission, from C. Raunkiaer. 1934. *The Life-Form of Plants and Statistical Plant Geography.* Oxford: Clarendon Press.

Fig. 5-12. Four of Raunkiaer's five life-forms: phanerophytes (1), chamaephytes (2–3), hemicryptophytes (4), and cryptophytes (5–9). The parts of the plant that die in the unfavorable season are unshaded; the persisting parts with surviving buds are shaded black.

    Hemicryptophytes – surviving buds or shoot-apices are situated at the soil surface; herbs growing in rosettes and tussocks.

    Chamaephytes – surviving buds or shoot-apices borne on shoots very close to but above the ground; creeping woody plants and herbs.

    Phanerophytes – surviving buds or shoot-apices borne on negatively geotropic shoots that project into the air; shrubs and trees.

Since the ability of a plant to survive in a given environment is dependent on its being adapted to that environment, and since the life form is a morphological adaptation, it should follow that given life forms would be more prevalent in some environments than in others. Indeed, in analyzing the life forms of various regions and comparing them with a "normal" spectrum based on one thousand species selected at random (Table 5-3), Raunkiaer found a predominance of phanerophytes in tropical moist regions; this is perhaps not unexpected, since the exposed buds are not subjected in this kind of environment to such adversities as cold temperature or aridity. Desert areas would require, among other drought-resisting adaptations discussed earlier, maximum protection of buds and regenerating parts from high temperatures and aridity; not surprisingly, one finds a high preponderance of therophytes and not insignificant proportions of chamaephytes and hemicryptophytes in such environments. Intermediate between these climate extremes, and their corresponding sharp differences in amount of protection afforded the propagative organ, is the moist-temperate region in which hemicryptophytes predominate, these affording an intermediate amount of protection.

Relative proportions of different life forms also occur on a much less global scale, as in the instance of a north- and a south-facing slope of a mountain (Table 5-3, part B). As will be shown shortly, the north slope is more cool and moist than the south slope and there is a vegetational response, in the way of life form, to this difference in microclimate. Finally, in yet another application, H. M. Hansen has applied the life form as an age indicator in considering fossil flora, from which he concluded that in the evolution of flowering plants, the progression has been from taller to shorter phanerophytes with a subsequent origin of hemicryptophytes, and most recently the development of chamaephytes, therophytes, and cryptophytes.

Inherent in the life-form approach is the idea of a vertical ordering or stratification of plants from the low-lying cryptophytes, therophytes, and hemicryptophytes to chamaephytes and phanerophytes of various heights. However, the emphasis on vegetative parts in the Raunkiaer system conveys little of the actual physiognomy of the community—how tall the plants are, what their spatial distribution is, what their leaf shape and texture is, etc. Can these aspects of the community be assessed without a fuller working knowledge of the various species comprising an area? That is, is it possible to develop an ecological classification that would not only convey the appearance but also indicate something of the function of a community, some categorization that would serve for analysis of communities in the way

TABLE 5-3. The Proportion of Life Forms, Based on the Raunkiaer Scheme, in Various Environments

Location	Phanero- phytes	Chamae- phytes	Hemicrypto- phytes	Crypto- phytes	Thero- phytes
A. Normal spectrum of 1000 sp.	46	9	26	6	13
Tropical climate	61–74	6–16	4–12	1–5	5–16
Tundra climate	0–1	22–26	57–68	4–15	2–4
Temperate—moist climate	8–15	2–7	49–52	15–25	9–20
Desert climate	9–26	7–21	18–20	5–8	42–50
B. Cushetunk Mountain, New Jersey					
North slope	41.8	1.2	41.8	15.2	0
South slope	32.1	1.8	46.4	12.5	7.1

Part A adapted, by permission, from Pierre Dansereau. Biogeography—An Ecological Perspective. Copyright © 1957. The Ronald Press Company, New York. Part B from J. Cantlon, 1953. Ecological Monographs 23: 241–270.

TABLE 5-4. Six Categories of a Structural Description of Vegetation Proposed by Pierre Dansereau

1. Life Form

T	◯	trees
F	◯	shrubs
H	▽	herbs
M	◠	bryoids
E	✡	epiphytes
L	⌬	lianas

2. Size

t	tall	(T: minimum 25 m)
		(F: 2–8 m)
		(H: minimum 2 m)
m	medium	(T: 10–25 m)
		(F, H: 0.5–2 m)
		(M: minimum 10 cm)
l	low	(T: 8–10 m)
		(F, H: maximum 50 cm)
		(M: maximum 10 cm)

3. Function

d	▢	deciduous
s	‖‖‖	semideciduous
e	▦	evergreen
j	▩	evergreen-succulent; or evergreen-leafless

4. Leaf Shape and Size

n	⬯	needle or spine
g	◊	graminoid
a	◇	medium or small
h	♡	broad
v	⋎	compound
q	◯	thalloid

5. Leaf Texture

f	▨	filmy
z	▢	membranous
x	▬	sclerophyll
k	⁝⁝⁝	succulent; or fungoid

6. Coverage

b		barren or very sparse
i		discontinuous
p		in tufts or groups
c		continuous

Reproduced, by permission, from P. Dansereau, 1951. Ecology 32: 172–229.

the trophic-level designations (producer, consumer, etc.) aid discussion of energy flow? A number of ecologists believe it is possible to do so. Dr. Pierre Dansereau, now of the Brooklyn Botanical Garden, is one such person. His scheme and its application will serve as an example of one of several possible approaches that have been employed.

Dansereau recognizes six major structural features to be assessed in describing a community and has proposed, in addition, a series of symbols that may be employed to represent the community in graphic form (Table 5-4). As can be seen from the tabulation, not only is the life form of the vegetation noted, but also its size and distribution or coverage, and several major characteristics of the leaf and leaf fall.

An application of the Dansereau scheme to a community in the Great Lakes area dominated by beech, maple, and hemlock is shown in Figure 5-13. The upper figure (a) represents a complete symbolic interpretation; the middle (b) a somewhat more conventional diagram of the same community. The appearance of this community can be described as follows (I have inserted the symbols indicated in Figure 5-13a for the reader's convenience of reference between the symbolic diagram and the chart of symbols): physiognomically, the area is dominated by a continuous cover (c) of tall (t), deciduous (d) trees (T) with broad (h) membranous (z) leaves. Of less significance among the tall trees are a few deciduous forms with compound leaves (v) and some sparsely distributed (b) needle-leaved (n) evergreens (e) with leaves of sclerophyllous texture (x). Deciduous (d) lianas (L) with small (a) membranous (z) leaves are sparsely distributed (b). One can then continue to describe in expanded form the other structural features of the shrub, herb, and bryoid layers of the community.

The advantage of a schema such as this one of Dansereau is the potential of permitting more ready comparison of communities (cf. Figure 5-13a and 5-13c). When it is tied to other functional features, such as productivity or mineral cycling, it is possible to detect some correlative and perhaps eventually causal relationships. Further, for the student or even the professional ecologist lacking sufficient training in taxonomic botany, a regrettable but increasingly prevalent situation, this approach obviates a major stumbling block. At certain levels of sophistication of vegetational analysis, such nontaxonomic schemes have a rightful and helpful place in community analysis.

The several diagrams just described indicate that the deciduous forest biome is dominated by deciduous trees—a tautology, of course. But this statement does not imply that only a given species is characteristic. Sugar maple, for example, is widely distributed in the eastern half of North America, but it is dominant only in the northern portion, sharing this status with basswood (*Tilia*) to the west and beech (*Fagus*) to the east (Figure 5-13). Although many of the deciduous tree species of the biome are widely distributed, their area of dominance is restricted and typically shared with

134
ECOLOGICAL COMMUNITIES

A. Life-form, size, function, leaf type and texture of a sugar maple—hemlock forest

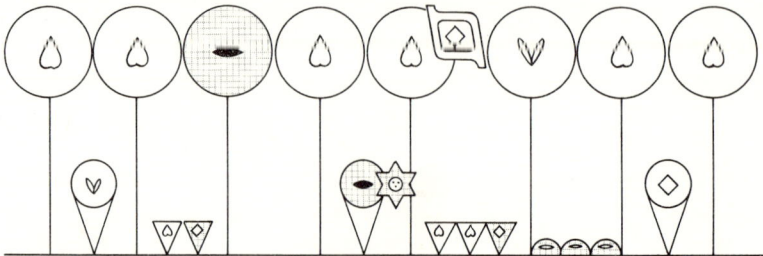

T t d h (v) z c (e n x b). L t d a z b. F m d a (v) z (e n x) i. E m e q k b. H l d h z (e a x) p. M l e n f p.

B. Semirealistic outline

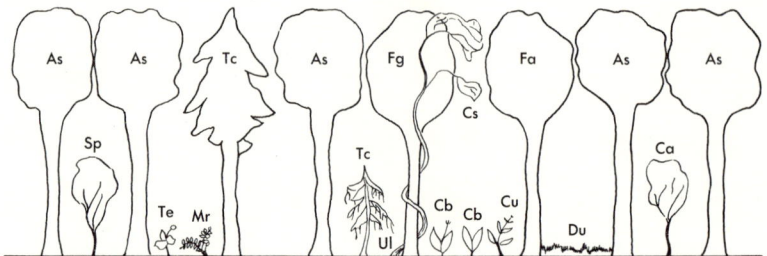

As, sugar maple; Tc, hemlock; Fa, ash; Fg, beech; Ca, dogwood; Sp, sambucus; Te, trillium; etc.

C. Structural diagram of a jack-pine barren

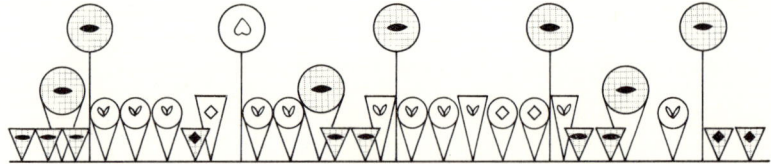

T l e n x l (d h z b). F m e n x i. F l d v (a) z p. H m d v (a) z b. H l e n (a) x p.

Redrawn, by permission, from Pierre Dansereau. 1951. Ecology 32: 172–229.

Fig. 5-13. Application of the Dansereau scheme for structural description of vegetation to a sugar maple-hemlock stand and a jack-pine stand.

one or more other species. This is well illustrated in the forest regions of eastern North America as described by Dr. E. Lucy Braun (Figure 5-14). The map suggests sharp discontinuities between forest types, but how discrete are these boundaries and, within each of these forest regions, how uniform are the communities? What are the regulative factors involved in these patterns? It is obvious that we need to turn from the more generalized vegetative and physiognomic description of structure to a consideration of

ECOLOGICAL COMMUNITIES

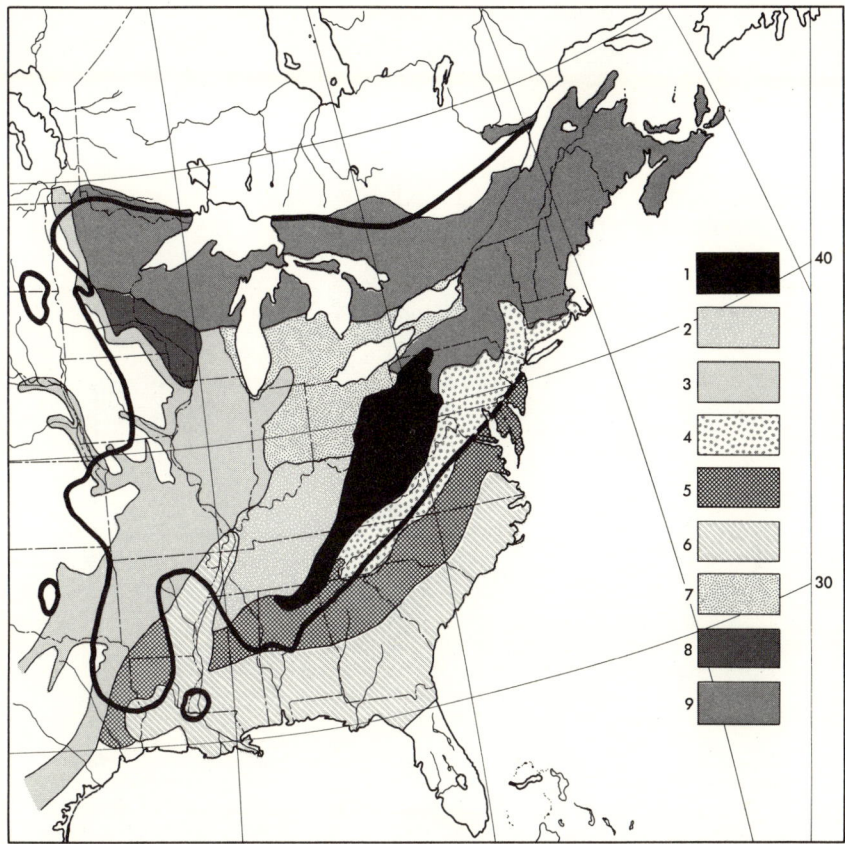

Redrawn, by permission, from Pierre Dansereau. 1957. Biogeography—An Ecological Perspective. Copyright © 1957. The Ronald Press Company, New York.

Fig. 5-14. Bioclimatic limits of sugar maple (heavy line) showing major forest regions recognized by E. Lucy Braun: (1) mixed mesophytic; (2) western mesophytic; (3) oak-hickory; (4) oak-chestnut; (5) oak-pine; (6) southeastern evergreen; (7) beech-maple; (8) maple-basswood; (9) hemlock-white pine-northern hardwoods.

species composition and to a consideration of the peculiar factors that dispose a particular organization of types to occur in particular regions.

Variation in Structure

Although each major forest ecosystem is typified by its characteristic assemblage, variation within the region may be considerable. An excellent illustration of the local regulation of community composition is shown in Figure 5-15. Although the portion of southern Ontario bordering the Great

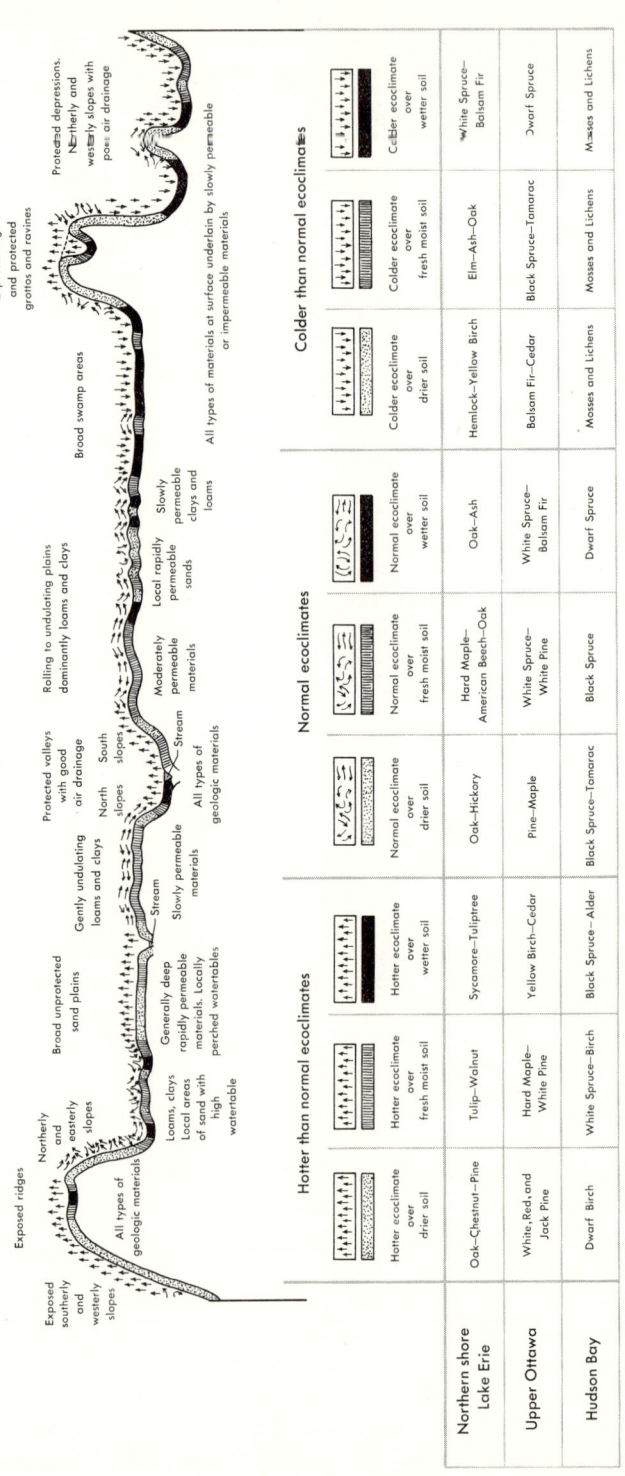

Redrawn, by permission, from G. A. Hills. 1952. Ontario: Department of Lands and Forests, Research Report No. 24: 1–41.

Fig. 5-15. The interrelation of microclimate, soil, and forest distribution in selected regions of Ontario.

Lakes is dominated by and characterized as being beech and maple, relatively slight variations in temperature and moisture and the interaction of these two gradients on the nature of the soil result in quite different species assemblages. Even casual observations either by the inveterate woods tramper or a sedentary auto passenger reveal the variability in vegetation observed in passing over even moderately rolling country interspersed with an occasional stream valley. Local topographic and microclimatological factors do seem to be involved in determining localized assemblages.

In an excellent study on this matter, John Cantlon showed a decided vegetational difference on the north and south slopes of Cushetunk Mountain in New Jersey, a difference tied directly to the local or microclimate. Cantlon found that the south slope had higher air and soil temperatures and a larger vapor pressure deficit, the latter being a measure of water availability and evaporation. For example, the average difference in the mean monthly temperature on the two slopes was 4.5°F at 4 cm below the soil surface, 6.0°F at 5 cm above the soil surface, and 3.5°F at 20 cm above the soil surface. These seemingly minor differences were responsible, however, for a striking difference in the vegetation of the two slopes, evidenced in part by the shift in life-form (Table 5-3, part B). In general, vegetation differences increased groundward, with the bryophyte or ground cover showing the most marked difference; the more moist and cool north slope had the greater amount of ground cover and higher occurrence of individuals of given species.

For a somewhat detailed example of the differences in slopes, consideration of only the tree layer will be instructive. First, the south slope had a greater density with 21,987 trees/3500 m^2 vs. 15,759 trees/3500 m^2 on the north slope. However, the total basal area of the south slope trees was less, 72.4 ft^2/3500 m^2 vs. 93.7 ft^2/3500 m^2; this results from the north slope having a greater proportion of larger individuals. Next, the most abundant species, in order of decreasing density, were not the same on the two slopes: on the south slope, the sequence of the first four was dogwood (*Cornus florida*), ash (*Fraxinus americana*), sassafras (*Sassafras albidum*), and tulip tree (*Liriodendron tulipfera*); on the north slope, the sequence was ash, witch hazel (*Hamamelis virginiana*), birch (*Betula lenta*), and maple (*Acer rubrum*). This particular species of maple was fourteenth in abundance on the south slope, the birch was ninth and witch hazel did not attain sufficient height (1 m) to be included in the tree canopy.

This contrast of the vegetation of a north and a south slope implies a sharp discontinuity based on exposure or orientation; the corresponding discontinuities observed in temperature and moisture may not, therefore, be so surprising. But if one were to conduct a study following a continuous transect from one of these slopes to the other, a continuous gradient of microclimate and vegetation rather than a discontinuity would be observed. In the Great Smoky Mountains of Tennessee and North Carolina, mean temperatures decrease with elevation at an average of 2.23°F for each 1000 ft; thus, high elevations in these mountains average 10 to 15° cooler than the base. Likewise, annual precipitation increases from about 125 cm in the lower valleys to about 200 cm at high elevations. These major environmental gradients dictate to a considerable extent the distribution and relative abundance of individual species and, in consequence, affect the composition of the plant communities and their associated ecosystem components. In a major study of this problem, Robert Whittaker plotted the distribution and abundance of the vegetation along a moisture gradient. Almost all species showed a bell-shaped curve of population distribution along the gradient, with broad overlap among the different populations (Figure 5-16).

Such patterns imply a gradual and progressive change in the structure of vegetation from one environmental extreme to another, a continuum in

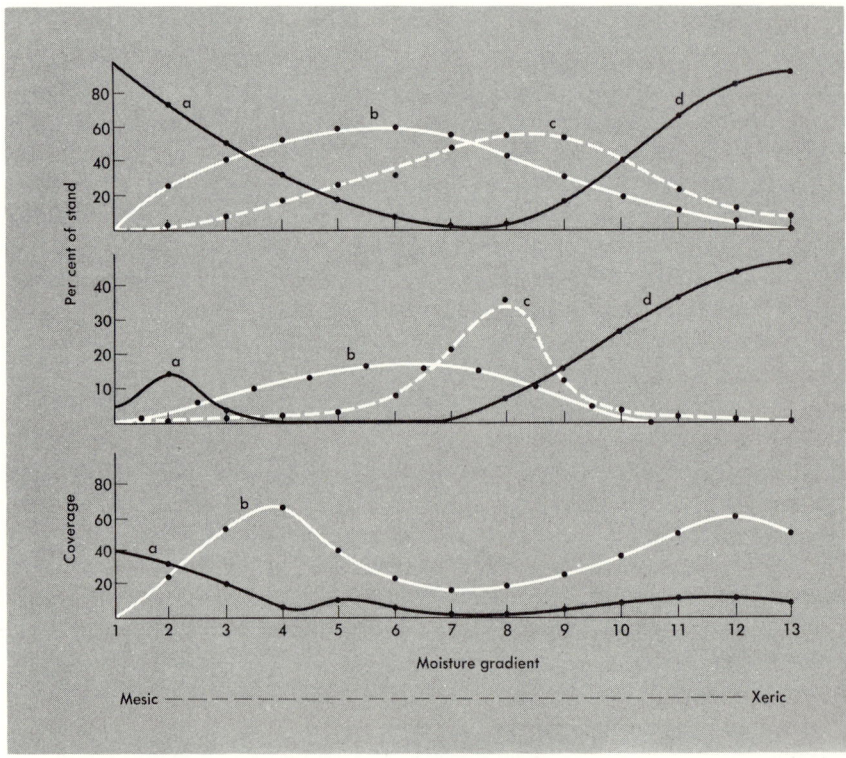

Redrawn, by permission, from R. H. Whittaker. 1956. Ecological Monographs 26: 1–80.

Fig. 5-16. Transect of the moisture gradient in the Great Smoky Mountains at 1500 to 2500 feet. Top curves are for tree classes: (a) mesic; (b) submesic; (c) subxeric; (d) xeric. Middle curves are for tree species: (a) birch (*Betula alleghaniensis*); (b) dogwood (*Cornus florida*); (c) oak (*Quercus prinus*); (d) pine (*Pinus virginiana*). Bottom curves are for the understory: (a) herbs; (b) shrubs.

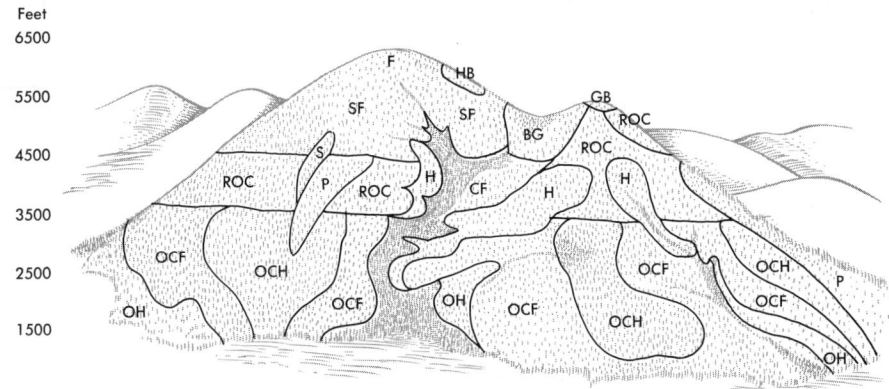

Redrawn, by permission, from R. H. Whittaker. 1956. Ecological Monographs 26: 1–80.

Fig. 5-17. Topographic distribution of vegetation types on an idealized west-facing mountain and valley in the Great Smoky Mountains. Vegetation types: BG, beech gap; CF, cove forest; F, Fraser fir forest; GB, grassy bald; H, hemlock forest; HB, heath bald; OCF, chestnut oak-chestnut forest; OCH, chestnut oak-chestnut heath; OH, oak-hickory forest; P, pine forest and pine heath; ROC, red oak-chestnut forest; S, spruce forest; SF, spruce-fir forest; WOC, white oak-chestnut forest.

which discrete subdivisions do not, in reality, exist. Nonetheless, the existence of the continuum does not preclude the recognition of major vegetation types over a broader area of the same region (Figure 5-17) or on the very broad scale of the biome (Figure 5-1). Whittaker had earlier demonstrated comparable patterns for some one hundred foliage-eating insects in the Smoky Mountains, and J. T. Curtis of the University of Wisconsin had shown such patterns in the upland forests of Wisconsin. Curtis concluded, in one of his studies: "... tree species occur in a continuously shifting series of combinations with a definite sequence or pattern, the resultant of a limited floristic complement acting on, and acted upon by, a limited range of physical environmental potentialities. Such a gradient of communities is here called a vegetational continuum. . . ." (*Ecology* **32**: 476–496. 1951.)

The nature of the community as implied by the continuum suggests that each community is distinct from all others, that it is individualistic. An historically important statement of the individualistic nature of the plant community is that of its foremost proponent, the American ecologist Henry Gleason:

> ...the vegetation of an area is merely the resultant of two factors, the fluctuating and fortuitous immigration of plants and an equally fluctuating and variable environment. As a result, there is no inherent reason why any two areas of the earth's surface should bear precisely the same vegetation, nor any reason for adhering to our old ideas of the definiteness and distinctness of plant associations. As a matter of fact, no two areas

of the earth's surface do bear precisely the same vegetation, except as a matter of chance, and that chance may be broken in another year by a continuance of the same variable migration and fluctuating environment which produced it.

(Bulletin of the Torrey Botanical Club **53**:7–26. 1926.)

This statement has misled some observers into thinking that Gleason meant that communities were random mixtures of species undetermined by environment—a position which is untenable and for which there is evidence that he did not hold it to be so. What is to be emphasized in the Gleason position is that species are individualistic in that no two are distributed alike. It follows, then, that since communities consist of individualistic and broadly overlapping species populations, they intergrade continuously—and each arbitrary isolate is, in fact, unique.

To be sure, there is no unanimity among plant or animal ecologists on this point regarding the nature of the community. On the other side of the ledger, there are those who contend that communities are discrete, discernible, describable entities. In this view, analysis will reveal that certain clusters of species reach their optimum in the same communities, and further that the species of one such grouping would never occur as important members of another group. In the more extreme development of this view, plant associations are viewed as having objective reality like an organism or a species and being capable of description in comparable ways. Major proponents of this view have been the American ecologist Frederick Clements and Josias Braun-Blanquet, of the Zurich-Montpellier "school" of phytosociologists. Clements' statement that "the developmental study of vegetation necessarily rests upon the assumption that the unit of climax formation is an organic entity" is indicative of this viewpoint.

To explore and provide complete evaluation of opposing "organismic" and "individualistic" views would take us well beyond the introductory nature of this text. What is important here is that ecology, like other fields within biology, has adherents to different positions, hypotheses if you will, and that likewise there is an arena in ecology for both vigorous debate and certainly much more collection and analysis of data. Now, having considered some of the structural aspects of the community, let us turn to a discussion of some aspects of its dynamics.

FUNCTIONAL ASPECTS OF THE DECIDUOUS FOREST

Periodism

In order to discuss vegetational structure, essential and characteristic features were abstracted to a kind of static model; in doing so, we may have obscured the dynamic, ever-changing aspect of physiognomy and composition. For example, although the rather sharp differences in vegetation on the north and south slopes of Cushetunk Mountain were discussed, variation in the time of occurrence of major vegetational events was not. On the north slope, which you may recall is cooler and moister, many of the herbs are about to bloom or are in bloom or fruit by late spring; however, the maximum period of herbaceous activity on the drier and warmer south slope is during early summer. Since the vegetational differences between the slopes were largely due to relative density, frequency, and cover and not to exclusive presence on one slope and absence on the other, the difference in flowering activity is occasioned by both subtle physiological variations within each species and by subtle but real microclimatological differences between the slopes.

Since each species has its own characteristic pattern of sequential development and flowering, a pattern that is largely attuned to and regulated by the major environmental climatic gradients, it is not surprising that whole communities demonstrate phenomena attuned to naturally recurring events. Thus, in the deciduous forest biome, spring brings release from dormancy and a resurgence of vegetative activity that culminates in leafing out in deciduous trees; fall brings the onset of dormancy and a curtailment of activity manifested in leaf color change and fall. Since there are natural geophysical phenomena that recur at different intervals, and since different species differentially respond to such stimuli, different rhythms would be expected, *a priori,* among different communities. Thus, the sugar maple community that leafs out in spring and undergoes leaf fall in autumn is responding to an annual rhythm, that of shifting day-length resulting from the shift of the earth on its axis. By the same token, this same group of plants responds during the growing season to the diurnal rhythm of alternating periods of light and darkness by undergoing photosynthesis during the day but not at night. It is not intended here to explore the phenomenon of animal, plant, and community periodism in its myriad facets; this is an intense area of investigation in its own right and has been well treated in a number of recent monographs. The interest here is in considering the phenomenon with respect to the larger issue of the ecological community. For example, we earlier discussed the regulation of the distribution of two species of barnacles by tidal periodicity, both that occurring daily as well as that occurring monthly. Our question now is the degree to which naturally recurring phenomena affect the structure and function of ecological communities. We shall consider (1) the regulatory effect of photoperiod on the growth, development, and flowering of a single species and thereby of the community of which it is a part, (2) the variation that exists within widely distributed species regarding the response to photoperiod and the concomitant effect on the ecosystems of which it is a part, and finally (3) the diurnal metabolic pattern of an ecosystem.

Spring and Sumacs. Onset of vegetative activity is the characteristic biological criterion of the beginning of spring, regardless of what the calendar may suggest. The sequence of these phenological events in sumac (*Rhus glabra*) has been well described by Elizabeth Gilbert (Figure 5-18). One of the striking characteristics of this onset stage of plant activity is that events that mark the initiation of development of an organ (e.g., bud elongation and opening, the appearance of the leaf, and inflorescence) are completed rather rapidly; in contrast, events dealing with completion of growth of an organ (cessation of growth of twig, leaf, and inflorescence) occur over a longer period of time. Comparisons of some nine clones of sumac showed great uniformity in the sequence of these phenological events, suggesting the most important control to be genetic, but the fact that slope exposure altered the time of onset implies an additional regulation by environmental gradients comparable to those on the two slopes of Cushetunk Mountain.

The release from inactivity and the onset of the sequence of phenological events described in sumac imply attunement to the shift in temperature and photoperiod that takes place seasonally. The evidence for a causal relationship between these environmental gradients and vegetative activity is indeed extensive. It is well-known that among annuals, for example, most seeds will not germinate until after a period of exposure to cold. This is particularly the case in those annuals characteristic of cold climates; a cold stimulus is also prerequisite to hatching in a number of insects. For desert

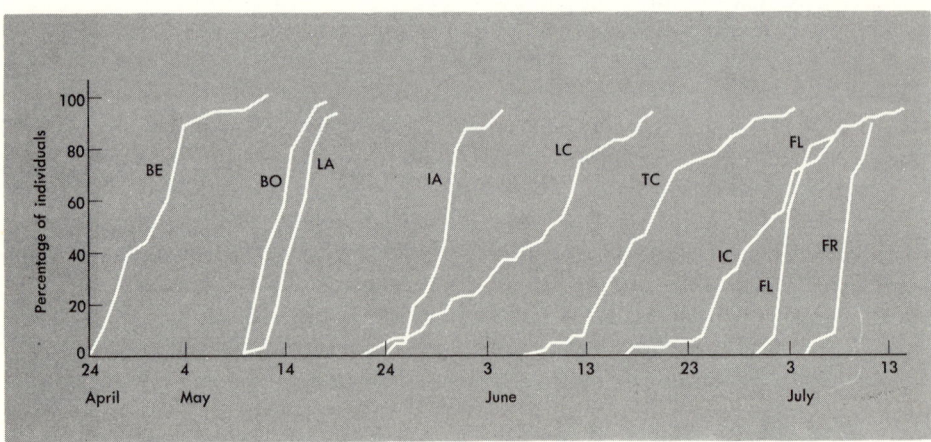

Redrawn, by permission, from E. F. Gilbert. 1961. *American Midland Naturalist* 66: 286–300.

Fig. 5-18. Progress of phenological events in sumac in southern Michigan. BE = bud elongation; BO = bud opening; LA = leaf appearance; IA = inflorescence appearance; LC = cessation of leaf growth; TC = cessation of twig growth; FL = first flower; FR = first fruit; IC = cessation of inflorescence growth.

annuals, the stimulus to release from dormancy is the occurrence of precipitation. Once germinated, however, the plant grows, matures, and reproduces in response to a variety of factors including the production of hormones, the direction and quality of light, and the length of day.

The regulatory influence of photoperiod, or, if your prefer, the differential sensitivity of species to the length of the day, was first demonstrated in 1918 by W. W. Garner and H. A. Allard. Their initial studies on tobacco were augmented by work on other species, and subsequently by many other investigators on yet many other species. From their studies, Garner and Allard concluded that there are "long-day" and "short-day" plants, the former flowering when the photoperiod exceeds a given minimum (usually 12 to 14 hours), the latter when the photoperiod is below a given maximum (usually 11 to 15 hours). In fairness to the nonconformists, some plants show no photoperiodic response; they are usually referred to as neutral-day or day-neutral plants.

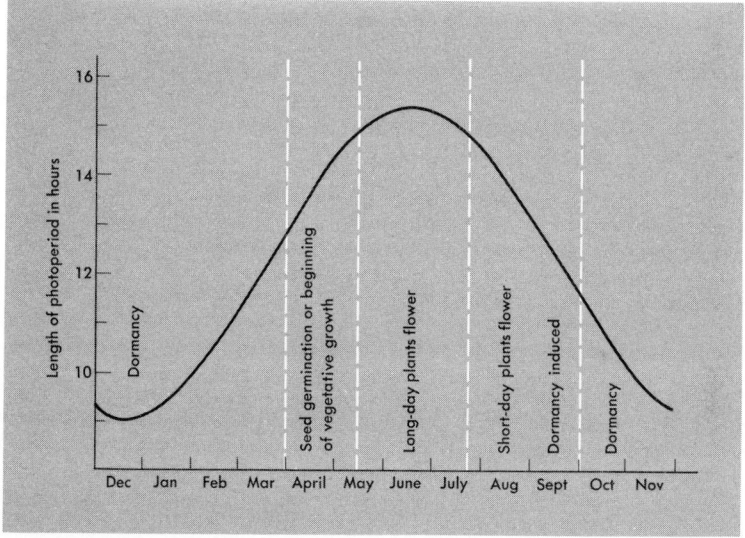

From The Living Plant by Peter M. Ray. Copyright © 1963 by Holt, Rinehart and Winston, Inc. Redrawn by permission of Holt, Rinehart and Winston, Inc.

Fig. 5-19. Yearly variation in length of the day at 43° north latitude and the correspondence to photoperiodic responses of plants.

The effect of this differential response by given species to temperature and to the quality and quantity of light in a given ecosystem is reflected in the seasonal progression of major events (Figure 5-19). Thus, we have come to another basis of ecological, or eco-physiological, categorizing of vegetation, not by their taxonomic but rather by their functional status.

Photoperiodism and Ecotypes

From this discussion it might be assumed that a given species has as specific a physiological response to photoperiod as it has a specific morphological adaptation to another environmental parameter. Thus, one might anticipate that over its extensive range (Figure 5-14) sugar maple would leaf-flower-fruit, etc. in any given area only when the critical temperature and photoperiod levels were reached. It would then follow that there should be a south-to-north progression in these phenological events corresponding to the progression in these environmental gradients. In a general way such patterns are recognized, for a one-degree northward shift in latitude amounts to about a difference in four days in the onset of a given phenological event. Spring is "earlier" to the south. Incidentally, this same effect is also generated by about a 400 foot change in altitude.

There is ample evidence, however, to suggest that widespread species are not physiologically identical in all parts of their range. In 1944, Charles Olmsted demonstrated that different populations of a common prairie grass known as side-oats grama (*Bouteloua curtipendula*) did not have identical responses to given photoperiods. Although essentially identical morphologically, populations from such northern areas as Canada and the Dakotas were shown to be long-day plants, demonstrating normal vegetative and flowering behavior only with photoperiods of 14 hours or longer; in contrast, populations from southern areas like Texas and Arizona were shown to be short-day plants, performing normally under 13 hours of light, but failing to flower on photoperiods longer than 14 hours. According to an extensive study of the ecology of alpine sorrel (*Oxyria digyna*), H. A. Mooney and W. D. Billings showed that populations from California, Colorado, and Wyoming require about 15 hours of light for flowering, but photoperiods of over 20 hours are necessary for flowering north of the Arctic Circle. These investigators also reported other physiological differences in populations at different latitudes, the more northern populations having more chlorophyll, higher respiratory rates at the same temperature, and an attainment of peak photosynthesis at lower temperatures.

In some instances, these ecological races, or *ecotypes* as they are called, may show little or no morphological difference concomitant with the physiological differences; sometimes they do. One of the striking examples of the latter is the variation of range and average height of different populations of a perennial herb, the yarrow (*Achillea*) (Figure 5-20). In extensive studies, Jens Clausen, David Keck, and William Hiesey compared populations of *Achillea* from widely different habitats by transplanting and growing them under one uniform condition; in other studies, they compared some fourteen populations from different habitats under uniform growing conditions of three different climatic types. As a result, they were able to show the

ECOLOGICAL COMMUNITIES

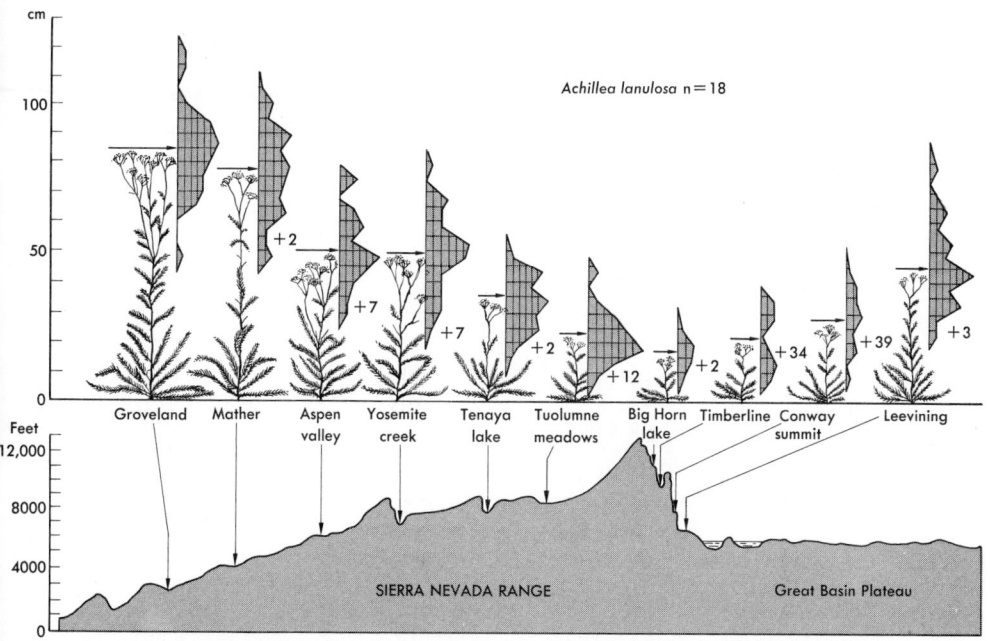

Fig. 5-20. Ecotypic variation in the height of *Achillea lanulosa* grown in a uniform garden at Stanford, California. The plants originated in the localities shown in the profile, a 100-mile transect across central California at approximately 38° north latitude. Each population sample represents about 60 individuals. The frequency diagrams show variation in height within each population: the horizontal lines separate class intervals of 5 cm according to the marginal scale, and the distance between vertical lines represents 2 individuals. The numbers to the right of some frequency diagrams indicate the nonflowering plants. The specimens represent plants of average height, and the arrows point to mean heights.

existence of considerable genetic variation and racial differences among plants of a single species.

Using the transplant garden procedure of Clausen, Keck, and Hiesey, Calvin McMillan studied the role of ecotypic variation in distribution of the central grasslands of North America. As many as twelve species of grass, including side-oats grama, in which Olmsted had previously reported photoperiod ecotypes, were studied from more than 40 sample sites ranging over the central grasslands from Montana, North Dakota, and Minnesota in the north to Oklahoma in the south. The transplant garden was at Lincoln, Nebraska, where responses under both natural and experimental light regimes were observed. McMillan observed not only geographic variation in photoperiod response in a number of species, but also both latitudinal and altitudinal gradients (Figure 5-21). In progressing southward some 825

ECOLOGICAL COMMUNITIES

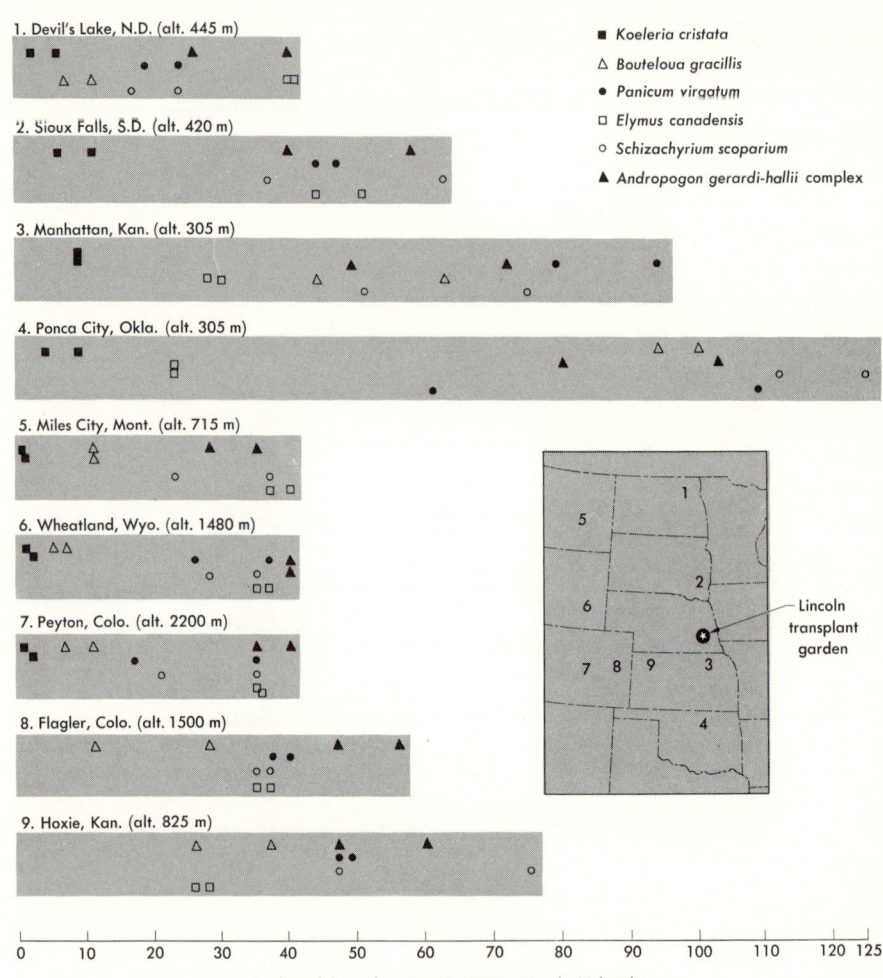

Redrawn, by permission, from C. McMillan. 1959. Ecological Monographs 29: 285–308.

Fig. 5-21. Comparison of community responses of various grassland species in a transplant garden at Lincoln, Nebraska in 1957. The symbols indicate the extremes of initial flowering time of population samples transplanted from the locations shown on the inset map.

miles, but with a change of only 150 m in elevation, from Devil's Lake, North Dakota to Ponca City, Oklahoma, the period during which initial flowering occurred in an experimental community consisting of six species increased from about 40 to about 125 days. By contrast, the period of initial flowering over the same range of latitude is strongly influenced by altitude. This is seen in the progression from Miles City, Montana at 715 m, to Wheatland, Wyoming at 1480 m, and Peyton, Colorado at 2200 m; all of these communities show an initial flowering period of 40 days, like that of

Devil's Lake to the north, but at different latitudes. At essentially the same latitude, however, altitude also affects the situation; there is a west-to-east altitudinal gradient at the same latitude comparable to a north-to-south latitudinal gradient at the same altitude. For example, the west-to-east transect involves a decrease in elevation from 2200 m at Peyton, Colorado, to 1500 m at Flagler, Colorado, to 825 m at Hoxie, Kansas, and to 310 m at Manhattan, Kansas and a corresponding lengthening of the period of initial flowering. This has, then, the same effect as a latitudinal gradient at the same altitude, as demonstrated by the Devil's Lake, North Dakota to Ponca City, Oklahoma transect.

Stating these results in another way, and coupled with other data obtained, a given species of grass in the northern part of the grassland biome consists of long-day plants that flower during the long days of midsummer; in the southern part of their range, the same species consists of populations of short-day plants that flower in early autumn. Likewise, populations of a given species occurring in the western part of the range at high altitude flower earlier than their eastern brethren at lower altitudes. In each instance, McMillan sees these ecotypes as attunements to the peculiar climatic conditions of their natural regions—a more northern community, for example, being attuned to a shorter frostfree period by a shorter period of flowering. Thus, it must be that there has been natural selection for aggregations of individuals of different species with characteristics of early maturity which allow survival under such conditions—a selection for entire ecosystems. It would thus be the case that the continuity of the grassland over a broad geographic area of admittedly nonuniform habitats is related to the ecotypic variation inherent in grasses, a variation which, in turn, is regulated by genetic gradients. Since the likelihood of identical habitats is low, a repetition of combinations of certain species over broad geographic ranges is almost certain to involve ecotypes of the species involved. The great central grassland from Texas to Alberta thus appears to be a physiognomically uniform vegetational unit in spite of habitat nonuniformity, primarily because grasses are grasses—because of their wide range of genetic and physiological adaptation.

Periodism and Temperature Effects

On a diurnal basis, there are a number of significant periodic phenomena which affect the function of a community. The strikingly extensive range of diurnal temperature on the desert floor is a case in point (Figure 5-22). In such situations, desert shrubs are differentially adapted to withstand daily changes of 100°F at the ground surface while simultaneously experiencing little or no change in their deeper roots and a quite considerable change of about 40°F a meter above the ground. Owing to the high specific heat

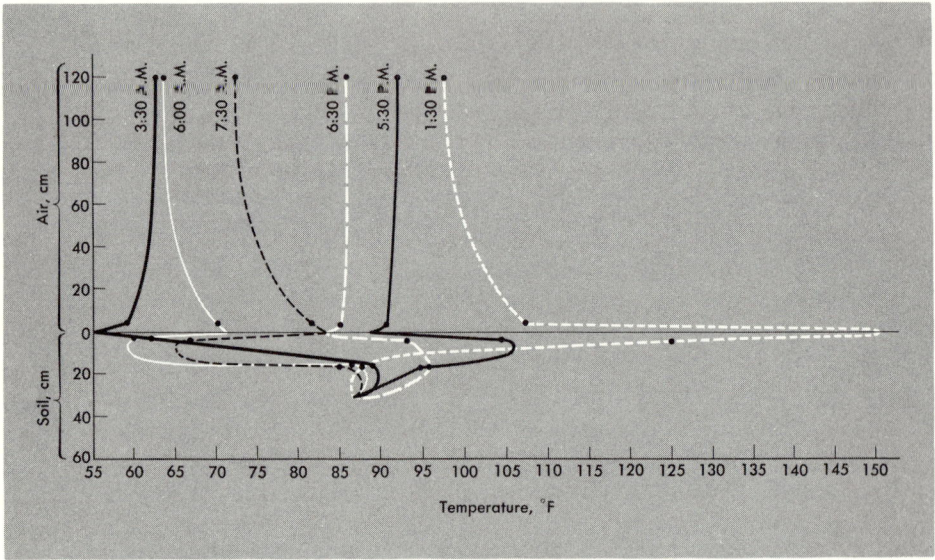

Redrawn, by permission of the publisher from Plants and the Ecosystem by W. D. Billings. Copyright 1964 by Wadsworth Publishing Company, Inc., Belmont, California.

Fig. 5-22. The daily cycle of air and soil temperatures from a vegetated sandy area in the Nevada desert on a clear day, July 31, 1953.

of water, diurnal temperature changes of such magnitude do not occur in the surface waters of aquatic ecosystems; over the course of a year, however, considerable changes in temperature do take place, particularly in the upper waters of temperate ecosystems (Figure 5-23).

The forces in this series of changes involve the changes in density of water with temperature and the action of wind. Since water is most dense at 4°C, warmer or colder water will float on top of a layer of this temperature. Thus, after the ice melts, the surface water warms and as it becomes more dense it sinks below the colder, less dense layer immediately beneath it. This overturning of water which, in the absence of wind, will occur at 4°C ultimately results in a temperature that is uniform from top to bottom. Subsequent heating of surface water, which is accompanied by a corresponding decrease in density, results in warmer water at the surface; wind action results in stirring of the surface waters, mixing them to depths according to the strength and direction of wind and relative to the exposure or orientation of the system. By midsummer, there is a relatively homogenous temperature layer, the *epilimnion,* often several meters deep, at the surface, followed by a zone of rapid temperature change, the *metalimnion,* and then a relatively stable region, the *hypolimnion,* extending to the bottom. As fall progresses, surface temperature changes with corresponding increases in density, eventually resulting in top-heavy conditions; in the absence of wind, turnover will, as mentioned before, occur at 4°C, but turnover may occur over a longer period of time and at higher temperatures. The end result in either case is the development of a uniform temperature profile from surface to bottom comparable to that of the spring.

The biological significance of this temperature cycle in temperate aquatic ecosystems is indeed broad. Not only are the activities of temperature-dependent organisms directly affected, but also the presence of an ice cover, especially when snow covered, severely affects light transmission with a resultant reduction of photosynthesis. Stability of water layers during the summer stratification reduces the amount of mixing, and thereby the hypolimnion tends to become depleted of oxygen even though it may be pro-

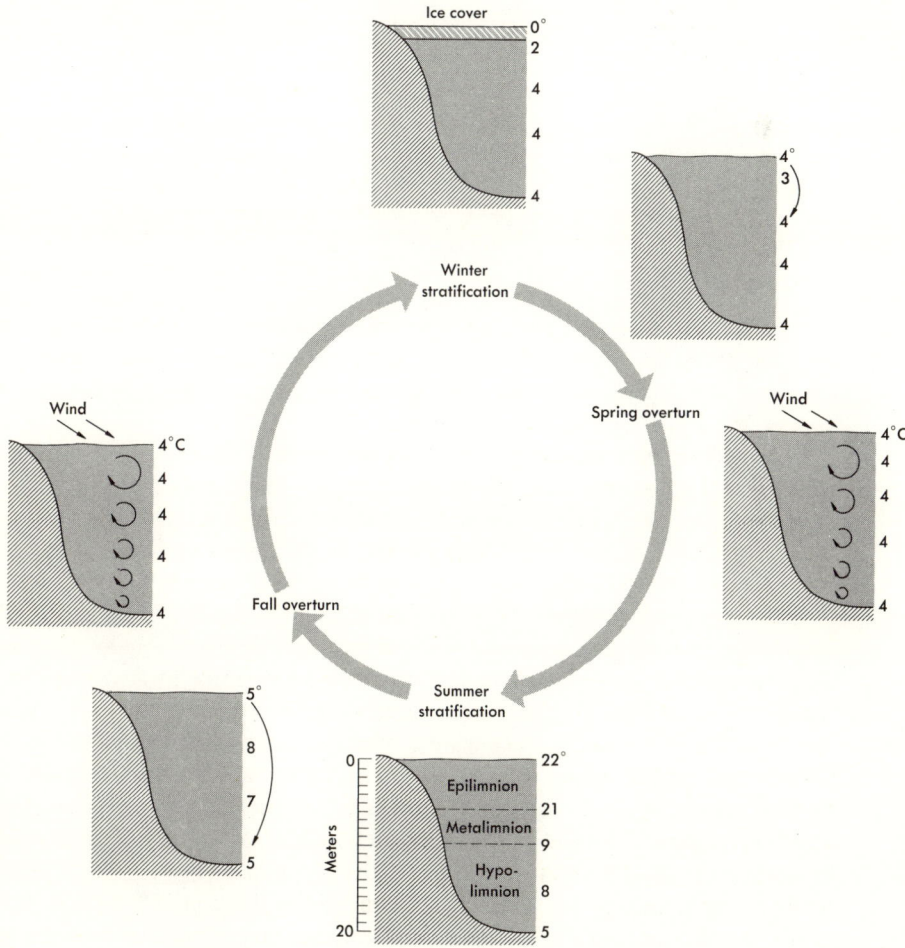

Fig. 5-23. The seasonal cycle of temperature in a temperate lake.

duced in abundance at the surface; that is, in the stratified condition, there is no atmospheric contact with the hypolimnion. We shall see the untoward effect of this oxygen depletion in a discussion of Lake Erie in Chapter 6. On the positive side, however, a significant result of the semiannual mixing of the entire body of water is that nutrients are also mixed and redistributed; those which became part of the lower water as a result of sinking of dead protoplasm are brought to the surface waters, where they are thus available for photosynthesis and other anabolic activities.

Not all aquatic systems experience such complete mixing. In a very few inland lakes, some water, typically in the lower portion, remains un-

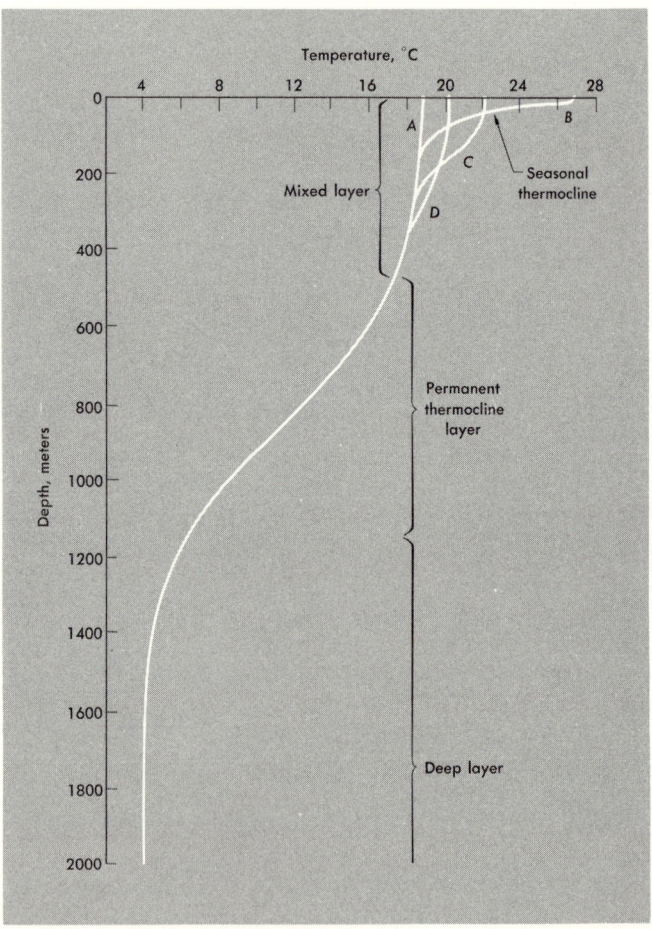

Redrawn, by permission, from G. L. Clarke. 1954. Elements of Ecology. New York: John Wiley and Sons.

Fig. 5-24. The vertical temperature structure in the north central part of the Atlantic Ocean. Seasonal changes in the upper layers are indicated as: A, April; B, August; C, December; D. February.

mixed with the main water mass during the circulation periods; failure to circulate thus largely contributes to the stagnation of nutrient cycling in such systems. In the case of the deep ocean, thermal mixing is restricted to the upper several hundred meters (Figure 5-24); this is largely the explanation of sedimentary stagnation of mineral cycling in the ocean discussed in Chapter 3. However, on the other side of the ledger, the ocean provides a highly temperature-stable environment. Organisms tolerant to a temperature of only 3° or 4°C have no problem whatsoever below about 1400 m; George Clarke has suggested that such a temperature-restricted organism could travel over 60 per cent of the globe without exposure to any significantly different temperature.

Periodism and Metabolism

Turning to yet another aspect of community dynamics, we can consider two similar but opposite processes of considerable importance, respiration and photosynthesis. All producers in the system contribute to the total or gross photosynthesis and the consequent output of both stored chemical energy in the form of biomass and the significant by-product, oxygen. All organisms in the system, producers included, utilize this stored energy and oxygen in metabolic activities associated with growth and reproduction, a complex of events subsumed under and measured as respiration. But whereas photosynthesis is dependent on light, respiration is not; it follows, then, that for an ecosystem to maintain itself—that is, to be balanced—the output of photosynthesis in a closed system must be at least equal to the respiratory demands of the system. It thus becomes important to consider the characteristics of these two opposing metabolic processes.

Robert Byers has investigated the metabolism of a number of highly diverse aquatic ecosystems under laboratory conditions, small counterparts of natural, and unnatural, systems which are conveniently referred to as microcosms. In his studies using a 12-hour photoperiod, he demonstrated that nighttime respiration is at a maximum within a few hours of darkness and drops progressively thereafter. Photosynthesis shows a similar pattern during the period of light, reaching its maximum within the first few hours and decreasing thereafter through the remainder of the day (Figure 5-25). A number of investigations under natural light conditions have shown that photosynthetic maxima occur in midmorning, in agreement with Byers' laboratory results. It is of importance to note, however, that under natural conditions, the photosynthetic maximum occurs several hours before noon, the time when energy input is at maximum. The lack of conformity of maximum energy input and rate of photosynthesis appears related to an actual inhibition of photosynthesis at higher light intensities that has been reported by a number of investigators.

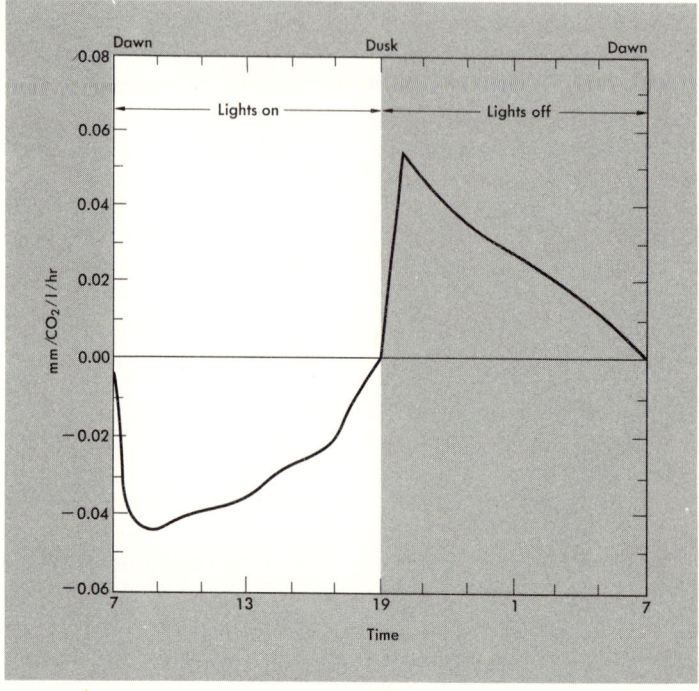

Redrawn, by permission, from R. J. Byers. 1966. In, C. S. Goldman, Primary Productivity in Aquatic Environments. Berkeley: University of California Press.

Fig. 5-25. The diurnal pattern of photosynthesis and respiration in freshwater ecosystems as reflected by the rate of change of dissolved carbon dioxide.

In his first major study of microcosm metabolism, Byers found that the average ratio of gross photosynthesis to respiration was 1.05. That is, there was a slight excess of photosynthetic activity sufficient to meet the respiratory demands of the systems—the systems were in balance. And there is evidence that suggests a rather close coupling of these processes in balanced or steady-state systems. For example, on cloudy days, not only does photosynthesis decrease, respiration does also. Byers' major professor, Howard Odum, has proposed a classification of ecosystems based on community metabolism, on the ratio of photosynthesis P to respiration R. According to this scheme, a stabilized system is one in which the ratio of photosynthesis to respiration is unity; that is, where $P/R = 1$. A system in which photosynthesis exceeds respiration, $P/R > 1$, is considered to be *autotrophic,* and one in which respiratory demand exceeds photosynthesis, i.e., $P/R < 1$, is said to be *heterotrophic* (Figure 5-26). In the autotrophic system, biological fertility is based on current production; in the heterotrophic system it is based on past production, organic matter accumulated over a period of time and often imported from another ecosystem.

Stability, it will be noted, however, is not contingent upon a given habitat (desert, grassland, forest, etc.) but rather on the dynamic interaction of the myriad forces involved in promoting given photosynthetic and respiratory rates. Nonetheless, the tendency is for systems to proceed toward stability ($P/R = 1$) and thus to maintain themselves, i.e., the diagonal line of the graph, over both the short and long term. It was noted above that even on a diurnal basis, a reduction in photosynthesis is coupled with a reduced community respiration. On an annual basis in temperate systems, the spring-summer autotrophism is offset to varying degrees by fall-winter heterotrophism.

The tendency to stability and the adjustments involved therein have been shown in a rather simple but elegant experiment by B. J. Copeland, who showed that an 85 per cent reduction in light intensity from 1500 to 230 foot-candles was followed, as expected, by a reduction in metabolism; the drop was to about $\frac{1}{6}$ of the previous level. Interestingly, even though

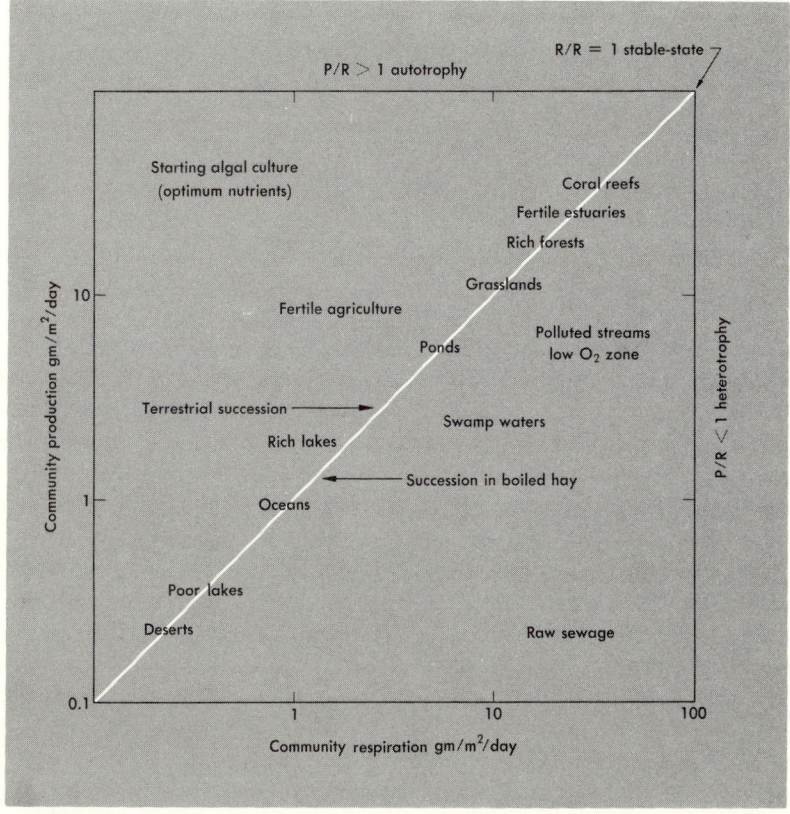

Redrawn, by permission, from E. P. Odum. 1959. Fundamentals of Ecology. Philadelphia: W. B. Saunders Co.

Fig. 5-26. Various types of communities classified on a basis of community metabolism.

the reduced light intensity persisted, the system recuperated, gradually increasing its metabolism until it reached the previous balanced level, all in a period of about 60 days. The recuperation, however, was accomplished by a change in the dominant producer, from turtle grass to blue-green algae. Copeland's ecosystem was disturbed but restabilized at about its previous level; other systems also show this tendency to stability, although they may do so at different levels along the diagonal, depending on the relative amounts of photosynthesis and respiration. This tendency to stability constitutes the focus of the next and final topic in this chapter.

ECOLOGICAL SUCCESSION

Although he was not an ecologist, the aphorism "Nature abhors a vacuum" expressed by the 17th century Dutch exponent of pantheism, Baruch Spinoza, quite aptly describes a major ecological phenomenon. Bare ground, either on land or under water, seldom remains that way for very long; "nature" in the form of vegetation moves in with dispatch. As characteristic as the colonization process itself is the subsequent series of sequential replacements that occur on the site, the successional changes that occur. The structural changes in an open field no longer cultivated, or in an unmanaged farm pond, are both marked and easily recognized; such structural changes have been well studied by ecologists. As a result, the sequence and timing of communities on given sites and in given regions can be predicted with considerable reliability. Thus, in the deciduous forest region of Indiana, the two foremost American students of community ecology in the first half of the 20th century, Frederick Clements and Victor Shelford, showed that the different communities initially present in such diverse habitats as flood plains, sand ridges, shallow and deep ponds, and clay banks all demonstrated a quite predictable series of changes and that each culminated in a stable ecosystem, a beech-maple forest. Whereas these structural changes are generally and commonly recognized, the associated functional changes are not. In part, this is because they are not so obvious to the untrained eye and, in part, because they acquire assessment of parameters not so readily accessible without adequate instrumentation. A discussion of the successional changes in an actual ecosystem can serve to sharpen the focus on the major structural and functional aspects of this dynamic community process.

Succession in Beach Ponds

Along the south shore of Lake Erie, at Erie, Pennsylvania, is a peninsula some four miles long known as Presque Isle (Figure 6-7). Owing to a combination of its sandy shore and its exposure to the violent storms and heavy wave action for which Lake Erie is notorious, the peninsula is subject to the frequent establishment of small beach ponds (Figure 5-27a). These are created when an elevated bar of sand develops, thereby isolating a small portion of the lake; the ponds are seldom more than 100 to 200 m long, 10 to 20 m wide and 1 m deep. Some of the ponds are wiped out days, months, or even a few years later by subsequent storms which either break down the sand bar or blow in enough sand to fill the basin. A better protected pond survives this geological fate only to be immediately subject to its biological fate, ecological succession (Figure 5-27b). Because of the geological history of the peninsula and the persistence of some beach ponds, it was possible for us to identify ponds of different chronological age and thereby to facilitate the study of some structural and functional changes that have occurred as the ponds progressed from an open water to a vegetated semi-terrestrial state.

From a structural standpoint, two major changes were observed in successively older ponds: (1) a change in species composition and (2) a change in variety or diversity (Figure 5-28). Some plant species that were present during the initial stages are missing from the more advanced stages; stonewort alga (*Chara*) and cattail (*Typha*) demonstrate this kind of change. By the same token, some species are not present until fairly late in succession, the yellow water lily (*Nuphar advena*), for example. Yet other species, of which the bulrushes (*Scirpus*) are prime examples, persist as major components of the system for much of its history. These differences are doubtless tied to the tolerance limits characteristic of each species as well as to the subtleties of interspecific competition (see Chapter 4). Comparable shifts of species composition in phytoplankton and, to a less marked degree, in the animals also were observed.

In addition to these kinds of changes in composition, there is a marked increase in the numbers and kinds of both autotrophs and heterotrophs. Sparseness of distribution and limitation of kinds mark the early ponds; increased density and heterogeneity characterize the older ponds. The relative simplicity of structure of the young pond is in striking contrast to the relative complexity of the more advanced in succession (Figure 5-28).

On the functional side, two major changes may be noted. One of these is a progressive increase in the amount of both living and dead organic matter. In part this biomass increase is expected from the already noted increase in numbers, and since the amount of living organic matter shows an increase, there would be an eventual increase in dead organic matter. The accumulation of organic matter on the bottom reaches the point, it may be noted, that the pond is progressively filled in. Measurements of other organic components such as plant pigments, and notably chlorophyll, also show a progressive increase with more advanced stages of succession.

The second major functional change deals with a shift in community

156
ECOLOGICAL COMMUNITIES

A.

Photos by author.

Fig. 5-27. Beach ponds on Presque Isle at Erie, Pennsylvania. (A) A newly formed beach pond less than one year old; (B) a beach pond about fifty years later.

B.

ECOLOGICAL COMMUNITIES

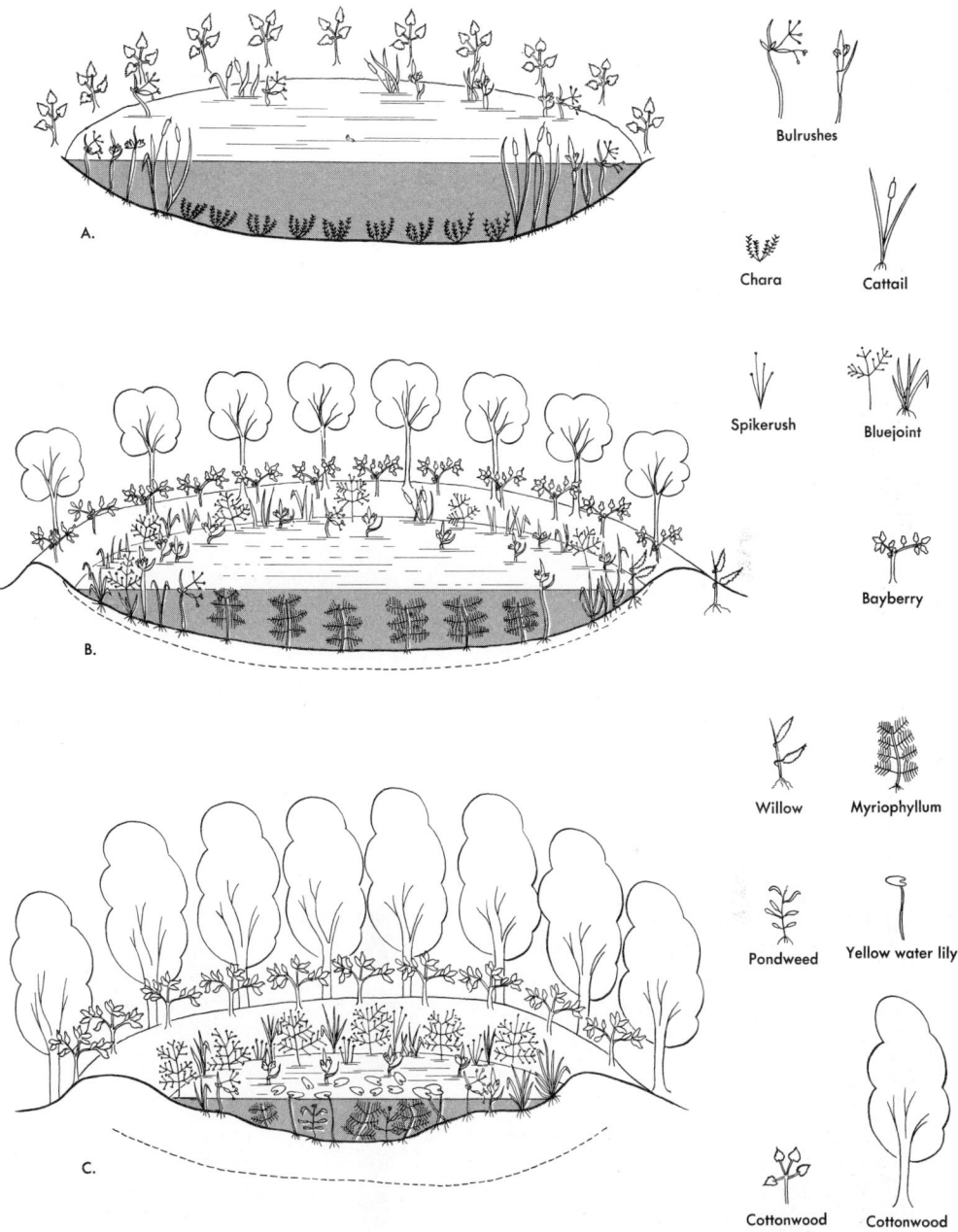

Fig. 5-28. Generalized stereo-profiles of beach ponds on Presque Isle at Erie, Pennsylvania, at (A) four years, (B) 50 years, and (C) 100 years of age. Note the changes in kind, distribution, and abundance of different species and the accumulation of organic matter filling in the bottom.

metabolism from young ponds, which are autotrophic ($P/R > 1$), to those which are stabilized ($P/R = 1$), and finally to a heterotrophic ($P/R < 1$) condition. Although the number and kind of primary producers increases and results in increased gross production, at least initially, the increasing respiratory demand of the system results in a progressive decrease in the metabolic ratio. The increasing heterotrophy of these aquatic systems applies to that phase of their succession in which they achieve a terrestrial condition. Although no studies have been conducted beyond this transitional stage, evidence elsewhere strongly indicates that such systems would continue to undergo terrestrial succession with an accompanying trend toward stability of their metabolic ratio.

These four major structural and functional attributes of ecological succession (increase in species diversity, increase in structural complexity, increase in organic matter, and tendency toward metabolic stability) are, in a sense, both causes and effects of the very processes of change and the eventual stability that characterize ecosystems in general. A newly available environment, like a beach pond or a plowed but unplanted field or a talus after an avalanche, is fair game for spores and seeds. But not all these spores and seeds can "play the game" in such a rigorous environment, where solar exposure is considerable and moisture is restricted. Those that succeed in becoming established also immediately begin chemically and physically to modify their environment by their metabolic and behavioral activity; they add their waste products and thereby chemically change the nature of the substrate; they may bore into the soil and thereby physically affect drainage, etc. Spinoza, to whom we referred at the start of this section, also noted a basic ecological principle (out of his context, to be sure) in stating that "nothing exists from whose nature some effect does not follow." Thus it is that each species alters its own environment and that of its associates such that it eventually precludes its own and sometimes others' existence but in so doing provides a new set of conditions within the tolerance range of yet other species. Thus, organic matter and various metabolites which increase are both a result of previous ecological activity and causative agents of subsequent changes.

If all this is so, then why eventually does an ecosystem achieve a kind of steady-state? This is a condition referred to as a climax community, an ecosystem that is self-perpetuating and in which the dynamic changes not only occur but are necessary for the maintenance of the community. On Presque Isle, the beach ponds ultimately fill in, undergo terrestrial succession, and terminate in a climax community, a beech-maple forest. The climax community results when no other combination of species is successful in outcompeting or replacing the climax community. In part, this is to be explained by the tolerance limits and optimum requirements inherent in each species. But stability of the climax is certainly not so simply explained. The answer lies in an as yet not fully understood property—diversity.

Professor G. Evelyn Hutchinson, of Yale University, in an essay with the intriguing title, "Homage to Santa Rosalia, or why are there so many kinds of animals?" has posed the question well; he and others have also suggested some answers. The argument, oversimplified, runs something like the following: the more advanced the system, the more complex its function by virtue of the increased number and availability of different ecological niches; the more niches, the more diversified the flora and fauna; the more diversified the biota, the less likelihood that any major shift in one component would adversely affect the system as a whole. Thus, if there are many kinds of producers, each overlapping to various degrees in their respective ability to utilize various wavelengths and intensities of light, a shift in spectral quality or quantity would tend to affect some but not all producers. The ecosystem would thereby be able to continue with little if any detectable disruption. The persistence of a major change would likely, however, result in new equilibrium levels and new combinations of associations of the "survivors." Copeland's study of the shift of the dominant producers from turtle grass to blue-green algae with a shift in light intensity is a case in point in the opposite direction. The absence of immediately available alternate routing of production resulted in a dramatic drop in output; recovery eventually came, but at the expense of some period of time. Highly integrated and complexly interrelated ecosystems, like those of the climax sort, are capable of responding quite readily to various kinds of short-term environmental insults and thereby reflect considerable stability.

It is thus current theory that the stability of the climax community is a function of its species diversity and that the aging phenomenon or succession in an ecosystem is well described as an evolution toward high diversity—a large number of ecological niches and its counterpart of a large number of species. The latter follows from the Gausian competitive-exclusion principle (see p. 98) that only one distinct species population can occupy one distinct niche, the latter being a unique multidimensional physical-chemical-biological function in the community. The number of ecological niches in a given ecosystem is a function of the history and evolution of the system and of its productivity; thus one becomes a measure of the other, productivity of diversity, diversity of productivity. Evidence presented earlier (Table 2-5, Figure 5-11) shows the tendency of productivity to increase from the poles to the tropics. In part this is related to differences in incident radiation (Figure 2-1), but it is also related to the higher diversity of species in the tropics (Table 5-5). It should follow, then, that a climax tropical forest would, by virtue of its higher species diversity, be relatively more stable than a climax deciduous forest, and the latter more stable than a climax in the tundra; the same environmental insult to each of these systems should have less consequence as one moves towards the tropics. Such predictions still demand adequate investigation, and there is little doubt that the general

TABLE 5-5. The Number of Species in Different Geographical Regions Showing a General Increase in Diversity with Decreasing Latitude

Insects	Beetles[2]		Ants[1]		Dragonflies[3]		
	Labrador	169	Alaska	7	Nearctic	59	
	Massachusetts	2000	Iowa	73	Neotropical	135	
	Florida	4000	Trinidad	134			
Molluscs	Nudibranchs[1]		Land Snails[2]		Lamellibranchs[1]		
	Arctic latitudes	10	Labrador	25	Newfoundland	30	
	Temperate latitudes	90	Massachusetts	100	Cape Hatteras	150	
	Tropical latitudes	130	Florida	250	South Florida	200	
Vertebrates	Coastal Marine Fish[2]		Snakes[1]		Nesting Birds[1]		
	Labrador	75	Canada	22	Greenland	56	
	Massachusetts	225	U.S.A.	126	New York	195	
	Florida	650	Mexico	293	Colombia	1395	
Plants	Flowering Plants[2]		Ferns and Clubmosses[2]		Endemic Genera of Flowering Plants[4]		
	Labrador	390	Baffin Land	11	North Temperate Zone	127	
	Massachusetts	1650	Labrador	31	Tropical Zones	465	
	Florida	2500	Massachusetts	70	South Temperate Zone	55	

Data adapted from: (1) A. G. Fischer, 1960. Evolution 14: 64–81. (2) G. L. Clarke, 1954. Elements of Ecology. New York: John Wiley and Sons, Inc. (3) C. B. Williams, 1964. Patterns in the Balance of Nature. New York: Academic Press. (4) R. Good, 1953. The Geography of Flowering Plants, 2nd ed. London: Longmans, Green and Company, Ltd.

topic of species diversity, patterns, and causes, and its role in ecosystem dynamics will occupy a central focus in ecological study for sometime to come.

Succession in the Past

Over the short term, minor fluctuations in environmental gradients have progressively less effect the farther along a system is in succession. The chestnut blight, although virtually eliminating the chestnut from dominant status, did not result in the demise of the mixed hardwood forests of the east; the system realigned its structure, adjusting rather quickly to the change. On a longer term basis, however, climax communities, adapted as they are to the prevailing climate as well as to the local microclimatic and edaphic conditions, do show change. This close identification of particular

ECOLOGICAL COMMUNITIES

communities with particular climates is the basis of an active aspect of ecology, paleoecology, which deals with determining and dating the chronology of climate in particular regions. As was noted in the discussion of beach pond succession, there is a progressive filling in by organic matter; among the constituents of this organic matter are pollen grains released both from the community incumbent in the pond and the surrounding area. By removing a core of the sediment and tabulating the percentages of pollen grains of each species in successive levels of the deposit, deductions can be

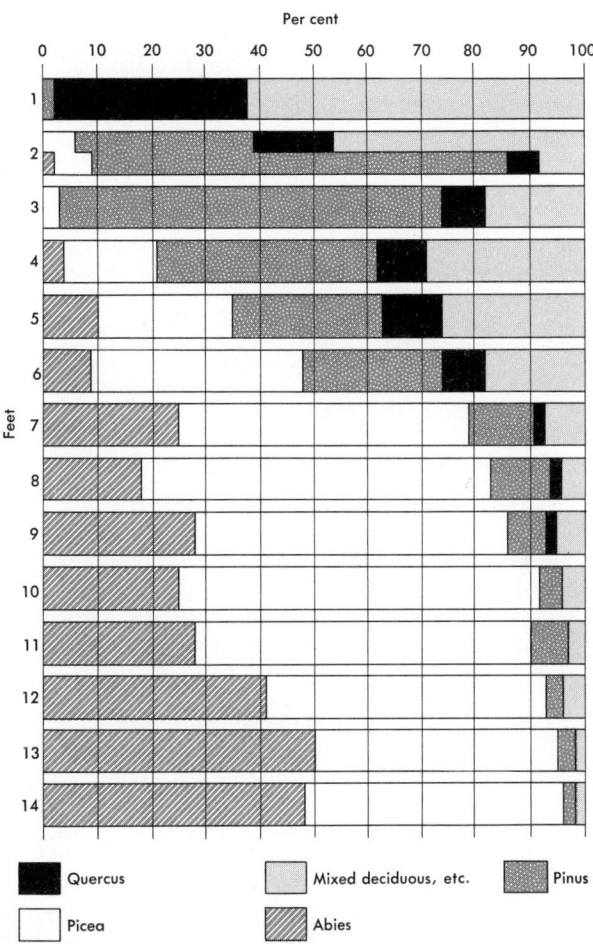

Redrawn, by permission, from P. B. Sears. 1930. Ohio Journal of Science 30: 205–217.

Fig. 5-29. Pollen diagram of Bucyrus Bog in northern Ohio showing the proportions of the major genera at each level. The investigator, Dr. Paul Sears, informs me, "What is labeled *Abies* was probably *Picea canadensis*, illustrating one of the difficulties encountered in early work, namely, the lack of reliable literature for pollen identification."

made of the community composition that prevailed at the time each level was deposited. The climate corresponding to each level is then inferred from the particular community composition.

This principle of determination of the chronology of forest composition and climate by pollen analysis had its initial development in Europe about 1915. One of its first applications in the United States was made in 1930 by Paul Sears (Figure 5-29). The reconstruction of this postglacial forest in northern Ohio enabled Sears to infer the following climatic sequence:

Depth in Feet	Climate
14–12	Cold, wet of northern Labrador
11–7	Gradual shift from oceanic to continental climate
6–4	Cool, dry climate of southern Manitoba
3–2	Period of maximum desiccation
2	Abrupt increase in humidity. Cool, moist climate of northern Great Lakes
1	Moderation of temperature and continued increase in humidity; present climate of north-central Ohio

Additional studies by Sears and by the many students and colleagues he stimulated to engage in this type of investigation have sharpened the picture of postglacial vegetation and climate in North America, in both glaciated and nonglaciated regions. The subsequent application, beginning in the 1950's, of radiocarbon dating of pollen and associated sediments has enabled assignment of a time scale to the chronology. Although there are, as would be expected from even limited acquaintance with distribution of extant communities, differences in the particular sequence of communities in different locales, and some disagreement among investigators about given events and interpretation, the postglacial sequence recognized by Dr. Sears is generally widely accepted. It is as follows:

I. A moist, cool period; maximum of spruce (*Abies*) and fir (*Picea*). About 11,000 years ago.
II. A dry, warmer period; maximum of pine (*Pinus*) with oaks (*Quercus*) almost always an accessory. About 9000 years ago.
III. A more humid, warm period; maximum of beech (*Fagus*), with hemlock (*Tsuga*) in some places. About 6000 years ago.
IV. A dry, warm period; maximum of oaks and hickory (*Carya*). About 3500 years ago.
V. A more moist and cool period; increase of more mesic genera [maples (*Acer*), hemlocks, chestnut (*Castanea*), pine]. The present.

Investigations in paleoecology are much broader in scope than might be implied by this discussion of pollen analysis. The principle of the relationship of climatic adaptation and community composition cannot be approached by a study of pollen in a marine situation, for example. Here, the relative distribution and abundance of key invertebrates, quite often molluscs, serve the same function as pollen in a bog sediment. Analysis of growth rings in trees, particularly long-lived species, also provides a key to past climate. However, it is not the purpose here to explore this exciting field in detail but rather to indicate two general points: (1) that the ecology of the past can be studied and offers as many if not more challenges to the investigator than a study of the ecology of the present—and certainly each will make and has already made substantial contributions to the other; (2) communities are indeed dynamic, ever-changing in composition and function in response to both immediate and long-term environmental changes. The seeming stability of present-day climax communities is indeed deceptive and likely to give a false sense of security. As a biological unit they remain stable by not being static.

REFERENCES

Correlated Readings

Kormondy, E. J., 1965. *Readings in Ecology.* Englewood Cliffs, New Jersey: Prentice-Hall, Inc. In addition to the section, "The Study of Communities," pp. 118–164, the following are of particular relevance:

Garner, W. W. and H. A. Allard, Further studies in photoperiodism, the response of the plant to relative length of day and night, p. 36.

Hutchinson, G. E., Homage to Santa Rosalia, or why are there so many kinds of animals?, p. 204.

MacArthur, R. H. and J. W., On bird species diversity, p. 208.

Margalef, R., On certain unifying principles in ecology, p. 215.

Odum, E. P., Relationships between structure and function in ecosystems, p. 211.

Oosting, H. J. and W. D. Billings, Factors effecting vegetational zonation on coastal dunes, p. 31.

Shelford, V. E., Physiological animal geography, p. 17.

Technical Monographs

Ager, D. V., 1963. *Paleoecology.* New York: McGraw-Hill Book Co., Inc.

Becking, R., 1957. The Zurich-Montpellier School of Phytosociology. *Botanical Review* **23**: 411–488.

Billings, W. D., 1964. *Plants and the Ecosystem*. Belmont, California: Wadsworth Publishing Co.

Biological Clocks, 1960. *Cold Spring Harbor Symposia on Quantitative Biology*, Vol. 25.

Byers, R. J., 1963. The metabolism of twelve aquatic laboratory microcosms. *Ecological Monographs* **33**: 281–306.

Eyre, S. R., 1963. *Vegetation and Soils*. Chicago: Aldine Publishing Company.

Kormondy, E., 1969. Comparative ecology of sandspit ponds. *American Midland Naturalist* 82(1): 28–61.

MacArthur, R. H., 1965. Patterns of species diversity. *Biological Reviews* **40**: 510–533.

Odum, E. P., 1963. *Ecology*. New York: Holt, Rinehart and Winston.

Oosting, H. J., 1950. *The Study of Plant Communities*. San Francisco: W. H. Freeman and Company.

Shelford, V. E., 1963. *The Ecology of North America*. Urbana: University of Illinois Press.

Whittaker, R. H., 1962. Classification of natural communities. *Botanical Review* **28**: 1–239.

According to current idiom, the world's ills involve the three P's—pollution, population, and poverty. The first two of these clearly fall within the professional concerns of the ecologist; all three are his concerns as a person. Pollution has been a concomitant of man's existence, as have the effects of population growth; poverty was contemporaneous with the development of socioeconomic hierarchies, which probably developed soon after man's biological origin. It is important at the outset to note that although pollution is not new, its recognition is of dramatic recency. Likewise, though problems of population growth and regulation existed beforehand, it was only 200 years ago that Malthus and others called attention to them; it is barely a quarter century since the consequences of unregulated growth really began to hit home. Finally, for whatever consolation it may have in the intensified and recent concern over poverty at home and abroad, a major religious figure once reminded his audience that "the poor always ye have with you."

The status of a problem is not determined by its antiquity but rather by its urgency and immediacy. A swollen stream does not await the training of engineers who in turn construct dams and diverge waterways; it warrants an immediate convergence of sandbags on the stream banks. With the flood crest passed, the sandbags may remain for sometime as a grim reminder of a torturous experience but most likely soon begin gradually to fall into disorder. The public is immediately satisfied, and generally becomes complacent or distracted by other concerns. The immediate problem of the flood is resolved, but the long-range problem of managing water resources is not, for without precautionary measures it could happen again. What has this to do with the ecologist? Simply that immediate problems can be solved, like stop-

ecology and man

CHAPTER 6

ping the discharge of industrial acid into a stream that serves as a source of potable water for a community downstream. The long-range problems of learning how to cope with the by-products of man's biology and culture require infinitely more patience and time, and training and experience. If man is not able to cope with these situations, some future articulate output of the evolutionary process may well be able to comment on man as man has on the inability of the dinosaur to have adapted to its environment.

THE HUMAN POPULATION

Human Population Growth

It is virtually impossible to read any newspaper or periodical without encountering the phrase "population explosion." The dramatic and devastating connotation of the epithet is no less searching than the expressions of worried frowns and sighs it elicits on the part of the reader, who then turns to the comic section or cartoons in solace. Instead of this well-worn expression, a historian colleague of mine at Oberlin has used the metaphor, "the mushroom crowd," in obvious allusion to the now-familiar symmetry of an above-ground atomic blast. The phrase is apt in some respects: the rapidity of mushroom, and population, growth; the collective quality implied, many hyphae forming the fruiting body, many people forming the population body, etc. However, to the biologist, the mushroom metaphor has an alternate meaning, that of a largely temporary and purely reproductive structure, and of organisms that are exclusively decompositional in activity. Populations are, however, more permanent, have a large amount of vegetative activity, and even occasionally some creative output. But this is not to the central point, namely, that many discussions of "the" population imply, if not assert, that there is a problem and then proceed to focus sharply on numerical aspects. A more scientific approach is to assess the situation and then decide whether there is a problem, define it, and seek its resolution. The end result may be the same—recognition of a problem—but the approach is quite different.

Since the matter is of global concern, it will be more appropriate to consider the world's population rather than to focus on that of a particular region or area. The growth of the world's population through 1965 (Figure 6-1) allows for speculation regarding its form: if it is sigmoidal, is it still in the positive acceleration phase, as suggested by the extended, theoretical lines, which show no real deceleration towards a leveling off, or is it J-shaped and subject to ultimate if not imminent collapse? It is not absolutely apparent which is the case, but there is little question but that world population is heading toward far greater numbers—and far greater problems in consequence. One of the things learned from the study of natural populations

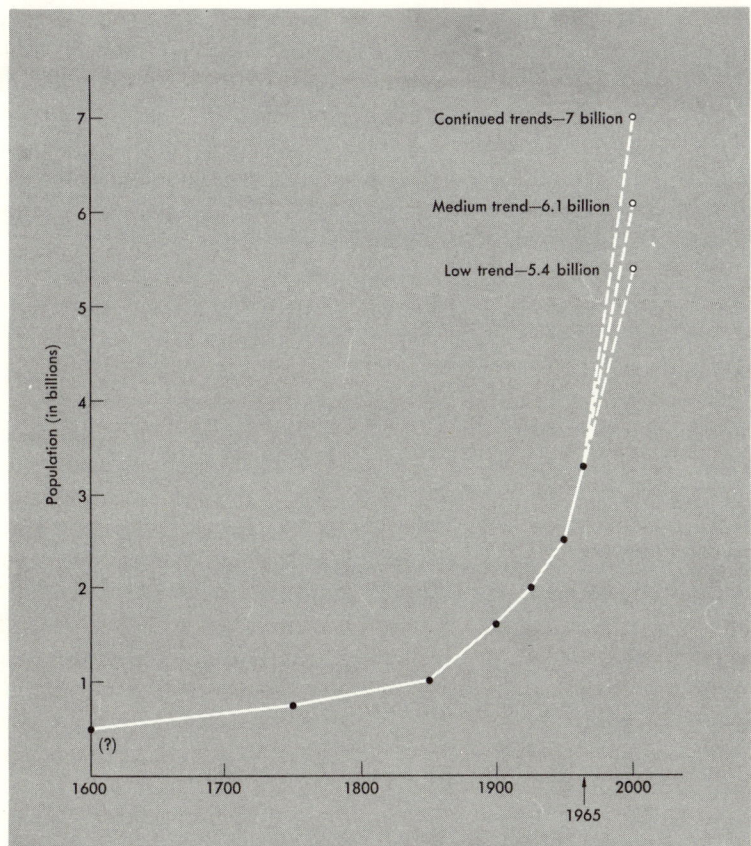

Fig. 6-1. Growth of world population, 1600–2000, based on various publications by the United Nations. The data prior to 1800 are estimates, those subsequent to 1965 are projections.

(Chapter 4) is that all populations initially follow a sigmoidal pattern and subsequently show a variety of patterns—J's, oscillations, fluctuations, and even a rather steady equilibrium. Most importantly, however, is another of the "lessons" that seem to be developing from the study of natural populations, namely, that all populations are inherently capable of self-regulation in the face of environmental change; whether that innate capacity is exercised fully or fast enough is another issue.

An expression of confidence in self-regulation should not be considered as being that of an assured and even benevolent Pollyanna ecologist; it is an assumption about human populations based on the study of other populations, but it does not assume, necessarily, the operation of any of the mechanisms employed by natural populations to effect self-regulation, some of which are at once undesirable and unwanted. Yet a little additional reflection makes one wonder about some of the mechanisms which have, historically if not contemporaneously, contributed to less rapid human population growth—disease, pestilence, and armed conflict, although the actual regulatory effect of the latter is debatable. The interpolation of conscious individual or family choice on procreation significantly alters both the problem and its resolution, as we shall see. But before judging and proposing, it is important that we assess the situation by looking at the evidence.

The pattern of world population growth to 1965 and the projections based on various growth trends (Figure 6-1) allow one to put it into a variety of perspectives. One can see, for example, the dramatic reduction in the time that has been and may be required for the population to increase in increments of one billion:

from 1 to 2 billion	–	1850–1925, or 75 years
from 2 to 3 billion	–	1925–1962, or 37 years
from 3 to 4 billion	–	1962–1977, or 15 years
from 4 to 5 billion	–	1977–1987, or 10 years

or the time it has taken or may be required to about double the population:

from 0.75 to 1.6 billion	–	1750–1900, or 150 years
from 1.6 to 3.3 billion	–	1900–1965, or 65 years
from 3.3 to 7.0± billion	–	1965–2000, or 35 years

Perhaps it may bring home the matter to the reader from the northeastern part of the United States to state that the tri-state area bounded by Trenton, New Jersey, Poughkeepsie, New York, and New Haven, Connecticut, which now has about 18 million residents, is expected to have 30 million residents by 2000.

But all regions of the world will not be like this tri-state area. In fact, the projections on a worldwide basis (Table 6-1) suggest that the 67 per cent population increase in this tri-state region is out of step with that of the more developed countries in general (47 per cent increase), but in line with North America (78 per cent), and half that of the less well-developed regions (130 per cent). These growth patterns are consonant with the kind of age structure in each of these regions (Figure 4-12). Although the numerical and percentage increases are dramatic, they do not suggest the amount of space involved; we have already seen that it is density which has much to say about the regulatory mechanisms in natural populations. Thus, it is the density of these various area and regional populations that is of considerable significance and to which attention needs to be given (Figure 6-2). Even

TABLE 6-1. Population Estimates in Millions, from 1960 to 2000, for Major Areas and Regions of the World Based on a Projection of Medium Growth

Major Areas and Regions	1960	1970	1980	1990	2000
World total	2998	3592	4330	5188	6130
More developed regions[1]	976	1082	1194	1318	1441
Less developed regions[2]	2021	2510	3136	3869	4688
East Asia	794	910	1041	1168	1287
South Asia	865	1107	1420	1782	2171
Europe	425	454	479	504	527
USSR	214	246	278	316	353
Africa	273	346	449	587	768
Northern America	199	227	262	306	354
Latin America	212	283	378	498	638
Oceania	16	19	23	27	32

Data from World Population Prospects as Assessed in 1963. United Nations Population Studies No. 41, 1966.
[1] Europe, USSR, Northern America, Japan, Temperate South America, Australia, New Zealand.
[2] All other countries.

the uninitiated should anticipate a different set of problems attendant to regions with low density but high growth rate (Africa, Latin America) as against those with low density and moderate growth rate (North America, USSR). A contemporary reading of the world's other ills suggests correlation, if not even causal connection, with regions of high growth rate, regardless of their present density.

It is difficult for most people to grasp the significance of these projections and their implications for the next several decades; numbers are numbers, and the larger or more infinitesimal the number, the less the ability to visualize it. If you doubt this, reflect a moment on a common measurement—the centimeter, 2.54 of which equal one inch. What conception do you really have of the diameter of a cell organelle measured in angstroms? (Each angstrom is 1/10,000 of a micron, the latter being 1/10,000 of a centimeter; hence, the angstrom is 1/100,000,000 of a centimeter.) Or, in the opposite direction, the meaning of the distance of a planet measured in light-years or millions or billions of miles? So it is with speaking of billions or even millions of people. A few years ago, William Vogt put the situation immediately at hand by suggesting that the reader count his pulse; if the pulse beat were normal, it would not quite keep up with the increase in world population, which was then about 50 million per year compared with about 38 million pulses per year. And even more telling, Vogt commented that the rate of increase at that time amounted to the equivalent of a city the size of Chicago, namely about 4 million persons, each month.

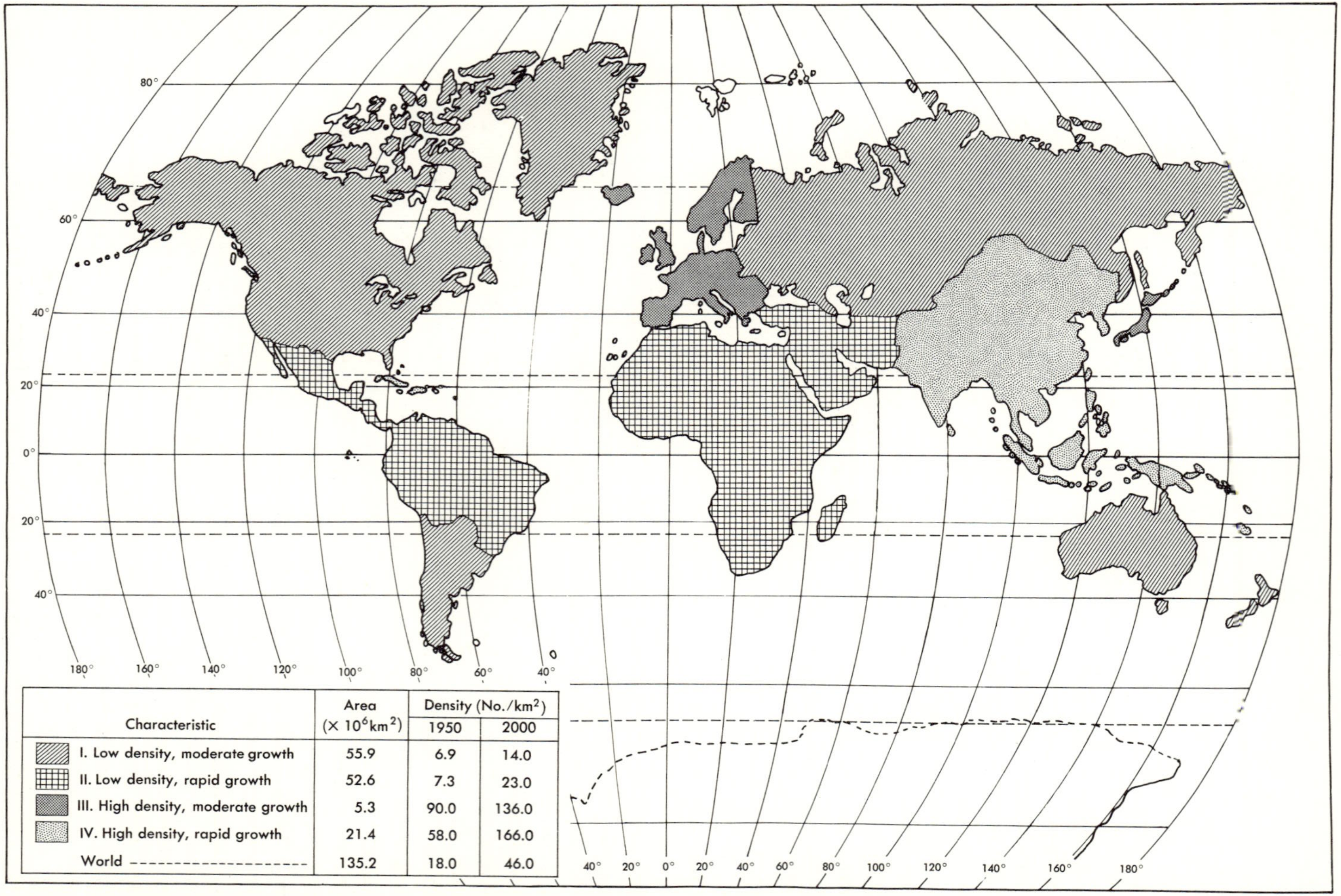

Characteristic	Area (× 10⁶ km²)	Density (No./km²) 1950	Density (No./km²) 2000
I. Low density, moderate growth	55.9	6.9	14.0
II. Low density, rapid growth	52.6	7.3	23.0
III. High density, moderate growth	5.3	90.0	136.0
IV. High density, rapid growth	21.4	58.0	166.0
World	135.2	18.0	46.0

Fig. 6-2. World regions by population density and rate of growth.

Redrawn, from United Nations Population Studies No. 28.

Natality and Mortality in Human Populations

With this profile and projection of population growth in hand, we can turn to an assessment of the forces prompting the direction of change. These are, as we saw in our earlier discussion, reducible to only two—natality and mortality, both of which are innately characteristic of a population but subject to myriad regulatory forces. There is little, if any, controversy regarding the relative importance of these two forces in the increase in human population; it is more largely the result of a reduction of mortality than an increase in natality. It is the case that about half of all the people alive in the world today have been born since 1945; the reason this group constitutes so large a segment of the population is not, as we shall see, the result of an increase in births but the truly phenomenal reduction in infant mortality accomplished through improved application of new medical (drugs, surgery) and environmental (sanitation, hygiene) technology. On the other hand, the reason this "born since 1945 group" constitutes no more than half of the population is the decrease in death rate of the "born before 1945 group" because of the same applied technology. Thus, in the short span since the founding fathers landed on Plymouth Rock, life expectancy in the United States has advanced from 33 to 70 years, and in the period from 1900 to 1965, the total death rate, all ages included, dropped from 17.2 to 9.4 per 1000. If demographers detect problems in the developing age structure of a growing population, other social scientists and medical people certainly are increasingly aware of the problems involved in the care of rising proportions and numbers of both younger and older persons in a population.

The mortality curve for man (Figures 4-6, 4-7), reflects a relatively high infant mortality, a low death rate until about 50, and then an increasing rate. In 1965, the infant mortality rate was 24.1, infant being defined as the interval between birth and one year of age, and the rate based on 1000; that is, 24.1 babies out of 1000 born died between birth and one year of age in 1965. According to data collected by Dublin, Lotka, and Spiegelman, this rate stood at 175.9 in 1900 for white males, 142.6 for white females, 369.3 for nonwhite males, and 299.5 for nonwhite females. This differential between the sexes and between whites and nonwhites persists today. In 1965, according to the Population Reference Bureau, the rates were: white males, 23.9; white females, 18.1; nonwhite males, 43.1; nonwhite females, 36.6. When compared on a global scale (Figure 6-3), the situation of infant mortality in the United States, a country supposedly so advanced medically and technologically, is of considerable concern. Although the United States compared favorably with the industrialized countries of Europe, it nonetheless ranked 15th in infant mortality rate in 1965, a rate more than twice that of Sweden. The rate among nonwhites (39.8), however, compares more closely with those of underdeveloped nations (Poland, 41.8; Brunei, 41.0; Jamaica,

ECOLOGY AND MAN

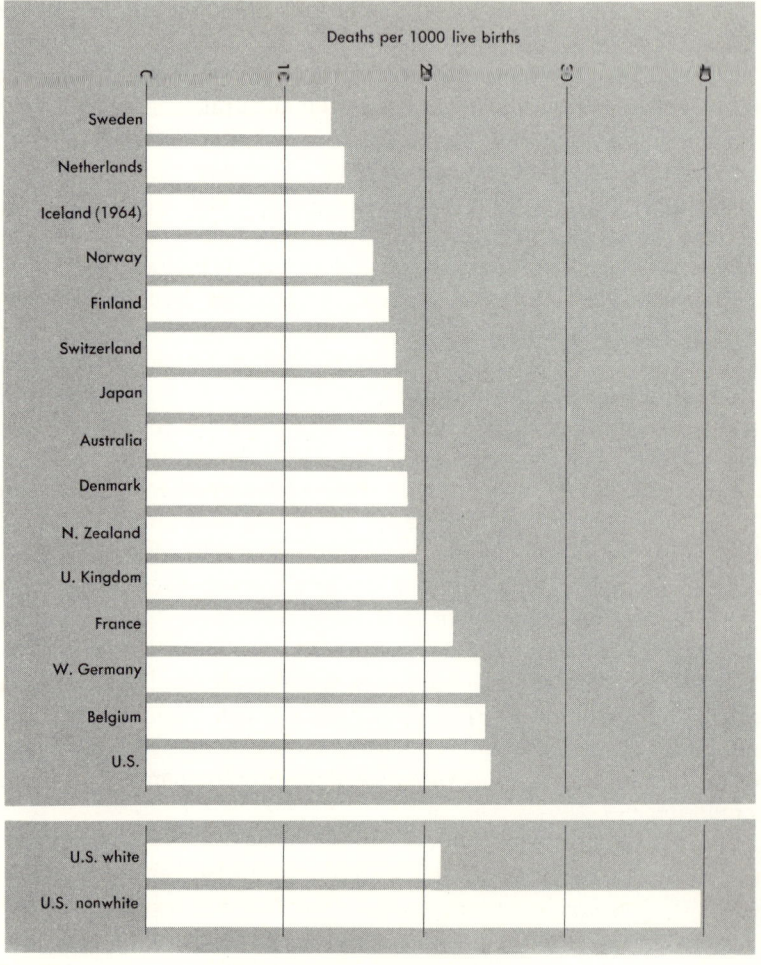

Redrawn, by permission, from Population, Profile, March 1967, published by Population Reference Bureau, Inc., Washington, D. C.

Fig. 6-3. Infant mortality rates in 1965.

36.7) but is less than some countries whose death rates are reminiscent of the early 1900's in this country. As these figures reflect, there have been truly dramatic reductions in infant and adult mortality; it is equally apparent, however, that the reduction has not yet affected the major undeveloped areas of the world. The subsequent effect on growth rate of the reductions in mortality that will certainly be forthcoming should need no further elaboration; they do demand a pause to reflect on the implications.

Natality was rather summarily dismissed above as being of less consequence in the relatively recent changes in human population age structure

ECOLOGY AND MAN

and size. While this is the case, it is also imperative to recognize that even no upward change in birth rate, if accompanied by a decrease in death rate, will produce a burgeoning population. A high birth rate with a high mortality has quite different consequences than a high birth rate with a low mortality. For example, the birth rate in economically advanced countries is generally about 15 to 20 per 1000 persons; in underdeveloped countries, the rate is about 40 per 1000 persons. Given the present high infant mortality in undeveloped countries, the situation of population size is markedly different from what it will be as mortality is reduced, especially if there is no downward change in natality. An assessment of the changes in natality that have occurred since 1910, their association with socioeconomic change, and their correlation with population growth in the United States (Figure 6-4) will be instructive on this point.

It is immediately and dramatically evident that while the United States population burgeoned between 1950 and 1967, the birth rate did not show a corresponding change, but rather one in the opposite direction (Figure 6-5); the increase was thus the result of reduced mortality. Had the high peak natality rates of the immediate post-World War II years (1946–47) been maintained and been coupled with the largely postwar reduction in mortality, the United States population would have reached some 370 million by the year 2000; present estimates suggest about 300 million persons. The seeming lack of relevance of economic conditions to birth rate can be seen by looking at the periods of the two lowest birth rates, of economic depression on the one hand (the 1930's) and of unprecedented prosperity (1958–1966) on the other. In Sweden, however, according to demographer Kingsley Davis, there is a consistency between the period of economic depression (1930–63) and a net reproduction rate below the replacement level, namely 0.81; here is a nation that has matched reduction in mortality by reduction in natality.

You may speculate that although the United States birth rate has dropped, the fact that there are more units of 1000 people, the base line of comparison, the total number of births would be up. In fact, the total number of live births did show an increase from a low of about 2.3 million in 1933 to a peak of 4.3 in 1957. Since 1957, however, there has been a steady decrease to about 3.6 million in 1965. This shift is best explained as a function of fertility rate, the number of live births per 1000 women between the ages of 15 and 44. In 1933 this rate was 76; it increased to 123 in 1957, and stood at 97 in 1965. Thus, although there were more women in the fertile age group in 1965 (some 40 million) as compared to 1933, they constituted a larger proportion of the 1933 population. During the next decade the "fertile female" group will increase to some 52 million, the result of the baby boom of the late 1940's; what effect this will have is, at the moment, enigmatic. However, many observers note that certain conditions have tended to accelerate a decline in birth rate—a rapid economic development, with manufacturing rising faster than agriculture or construction, has

174
ECOLOGY AND MAN

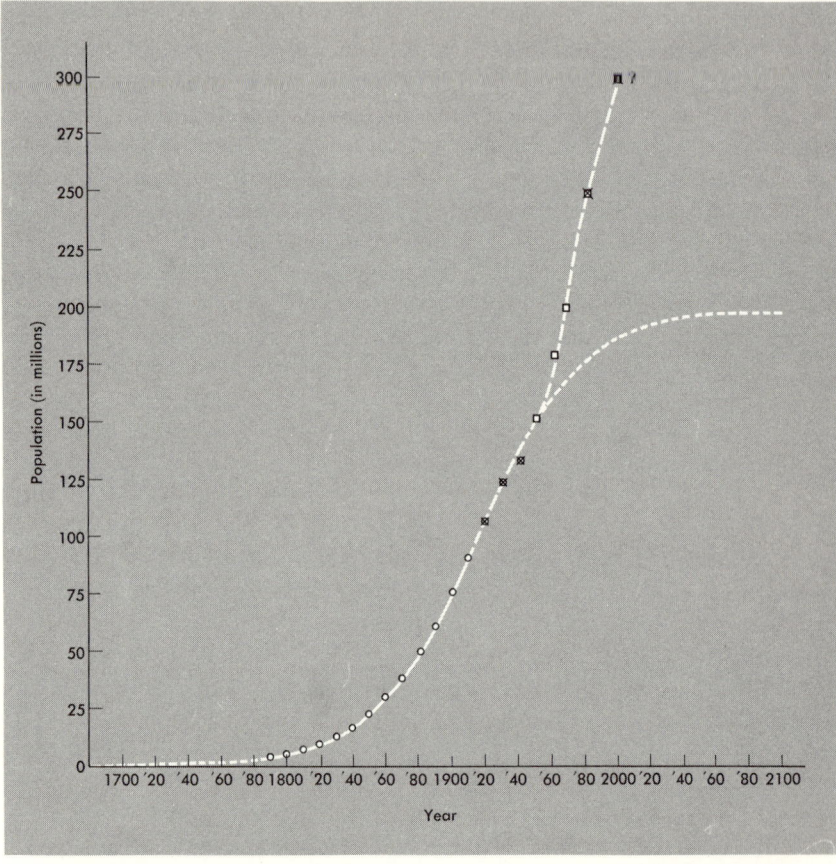

Basic graph, by permission, from R. Pearl, L. J. Reed and J. F. Kish. 1940. Science 92: 486–488; projections beyond 1967 are those of the United Nations.

Fig. 6-4. The census counts of the population of the United States from 1790 to 1940, inclusive (given by circles). The smooth curve is the logistic equation fitted to the census counts from 1790 to 1910 inclusive. The broken lines are extrapolations of the curve beyond the data to which it was fitted: the dashed portion from 1910 to 1940 is the part of the extrapolation that was tested by census counts (crossed circles) made since the logistic was originally fitted; the short dashed line shows the further extrapolation of the same curve; the squares and long dashed line represent the actual growth of population from 1950 through 1967; crossed squares and long dashed line represent present projections at a moderate growth rate.

as a consequence increasing urbanization in limited space and a resulting relative disadvantage for large families. The downward trends of both fertility and birth rates in the United States strongly indicate there has been a self-imposed control on birth rate; most interestingly, these trends were underway some five or more years before the contraceptive pill became widely available or the intrauterine device (I.U.D.) widely used. As most readers

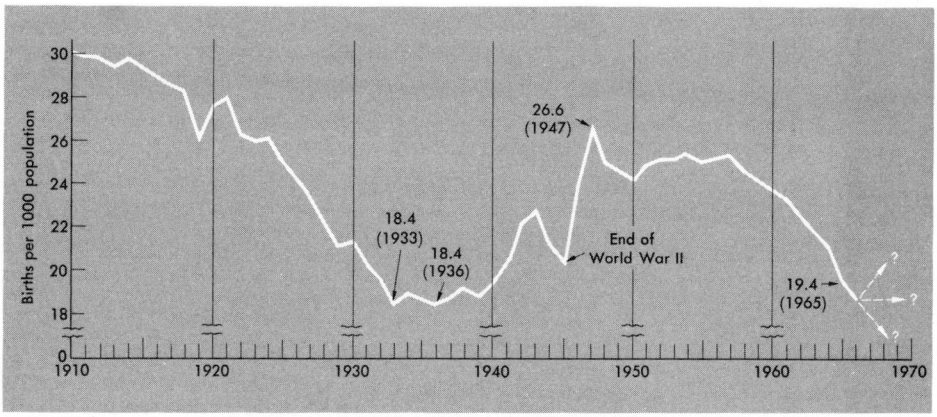

Redrawn, by permission, from Population Profile, March 1967, published by Population Reference Bureau, Inc., Washington, D. C.

Fig. 6-5. Birth rate in the United States, 1910–1966.

are doubtless aware, legalized abortion rather than widespread contraception in Sweden and Japan has resulted, particularly in the latter country, in dramatic reductions of birth rate.

Questions, Problems, and Resolutions

The questions that should be generating as a result of this brief consideration of aspects of mortality and natality in human population growth include the extent to which generalizations can be made regarding long-range trends, particularly as they affect so-called developing nations and regions. Will a self-imposed natality, comparable to that which seems to have developed in the United States, develop in other countries as their socioeconomic status improves? Or, since many critical observers see western-oriented contraceptive methods impractical or improvident in orient-oriented cultures, does the regulation of these regions lie partly in the sanctioning of abortion? There is no question but what improved medical and environmental technology will continue to depress mortality rates in all age groups, particularly in the early years of life, including the prenatal years. Then, if growth rates are to be decelerated, the only acceptable mechanism of control is at the input side—natality—for, although euthanasia has its proponents, wide-scale acceptance of it or of cannibalism, a practice employed by weevils, is not in the humane tradition.

It is precisely here, as Kingsley Davis has noted (see references) that society runs amuck. Virtually all proponents of population control have directed attention to family planning on the assumption that it is an effective means of regulating growth and have expended millions of dollars in the effort. Now there is no question but what population growth can be regulated by restraints on family size, but the paradox is that the principle of family planning stresses the right of parents to have the number of children they want, not the right of society to have the number of children it needs. This situation creates the dilemma that so long as families want more children than the number required for mere replacement (a net reproductive rate of 1; see p. 73), a population will continue to grow. For example, a 1966 survey of white women over 21 years of age in the United States indicated a desire for an average of 3.4 children—1.4 more than enough to replace the parents. In Tunisia and Java the desired number was 4.3; in Latin America the range was 2.7–4.2, although in seven Latin American capitals the ideal was considered to be 3.4. Thus, there is little question that so long as the family is "free" to plan its size, there will be increased population growth, and that as death control expands to undeveloped nations, there will be an even greater increase in population growth.

At least for the present, then, the resolution is not really one of control but rather of coping with ever increasing numbers. A redirection of population policy aimed toward making more children less desirable is at the moment so remote that attention must be placed on the immediate and imminent problems with, at least on my part, a fervent hope for real effort on the long-range problem.

As regards the population problem, we would contend that numbers alone, the "population avalanche" as biologist René Dubos has put it, are not the critical matter *per se;* the concomitant of numbers, density, is. On this point, Philip Hauser has calculated that at the present rate of world population increase, namely 2 per cent, population density will reach one person per square foot in $6\frac{1}{2}$ centuries. Thus, the really crucial issues seem to turn on spatial distance between people and the carrying capacity of the environment. How near to each other can people bear to be and how many people can the world support? Estimates on this by thoughtful people range from 50 to 200 billion to be reached in 250 to 300 years, and to unlimited numbers by those who see in our present and future technology the means of meeting the needs of an essentially unlimited population. Even this question is fraught with problems, largely turning on the matter of determining the minimum, optimum, or maximum in standards of living—how much space per person, how much energy (i.e., food) per person—let alone the more socioeconomically oriented questions concerned with clothing, housing, schooling, waste disposal, etc. To assume that some agreement could be easily reached on such matters is a major assumption, indeed, in view of man's inability to resolve issues of minuscule significance by comparison.

Some perspective can be brought to bear on carrying capacity by some substantive information. You may recall from the discussion on energetics that Vallentyne has estimated total annual net productivity to be 5.0 to

13.5×10^{16} kcal for the oceans and 5.0 to 7.2×10^{16} for the land, for a total of 1 to 2×10^{17} kcal per year. If the present human population of approximately 3 billion were exclusively herbivorous, and each person requires an average of 2200 kcal per day, or 8×10^5 kcal per year, the total energy requirement would be 2.4×10^{15} kcal. This is about 1 per cent of current net energy capture. As an aside, Julian Huxley recently estimated that more than two-thirds of the world population do not meet this minimum daily level. Thus relieved, you might jump to the happy thought of a population 100 times larger than at present—namely, 300 billion—supported by current net production. The matter is compounded, however, by several factors: man is not exclusively an herbivore, there are numerous other herbivores, assimilation is not 100 per cent efficient, and some 60 to 80 per cent of total plant production is in the ocean—the major untapped, unmanaged, and, so far, largely unpalatable plant production resource on the planet.

To try another perspective, assume man to be completely carnivorous. The interjection of another trophic level, the herbivore, implies a substantial reduction in energy that will then be available to carnivore man. From the earlier discussion of this trophic-level energy transfer, one can expect an energy loss on the order of 75 to 90 per cent from the net production of herbivores. Thus the 1 to 2×10^{17} kcal of net plant production would amount to 2 to 16×10^{16}, if a generous reduction of only 80 per cent is assumed. At this level of energy utilization, the carnivore need (2.4×10^{15}) would allow for a total human population of 30 to 50 billion. But in this calculation we have assumed no other carnivores and 100 per cent energy utilization, both outright prevarications of the natural scene. And in both manipulations we have assumed yet another travesty on nature—food is not equally distributed throughout the world.

Such speculations and predictions are a kind of scientific fun, if for no other reason than to manipulate a slide rule and refresh one's use of exponents. They lead back to fundamental principles, and that is one of the prime reasons that there is real enjoyment in such matters to the scientist, though their conclusions have little comfort for the scientist as a humanist. Some aspects of these basic energetics allow for manipulation by man; others, like the basic "givens" of efficiency of energy conversion, allow little if any leeway. To begin with, there are the matters of efficiency of primary energy capture and total amounts of primary production by different types of ecosystems. Most, as was noted earlier, are notoriously inefficient, utilizing only 1 to 3 per cent of total available energy. Studies on the selection for and management of the most efficient producer communities are in progress in various laboratories and show considerable promise; among these are communities of marine algae whose protoplasm is dried and powdered into a very palatable and functional flour. Improved management and greater acceptance and utilization of the natural communities that already have high production rates, with or without high efficiencies, such as reed swamps, estuaries, and coral reefs (Figure 2-4 and Table 2-5), offer yet additional promise. In effect, the vegetarian diet of the large mass of people in the Far East, though well below a minimum daily energy requirement, is supported by a reed-swamp type of ecosystem, the rice paddy.

By further judicious (when we have the knowledge that precedes wisdom) control and selection of the herbivores on which man could come to depend as intermediaries in energy flow, there is potential for increased efficiency and production at that level. This is an important point, for meeting the world's food needs is not only a quantitative but a qualitative matter, with protein being the most difficult to meet. For in spite of efforts to meet caloric requirements based on agricultural output, the potential would still exist for serious protein deficiency. To obviate this, man may have to adjust his cultural attitudes to adopt some methods and sources of meeting his protein needs which at present are considered unorthodox. Among unconventional food sources that have been suggested and upon which research is being conducted are the freshwater manatee, the marine dugong, the capybara, a large South American rodent—all of which feed on aquatic weeds that contribute little to human nutrition—and the eland, an African antelope that is adapted to grazing on marginal lands not suited to agriculture. Alternately, the protein-rich residue left when oil is removed from soya, cottonseed, and sunflower, which is now used as animal feed or fertilizer, shows considerable potential as a protein source through improved extraction procedures. Still another unorthodox source, besides the use of algae and synthetic foods produced in the laboratory, is the use of microorganisms as food, microbes that grow on substrates such as sawdust, petroleum, and coal, substrates that are otherwise unusable directly in meeting man's food needs.

It is important to recognize that these last few paragraphs have been directed toward immediate resolution of problems of population growth rather than toward long-range control of causes; further, attention has been focused only on the energetics involved. Now it is relevant to consider another ecological dimension, that of coping with the waste products of man's biology and culture—pollution.

POLLUTION

One hundred twenty-five million tons of urban solid wastes including 48 billion cans, 26 billion bottles and jars, and 65 billion metal and plastic caps, costing 3 billion dollars to collect and dispose; 3 billion tons of waste rock and milltailings from mines; 400 to 500 new chemical substances created for use each year. These are some annual figures for the United States in the mid-1960's; it is a matter of simple arithmetic to project these amounts into the future in correspondence with projected population increases. But these few figures do not include human and farm animal excreta, pesticides and herbicides, automobile exhausts, and industrial sewage. These are some of the agents that lie behind the "Beach closed for swimming" and "Water unfit for drinking" and needed, but never posted, "Air unfit for breathing" signs that increasingly mark the American landscape. The very by-products of man's biological and cultural processes have established the pollution milieu in which he finds himself—in the words of the proverb, "he who makes his bed must lie in it."

This kind of broad fire may lead to acknowledgment, recognition, and even further denigration of man but does not lead to perspective, understanding, and resolution. The topic of pollution warrants consideration to promote an ecological understanding of the matter by placing it in the perspective of the principles developed in earlier chapters; we need first to define our terms, to consider the matter in the context of ecosystems, and, as in the consideration of human populations, to determine what the problem is before attempting to determine courses for resolving it.

Defining Pollution

"To make or render unclean; to defile; desecrate; profane"—this is according to *Webster's New Collegiate Dictionary*. These are strong words, crisp and lucid. They are more direct but less informative than the following definition adopted by the Environmental Pollution Panel, of the President's Science Advisory Committee, in its report, "Restoring the Quality of Our Environment," in November, 1965:

> Environmental pollution is the unfavorable alteration of our surroundings, wholly or largely as a by-product of man's actions, through direct or indirect effects of changes in energy patterns, radiation levels, chemical and physical constitution and abundances of organisms. These changes may affect man directly, or through his supplies of water and of agricultural and other biological products, his physical objects or possessions, or his opportunities for recreation and appreciation of nature.

The key phrase here, "unfavorable alteration," is one to which we shall return subsequently and consider at length. First, let us consider in more detail the nature of the pollutant itself.

The production of pollutants comes as the "by-product of man's actions"—they are the residues of things he makes, uses, and throws away. They are concomitants of a technological society with a high standard of living. They increase both because of population increase and because of an increasing expectation for higher living standards; more is made, used, and thrown away. But, as the Committee on Pollution of the National Academy of Science noted in 1966, "As the earth becomes more crowded, there is no longer an 'away.' One person's trash basket is another's living space." Seen in this perspective, a pollutant is not something apart from man, but inherent in his very biology and culture; it is a result of his peculiar adaptations and attributes. In this framework, then, why should a "natural" by-product be considered "unnatural"—that is, polluting? According to our discussions of basic ecological principles, the biogenic cycle is requisite to and inherent in ecosystem dynamics and regulation; waste products are utilized and returned to the system for storage and/or reutilization.

This is an important point to bear in mind; the so-called pollutants, a value- and emotion-laden word in today's society, are in fact normal by-products of man as a purely biological organism and as a creative social being. They are the inorganic and organic wastes of his metabolic and digestive processes, and of his creativity in protecting and augmenting the production of his crops, of warming his home, clothing his body, of harnassing the atom. The problem is not in the natural elaboration of by-products; it is in the disposition of them. As the National Academy of Sciences Committee aptly stated, the problem is a case of "a resource out of place"—too much of a resource in one system, not enough in another. The problem is a resource being present in a system that is not adapted to it and thus constituting an unaccustomed stimulus, or, as a colleague of mine has put it, an "insult" to that system. These are stimulants, or insults, that may terminate some or initiate other biological processes, alter efficiency, affect species composition and structure, and in general thereby alter the dynamics of an ecosystem.

By-products, like the adage about the poor, will always be with us; they will increase as our technology and living standard increase, they will become more concentrated as urbanization proceeds and more people live in smaller areas. The answers do not and cannot lie solely in removing the cause, because so long as man exists he will have by-products; rather, the answers lie in intelligent management of that production through regulating the "unfavorable alteration of our surroundings." But we have moved too fast toward solution without first having discussed effects of misplaced resources, or pollutants, in the context of actual ecological systems and as they affect the three major environmental media—air, soil, and water. We shall begin with the Great Lakes.

Water Pollution and the Great Lakes

The greatest reservoir of fresh water on the earth's surface—a shore line of 10,500 km, an area of 245,000 km^2, and a volume of 25,000 km^3, with a waterway extending 1600 miles from Minnesota to the Atlantic

Ocean—this describes the St. Lawrence Great Lakes, one of man's greatest natural resources for water, transportation, hydroelectric power, food, and recreation (Table 6-2). It not only houses in its basin about one-eighth of the total population of North America; it is subject to their biologic and cultural by-products. What, in fact, can be said about environmental changes wrought by man's presence in the region of the Great Lakes and what concomitant changes have ensued on the structure and dynamics of these five great connected ecosystems—Lakes Superior, Michigan, Huron, Erie and Ontario?

Before we discuss these matters, however, it is important to be reminded of a major principle about ecosystems—they age. They undergo succession. An aquatic ecosystem proceeds inexorably, predictably, and ultimately to a semiterrestrial or fully terrestrial state. They initiate typically as nutrient-deficient, and hence unproductive and detritus-free systems, and develop to ones with increasing amounts of nutrients, and hence to productive systems with considerable deposits of organic materials. This aging process from low production, or oligotrophy, to high production, or eutrophy, as a result of enrichment is often referred to as *eutrophication*. Successional change, including the eutrophication of lakes, is, then, as natural a process as is individual development or population growth.

As we have already seen in Chapter 5, succession is accompanied by significant changes in structure and function, both biotic and abiotic. Some nutrients increase or become more readily available, and others are depleted through long-term storage; dissolved oxygen tends to be decreased, especially in deeper water; electrical conductivity and thermal properties are altered. There are, of course, corresponding changes in the biota, with the two major or at lease obvious changes involving plankton and fish. Plankton, composed of microscopic or near-microscopic plants and animals of open water, are sparse in oligotrophic lakes; their absence is responsible for the

TABLE 6-2. Morphometric Data for the St. Lawrence Great Lakes

Lake	Area (km^2)	Maximum Depth (m)	Mean Depth (m)	Volume (km^3)	Shore Line Length (km)	Mean Elevation Above Sea Level (m)
Superior	83,300	307	145	12,000	3000	183
Huron	59,510	223	76	4600	2700	177
Michigan	57,850	265	99	5760	2210	177
Erie	25,820	60	21	540	1200	174
Ontario	18,760	225	91	1720	1380	75

Data on area, depth, volume, and shore line, by permission, from G. E. Hutchinson, 1957. Treatise on Limnology. New York: John Wiley and Sons, Inc. Data on elevation: U. S. Army Corps of Engineers, U. S. Lake Survey Chart. 1955.

characteristic deep blue of such lakes, since there is nothing to reflect the shorter wavelengths of light back to the surface. As enrichment proceeds through the import of nutrients from surrounding watersheds and by wind-blown dust coupled with internal mineral-fixation processes, the original dominant phytoplankters, the desmids, are replaced by diatoms, then by flagellates and other green algae, and finally by blue-green algae. Major population blooms of the blue-green algae create most of the problems in water works: they clog filters, release obnoxious and objectionable aromas and flavors, and turn away even the most inveterate swimmer from the pea-soup consistency of his favorite swimming hole. Thus, from a utilitarian view, eutrophic water, at least in this condition, is unusable without major and typically expensive remedial treatment. Almost everyone has observed such eutrophication if only in a puddle persisting in a rut made by an automobile tire on a front lawn.

Oligotrophic lakes are the source of many of man's most favored fish—trout, char, chub or lake herring, and whitefish. As eutrophication proceeds, these gourmet delights are replaced by progressively less relished forms, such as bass, perch, and pike, and still later by generally much less favored types such as carp and sunfish.

The eutrophication process is, as is true of ecological succession in general, one that is measured on a geological time scale; the amount of natural eutrophication in a moderate-sized lake during a human lifetime is virtually imperceptible. The changes are slow, but nonetheless inexorable, the result of dynamic interactions between the components of the ecosystems, and subject to the influences of surrounding ecosystems and the major environmental gradients. In the Great Lakes, as in many other bodies of water, the natural process of eutrophication has been accelerated to a considerable degree by pollution, by man's misplacement of natural resources. Analysis of records from as far back as 1850 indicate that the effect has largely been since about 1910 and that it has been greatest in those lakes (Erie, Ontario, and Michigan) which have had the largest population growth within their drainage areas. Let us consider a few of the many changes, abiotic and biotic, that have taken place in Lake Erie.

Lake Erie is the shallowest and smallest of the Great Lakes (Table 6-2). Extending 240 miles from Toledo to Buffalo, its major source of water (about 80 per cent) is Lake Huron, via a river system that services industrial Detroit (Figure 6-7); additional water is derived from numerous rivers which drain agricultural land and also serve such major industrial cities as Toledo, Cleveland, Erie, and Buffalo.

Over the last 100 or so years, there has been a significant increase in the amount of calcium, sodium, potassium, and chlorides and sulfates in Lake Erie (Figure 6-6). There has also been a corresponding increase in the total dissolved solids (soluble inorganic substances) from about 140 parts per million in 1900 to nearly 190 in 1960. In both instances, the increase

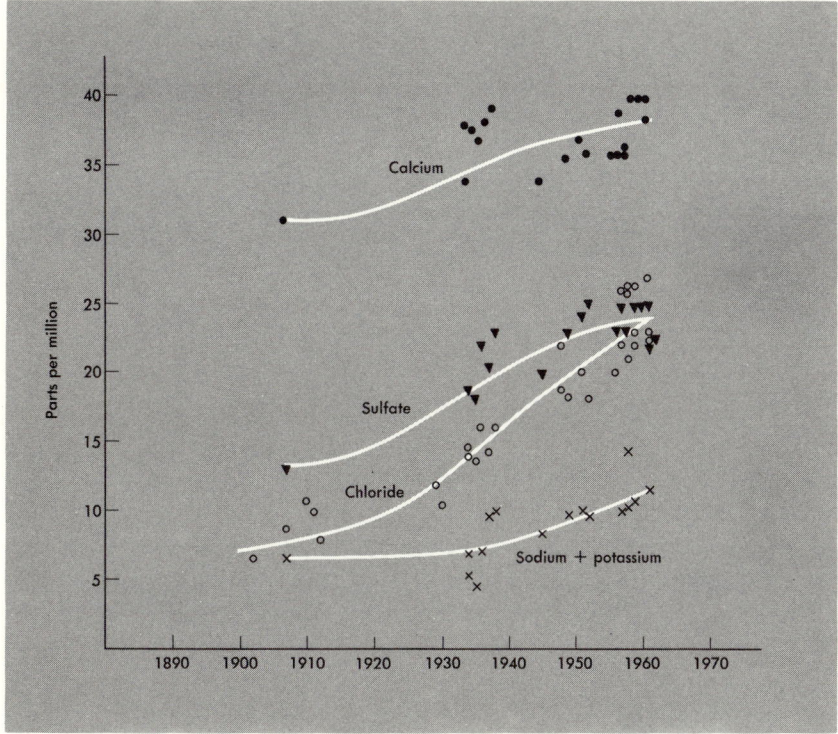

Redrawn, by permission, from A. M. Beeton. 1965. Limnology and Oceanography 10: 240–254.
Fig. 6-6. Chemical changes in Lake Erie, 1890–1960.

in these chemicals is most striking since about 1910, the time at which population growth in the region accelerated markedly. The fact that chloride and sulfate are important constituents of industrial and human sewage readily accounts for its significant increase in the lake. Of the other Great Lakes, only Ontario shows such a comparable increase. Significant increases in phosphates, which, as was noted in Chapters 3 and 4, are limiting factors, are attributable to two major sources, some 60 per cent from household sewage—laundry detergents—and some 40 per cent from fertilizers washed off the agricultural land of the region.

Substantial changes in the amount of dissolved oxygen in the western and eastern portions of the lake do not appear to have occurred since about 1930; in general, the shallow western end of the lake (average depth, 7.3 m) is subject to sufficient mixing of surface waters so that the hypolimnion is generally 80 per cent saturated. Occasional stratification occurs and has resulted in a rather quick depletion of oxygen in the hypolimnion. The deep eastern end (maximum depth, 60 m; average depth, 24 m) averages 60–70 per cent oxygen saturation. The central basin (average depth, 18 m), how-

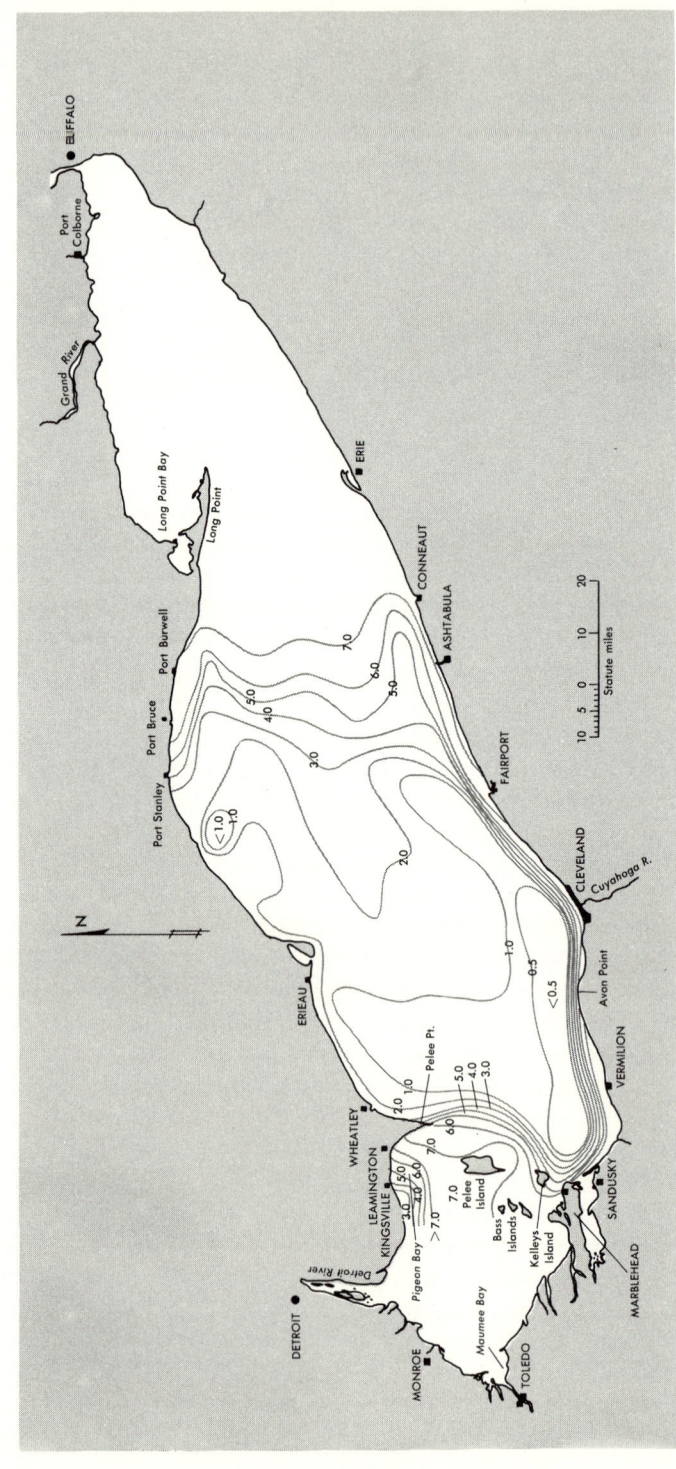

From A. M. Beeton. 1963. *Great Lakes Fisheries Commission Technical Report No. 6.*

Fig. 6-7. Distribution of dissolved oxygen in the bottom waters of Lake Erie, 1959.

ever, appears to be subject to severe oxygen depletion involving many hundreds of square miles, affecting about 70 per cent of the bottom water (Figure 6-7). The frequency of these low oxygen periods is yet uncertain, but evidence over a 33-year period indicates that the severity of the depletion is more frequent and the area involved is greater now than in the past.

On the biological side, evidence of eutrophic changes may be sought in their effects on bacteria, plankton, bottom fauna, and fish. Unfortunately, the published studies on plankton do not allow the kind of valid comparison which was made above for chemical changes in the lake; however, the data that do exist provide evidence of recent eutrophication by changes in the composition and abundance of both phytoplankton and zooplankton, particularly in the western and central basins. For example, from the records of the water filtration plant of Cleveland, Charles C. Davis found an average increase in phytoplankton counts from 81 per ml in 1929 to 2423 in 1962. The bacterial situation is even more markedly different. Between 1913 and 1946, when the population on the area of the western end of Lake Erie grew from 1 million to 3.5 million, the coliform bacteria (*Escherichia coli*) count increased nearly threefold, from 175.2 per 100 ml to 448.9. The eastern end of the lake experienced no change in the same period. In recent summers as many as three-quarters of the swimming beaches along the southern shore line of the lake have been closed because the coliform bacteria count exceeded the safety level for public health: in 1967 out of 83 beaches in Michigan, Ohio, Pennsylvania, and New York, 27 were unsafe for swimming for the whole season, 28 only periodically safe. It will be of interest to some to note that *Escherichia coli,* the index organism for aquatic pollution, is itself a nonpathogenic bacterium of the intestine. Pathogenic bacteria are difficult to detect but are often intestinal associates of *E. coli.* Since the latter is discharged with body wastes and dies off outside the body more slowly than pathogens and can be detected by a fairly simple technique, it is used as an indirect assessment of the pathogenic bacteria. The operating assumption is that as long as *E. coli* is present, there is a chance that some pathogenic bacteria are also present.

Significant changes in the distribution and abundance of the bottom fauna of western Lake Erie were detected in the period from 1930 to 1961 by John F. Carr and Jarl K. Hiltunen (Table 6-3). In 1961, the tubificid worm, an oligochaete typical of low oxygen conditions and hence an empirical criterion of pollution, constituted 84 per cent of the total bottom-dwelling organisms collected, a ninefold increase over a period of thirty years. Not so for the burrowing mayfly, *Hexagenia,* once so abundant that its synchronized emergence constituted a major nuisance. Highways were made slick by thousands of their bodies, and shovels were required to remove them from sidewalks. The mayfly population has been reduced almost to extinction, a direct result of its inability to withstand low oxygen conditions. These direct comparisons with the most striking changes in tubificids, midges,

TABLE 6-3. Average Density (number/m^2) of Bottom Organisms in Western Lake Erie in 1930 and 1961

Group	Number of Stations Compared	1930	1961	Ratio of Numbers 1961/1930
Oligochaeta (tubificid worms)	33	677	5949	8.79
Hexagenia sp. (mayflies)	33	139	1	0.01
Tendipedidae (midges)	23	73	322	4.41
Sphaeriidae (finger nail clams)	23	221	438	1.98
Gastropoda (snails)	16	40	221	5.52

Reproduced, by permission, from J. F. Carr and J. K. Hiltunen, 1965. Limnology and Oceanography 10: 551–569.

and mayflies indicate a sharp expansion of oxygen-demanding wastes between 1930 and 1961. In 1930, 263 km^2 or 26 per cent of the area was classed as polluted; in 1961, the entire area (1020 km^2) was so classed: 26 per cent lightly, 51 per cent moderately, and 23 per cent heavily. The area of heavy pollution increased ninefold, from 26 km^2 in 1930 to 263 km^2 in 1961 (Figure 6-8); the relationships of this area to major centers of habitation and industry are patent.

Marked changes have also occurred in the composition and abundance of both commercial and sport fish over the past 30 to 60 years. Lake herring, sauger, blue pike, whitefish, walleye—all commercially significant and gastronomically satisfying—have declined dramatically (Figure 6-9): lake herring from a high of 48.8 million pounds in 1918 to 1000 pounds in 1965; sauger from a high of 6.2 million pounds in 1916 to less than 500 pounds in 1965; blue pike from a high of 26.8 million pounds in 1936 to less than 500 pounds in 1965; whitefish from a high of 7.1 million pounds in 1949 to 6000 pounds in 1965; walleye from a high of 15.4 million pounds in 1956 to 783,000 pounds in 1965. This is not a consequence of sea lamprey, which has not been so important in Lake Erie as in the other lakes; Lake Erie tributaries provide unfavorable spawning grounds for lamprey. The explanation is directly tied to shifted environmental factors that have resulted in conditions in which desirable species fail to reproduce. Although total fish production in the lake continues to be about 50 million pounds, it is of the less table-favored forms—sheepshead, carp, yellow perch, and smelt.

This brief synopsis of changes in certain major physical, chemical, and biotic aspects of the Lake Erie ecosystem indicate that this is a system in

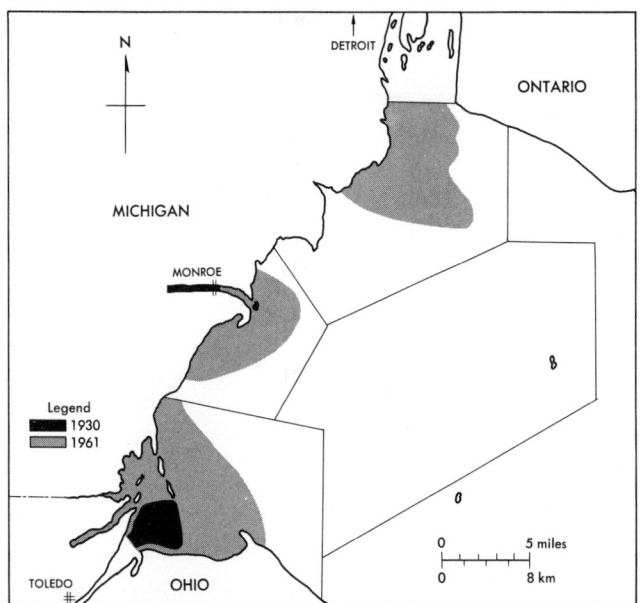

Redrawn, by permission, from J. F. Carr and J. K. Hiltunen. 1965. *Limnology and Oceanography* 10: 551–569.

Fig. 6-8. Zones of heavy pollution in western Lake Erie in 1930 and in 1961.

which, in the earlier words of the chapter, there are "resources out of place," as a result of which the system is experiencing an "unfavorable alteration." But one is also admonished to remember the other significant point made at the beginning of this discussion on water pollution concerning the natural aging, or eutrophication, which is a consequence of the dynamics of ecosystems. The problem in Lake Erie may be put in the words of the Federal Water Pollution Control Administration, in its statement before a Subcommittee on Government Operations of the House of Representatives of the 89th Congress: "The main body of the lake is deteriorating in quality at a rate greater than that of normal aging due to inputs of pollution resulting from the activities of man." And if pollution were to be discontinued, how long would it take to rid the system of the pollutants currently present? According to Robert Rainey, at the natural flow of water, it would take about 20 years for 90 percent of the wastes to be cleared from Lakes Erie and Ontario, and hundreds of years from Lakes Superior and Michigan.

Not all "unfavorable alterations" resulting from "resources out of place" are in the direction of accelerating natural successional processes, however. Some environmental insults to an ecosystem result not in progression but regression. Snow "in its place," as in melting, adds moisture to the soil; snow "out of place," as in an avalanche, reduces the landscape

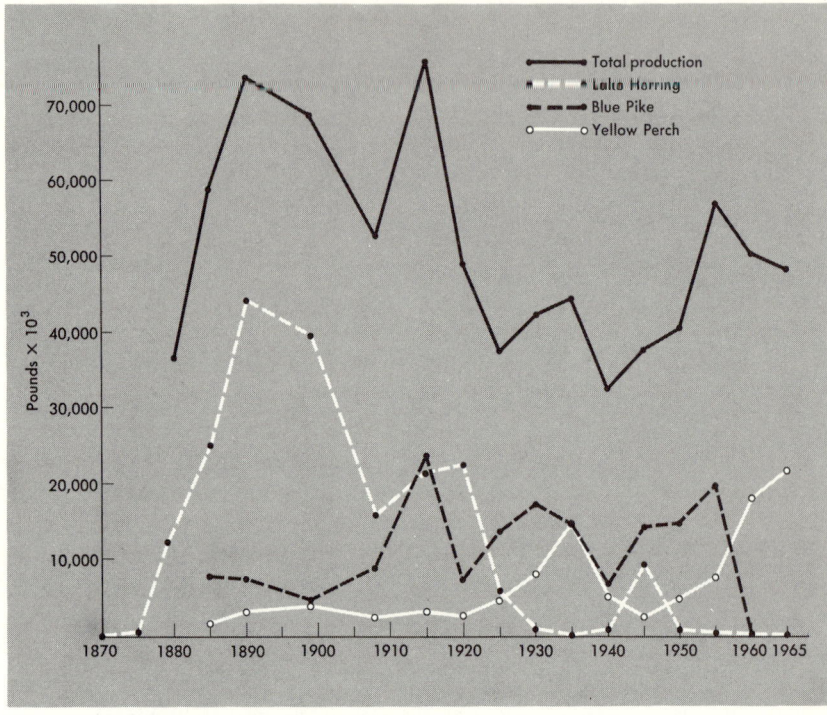

From data in N. S. Baldwin and R. W. Saalfield. 1962. Great Lakes Fisheries Commission Technical Report No. 3 plus supplement, 1966.

Fig. 6-9. Changes in the total catch of selected fish population in Lake Erie from 1867 to 1965.

to an earlier stage of its ecological history. Strontium "in its place" as a stable isotope is harmless to organisms; strontium "out of place" as the radioactive isotope can induce leukemia and perhaps result in death. Ionizing radiation "in its place," as in the sun and mineral deposits in the lithosphere, constitutes the background radiation of about 0.5 roentgen per year which geneticists believe to be at least partially responsible for spontaneous mutation, the very tool of evolutionary adaptation; ionizing radiation "out of place" in the form of atomic and hydrogen blasts can not only directly cause death but, more significantly, increased rates of and kinds of mutation which are more likely to be detrimental to an organism adapted to its current environment. But since man will increasingly be of the atomic age as it assumes more dominance in heating homes, preserving food, powering industry, and fueling transportation, a brief discussion of a few ecological considerations of ionizing radiation and of radioisotopes as environmental pollutants are in order.

Ionizing Radiation and Terrestrial Ecosystems

At the outset it is important to note the recency of this concern and of its study. The untoward ecological consequences of an atomic explosion were publicly recognized much later than were the immediate medical and military by-products. At this writing, not quite twenty years have elapsed since sources of ionizing radiation were available for the study of natural systems. Thus, few quantitative studies of the effects of ionizing radiation on ecosystems are available; the most significant to date have been conducted by George Woodwell and his associates at the Brookhaven National Laboratory on Long Island, New York, by Robert Platt, of Emory University, and his students, at the Dawsonville Lockheed reactor in northern Georgia, and by Howard T. Odum and associates in tropical forests in Puerto Rico.

At the Brookhaven Laboratory, a 9500-curie source of gamma irradiation, cesium-137, is centrally located in a stand of scarlet and black oaks and pitch pine, a part of the eastern pine-oak biome. The oaks are about 40-45 years old, with none over 64; some of the pines are as much as 100 years old. Exposure to the cesium source ranges from several thousand roentgens (r) per day a few meters away to 1.5 r at 125 m and to background levels at greater distances; lowering the source into a lead shield enables investigators to work in the forest with immunity. Within six months of the beginning of the radiation exposure, five vegetation zones were apparent; each widened appreciably over a three-year period. Nearest the source where the exposure was greater than 200 r/day was a zone in which all woody plants and most herbaceous plants were killed within the first year. For perspective, the lethal dosage of radiation required to kill 50 out of 100 persons, the so-called LD_{50}, is about 400 r. The sedge, *Carex pensylvanica,* survived in this same zone, to within 18 m of the source, where it received 200-300 r/day, and there has been some succession of herbaceous plants during the three years; shielded in the "shadow" of large trees, *Carex* survived much nearer the source. Away from this "devastated zone," as Woodwell refers to it, is a zone dominated by *Carex pensylvanica* with other low herbs, followed by a shrub zone dominated by ericaceous shrubs, which had exposures from 40 to 150 r/day, an oak forest with exposures of 12 to 40 r/day, and finally, a pine-oak forest where exposure was less than 12 r/day in 1962, 7 r/day in 1963, and 4.2 r/day in 1964.

It is immediately evident that the zonation pattern is related to stratification of the vegetation, trees being more sensitive than the shrubs, pines more sensitive than oaks, and the ground layer being least sensitive. This effect, according to a hypothesis of Dr. Arnold Sparrow of the Brookhaven Laboratory, is directly related to the average volume of chromosomes (i.e., the larger the volume, the more sensitive the plant—namely, a bigger target) and to the amount of bud shielding afforded by the plant itself (i.e., the larger the tree and/or the more buds, the more shielding). It is not unexpected that one of the corollaries of the observed zonation is a reduction in species diversity with increasing dosage (Figure 6-10). The untoward consequences of reduced diversity on community stability were discussed earlier. This zonation pattern and its concomitant reduction in species diversity has been shown in other studies of radiation effects and raises intriguing questions as one considers the parallel to the gradation of life forms and species diversity from tundra to tropics (Table 5-5). It would appear, as Woodwell states, "that the gross patterns of radiation effects on vegetation are by no means unique but have abundant precedent in nature. . . . This means that evolution of radiosensitivity in all of its various ramifications has been controlled not by radiation but by other factors, or combination of factors, that have had the same selective influence that ionizing radiation might have had." (1967. *Ecological Monographs* **37**: 53–69.)

There are hazards of high order in extrapolating from studies like these to the effects that might result from a bomb or reactor explosion. Of

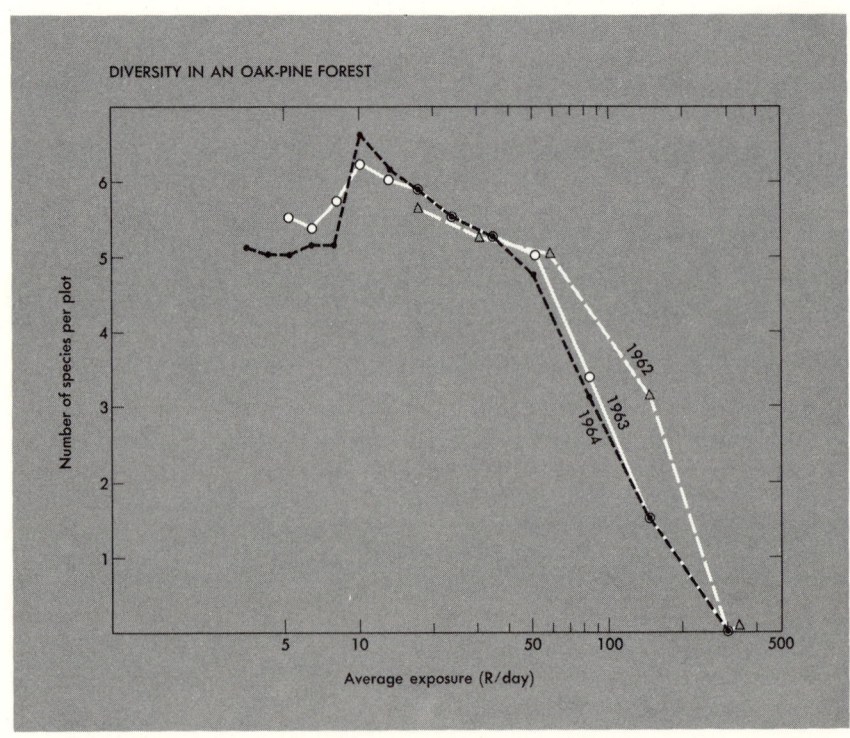

Redrawn, by permission, from G. M. Woodwell and A. L. Rebuck. 1967. *Ecological Monographs* 37: 53–69.

Fig. 6-10. Effect of chronic irradiation on species diversity in an oak-pine forest.

significant difference, the latter produce a short pulse of neutrons and both gamma and beta emitters instead of a chronic emission of gamma radiation such as has been typically employed in studies to date. Nonetheless, Dr. Platt has suggested that in the event of a 20,000-megaton atomic attack on the United States with 100 per cent fission, 2 to 5 per cent of the country would receive 15,000 r or more within 2 weeks, and 10 per cent would receive 5000 to 10,000 r. Of the remaining 85 to 88 per cent, the greatest percentage would receive 1000 to 2000 r. On this basis, Platt speculates that

> From 5 to 20% of the forest ecosystems may have the tree overstory seriously damaged or killed. Another 20% may be visibly affected, but without loss of the overstory; recovery for this percentage would be relatively fast. . . . For the rest of the country (grasslands, deserts, and tundra), temporary changes may occur in the species composition in 1 to 10% of the area, the remainder being relatively little affected.
>
> Therefore, direct radiation effects from nuclear war on vegetation are not likely to seriously limit man's reconstruction of his renewable resources. Other ecological effects may be far more limiting, such as radioactive contamination or effects on animal and food resources.
>
> —Ionizing radiation and homeostasis of ecosystems. *In* G. M. Woodwell (ed.), 1965. *Ecological Effects of Nuclear War.* Brookhaven National Laboratory Publ. 917 (C-43).

This final comment concerning radioactive contamination of ecosystems warrants further consideration.

Pollution by Radioactive Elements and Pesticides

Fission by-products both of nuclear detonation and water-cooled atomic power reactors do indeed constitute more of a potential hazard than direct ionizing radiation, because they follow biogeochemical pathways. So also do most of the pesticides that man has developed to regulate or eliminate bothersome insects and plants. Radioactive iodine, which is produced as a by-product of nuclear detonation; for example, is carried aloft into the atmosphere and through normal meteorological processes is transported for some distance and deposited on the vegetation and soil as "fall-out." Because the decay rate (i.e., half-life) of iodine is fast (8 days), that which falls on the soil is unimportant—it decays before normal edaphic processes can get it into the plants. However, that which falls on the leaves is important, for plants incorporate it and through grazing pass it on to cows and subsequently to man through the cow's milk. Behaving in typical iodine fashion, the radioisotope then concentrates in thyroid tissue, where its radiations can disrupt and damage the normal metabolism and growth of this endocrine gland. An unhappy example of this is seen in the consequences of the 1954 atomic bomb test on Bikini, at the western end of the Marshall Islands. An unexpected wind shift carried fallout back onto the eastern islands, notably on Rongelap. As of 1968, 17 of 19 children on Rongelap who were under 10 years of age at the time of the test had developed thyroid abnormalities, many cancerous; most of the victims, now between 15 and 24 years of age, show retarded growth.

The actual fate of different radioactive elements has been demonstrated in a number of organisms. Our concern here is not only with one organism but with ecosystems. The disposition of cesium (cesium-134) in white oak discussed earlier (p. 55) is particularly instructive in this connection because of the eventual losses from the plant to the ecosystem through the normal processes of leaf fall and rain leaching. This amount, about 19 per cent of the original input, is subject to recycling through normal biogeochemical processes back into the tree or into other vegetation and through grazing and detritus feeding to other components of the food web.

On a much larger scale, recent studies in the relatively simple tundra ecosystems of Alaska and Finland are particularly revealing. Reports by J. K. Miettinen, of the University of Helsinki, indicate that, in 1965, Laplanders had reached the highest radiation exposure of any human population through dietary uptake of such radioactive elements as strontium, cesium, polonium, and iron. Although the total fallout of radioactive material in Lapland is about half that in Helsinki, the greater radiation exposure, which is in the order of 55 times, is a direct result of ecological processes. Radioactive elements constitute a source of enrichment for the nutrient-deficient soils and waters of Lapland. Some of these elements are synthesized into protoplasm in lieu of the normal element that it simulates chemically (e.g., strontium-90 in place of stable calcium, cesium-137 in place of potassium), and others become physically adsorbed onto surface tissues (e.g., zinc-65). As an aside, this latter point, physical adsorption of nutrients, is of considerable significance; much recent work, particularly in aquatic ecosystems, indicates that major uptake of radioactive elements, and hence probably of stable forms as well, is not by way of metabolic incorporation, but by way of these nonbiological physical and chemical processes.

For the Laplander, however, radiation exposure is directly dietary in origin. They depend heavily upon reindeer meat, and the reindeer, in turn, depend heavily on the abundant and widespread lichen known as reindeer moss (*Cladonia*). Reindeer moss concentrates the fallout radioisotopes both biologically and physically, and these are, in turn, transferred to reindeer as they graze. The directness of this transfer is shown by the fact that the concentration of particular radioisotopes increased by four times in both lichens and reindeer meat between 1961 and 1964. At this point as much as 99 per cent of the strontium-90 goes no farther than the reindeer; it becomes trapped in bone. Not so, however, with other elements, which get passed directly to man as a result of his carnivorous and milk-drinking habits. If these elements are not metabolized or excreted, they become concentrated to levels considerably above the base level measured at the ground surface. For example, in a study of cesium-137 in the lichen-caribou-Eskimo food chain, it was shown that the Eskimo had twice the concentration of the caribou and that wolves and caribou had as much as three times the concentration of the lichen.

The high concentration ability of some organisms, some of which are in the order of thousands of times above the environmental level, has led to a suggestion of employing such species to decontaminate a system. They could be introduced, allowed to concentrate the pollutant, and be periodically harvested and disposed of in some appropriate fashion. But, in discussing the situation in Lapland, another clue for the potential management of these contaminants presented itself, dealing with the nutrient status of the soil and water. The nutrient-deficient soils and waters of Lapland lap up these introduced isotopes like long-lost friends. But a number of studies have shown that the uptake of given elements can be regulated by the mere presence of other elements. For example, the biological uptake of strontium-90 bears an indirect relationship to the amount of calcium present. In a situation in which the ratio of calcium to strontium-90 is above a certain level, plants will preferentially take up the calcium, even though the actual abundance of the strontium is considerable. This is a promising line of resource management, but far from being well understood.

The situation with pesticides is, in many respects, similar to that of radioisotopes; they too are environmental resources out of place but nonetheless subject to normal ecological processes. By virtue of biogeochemical cycling, the DDT that is used to control mosquitoes has a potential and often an actual regulatory effect on other biotic components of ecosystems. Some pesticides are subject to normal biological degradation by soil and water bacteria: the commonly used weed-killer 2,4-D is one of these—it is quite quickly destroyed in the soil. This particular compound is a synthesized growth regulator and simulates many of the naturally occurring ones; it is not surprising, then, that such natural, or pseudonatural, products are ecologically accommodated in normal ecosystem dynamics. On the other hand, other plant growth regulators and insecticides are quite resistant to biological decomposition. If such bioundegradable compounds should become "fixed" by the soil by being bound to the clay or humus fractions, they are of less consequence to an ecosystem; dieldrin and DDT, both widely used insecticides, tend to be fixed by some types of soils, particularly those rich in clay, and thus are less available under given conditions.

It is significant to note, however, that a substantial proportion of insecticides are not permanently fixed by the soil; also, they collect on plant surfaces and can thus be passed directly along a food chain. And importantly, because of differential metabolic and retention capacities of organisms, residue levels tend to increase with higher trophic levels. For example, in a study of DDT concentrations in organisms along the south shore of Long Island, where this insecticide has been used to control mosquitoes for some twenty years, some carnivores had concentrated it by a factor of more than 1000 over the organisms at the base of the food chain.

Even more concern must be registered when substantial amounts of DDT are found in organisms remote from possible sources of direct contamination. The Bermuda petrel (*Pterodroma cahow*) is a case in point: among the world's rarest birds, with a population of about 100, the petrel feeds at sea and visits land only to breed, and breeds only on Bermuda. Yet Charles F. Wurster has reported finding significant levels of DDT (6.44 ppm) in unhatched eggs and dead chicks. The only source of the insecticide is its oceanic food chain, and the only access to the latter is by runoff from the mainland some 650 miles away. In itself this distance from the direct source of contamination is striking, but more significant is the fact that various lines of evidence implicate the DDT as the probable major cause of declining reproduction in the petrel at a rate at which reproduction will fail completely by 1978. The correlation between DDT and diminishing reproduction is based on rather considerable and diversified evidence: as one example, of several that might be cited, healthy osprey produce 2.2 to 2.5 young per nest, but a Maryland colony containing a DDT level of 3 ppm in its eggs produced only 1.1 young per nest. There is some evidence to suggest that the DDT interferes with calcium metabolism, resulting in symptoms of calcium deficiency, as well as creating hormonal disturbance resulting in delayed ovulation and inhibition of gonad development; these disturbances may prove to be interrelated, and to be related to unsuccessful reproduction. It is important to note that a statistically significant decrease in calcium content of eggshells occurred between 1946 and 1950 in several species of carnivorous birds (peregrine falcon, golden eagle, sparrowhawk)—a period in which there was widespread introduction of DDT into the environment.

This is, of course, dramatic—but, after all, these are only birds, not man. Alas, the story for man is no less comforting. According to analyses by the Food and Drug Administration, residues of pesticide chemicals are found in about half of the thousands of samples of food examined each year, and about 3 per cent of the samples contain levels in excess of, or not authorized by, legal tolerances. In a study based on the period June 1964 through April 1966, residues of chlorinated organic pesticides (DDT, dieldrin, lindane, etc.) were commonly found in all diet samples and all kinds of food except beverages; meat, fish, poultry, and dairy products accounted for more than half of the intake, even though there is little direct application of pesticides to these products—they get there by the food chain. Further, DDT accounts for one-third of the total. Yet, as the study noted, the producing area for the food was typically outside the purchasing or consuming area—a situation not unlike the petrel and its DDT intake. Although the DDT levels (about 0.0014 mg per kilogram body weight) are well below the acceptable daily intake level (0.01 mg/kg body weight) established in 1965 by the World Health Organization Expert Committee on Pesticide Residues and the Food and Agriculture Organization of the United Nations, no self-respecting ecologist can fail to note the high frequency of contamination (more than half the samples over the last several years), the accelerating use of DDT (and of other pesticides), and the concentration phenomenon of DDT and other pesticides in the food chain. Not only is continued surveillance of pesticide levels a must as a matter of human health and safety, but investigations are needed of the effects of pesticides in all kinds of populations, including the human one.

****

EPILOGUE

From the kinds of case histories presented in the last few pages, it is relatively easy to be caught up in the emotion elicited by the term pollution—and I would be derelict to my profession if I were to castigate such a response. What is important, however, is to realize again that what we are dealing with are by-products, the wastes of a natural ecological agent—man. He is, and his wastes are, as much a part of the living world as the microbe and its wastes. But man has a peculiar and potential dominance over his ecosystem even though he is in no way independent of it; when he insults an ecosystem, he can expect to be slapped back. As he puts resources out of place, he can expect changes—undesirable concentrations of toxic substances, consequent reductions in the number and abundance of species, and a resultant and consequential community instability. He cannot, nor can any organism, exist without producing wastes. The problem, then, is intelligent and resourceful management. The quality of our environment will be a reflection of man's capacity to manage it. It will require much more understanding of ecological ramifications than are presently known and much more interplay of the myriad facets of a complex society in their resolution.

Solutions to the problems discussed in this chapter as well as to the many not discussed—air pollution, strip-mine wastes, open-pit mining, etc.—will certainly not come with ease. For many of them, we do not have the scientific wisdom to make reliable predictions and, if we did, we often lack the data on which to do so. These problems, and others which might have been discussed, are not ecological only. They are sociological, economic, governmental, psychological, and, in the final analysis, moral as well.

These problems will not be put down by a cry to return to a by-gone day, to some Camelot, nor to maintain the status quo. No ecologist worth his salt can argue for either; to do so would be a controversion of the most basic of ecological principles—dynamic and adaptive change. The landscape of America was indeed changed as man came to it, but it had changed before. Where I sit today in northern Ohio was formerly forest, but it was also formerly ocean and formerly glacier. Change is the essence of nature, both the gradual change that transforms a pond to a forest, or a tundra to a taiga, and the devastating kind by which a tornadic wind denudes a landscape. Man's hopes and chances, however, lie in the regulation of the changes that he, as a natural and integral part of the landscape, induces. He is a partner with other natural processes in the management of his resources and of his cultural and biological wastes. The future depends on man's intelligence to develop a body of knowledge about such management and on the wisdom which few now have to apply that knowledge. This demands a rethinking of man's place in nature, a rethinking of attitudes about the total environment—in the words of Aldo Leopold, the development of a new ethic for the land. The roots of the crisis in which man finds himself are deep in the outlook western man, in particular, has had about the land—land as his adversary to be conquered, as his servant to be exploited for his own ends, as a possession of rightful and eminent domain and, most importantly, land of unlimited capacity. These concepts must give ground to an ecological conscience, to a love, respect, admiration, and understanding for the total ecosystem of which we are part; our course, otherwise, is one of collision, an inexorable Armageddon.

REFERENCES

General

Bresler, J. B., 1966. *Human Ecology, Collected Readings.* Reading, Mass: Addison-Wesley.

Darling, F. F., 1964. Conservation and ecological theory. *Journal of Ecology* **52** (Suppl.): 39–45.

Krutch, J. W., 1954. "Conservation is not enough" and "The mystique of the desert," in *The Voice of the Desert.* New York: William Sloane Associates.

Leopold, A., 1949. "The land ethic," in *A Sand County Almanac.* New York: Oxford University Press.

Udall, S., 1963. *The Quiet Crisis.* New York: Holt, Rinehart and Winston.

Watt, K. E. F., 1968. *Ecology and Resource Management. A Quantitative Approach.* New York: McGraw-Hill Book Co.

White, L., 1967. The historical roots of our ecological crisis. *Science* **155**: 1203–1207.

Human Populations

Davis, K., 1967. Population policy: will current programs succeed? *Science* **158**: 730–739.

Markert, C. L., 1966. Biological limits on population growth. *BioScience* **16**: 859–862.

National Academy of Sciences—National Research Council, 1963. The growth of world population. Publ. 1091.

Pirie, N. W., 1967. Orthodox and unorthodox methods of meeting world food needs. *Scientific American* **216** (February): 27–35.

Population Bulletin, published 6 times yearly by the Population Reference Bureau, has timely information and provocative issues on this general topic.

Population Crisis, 1966. Hearings before the Subcommittee on Foreign Aid Expenditures of the Committee on Government Operations, United States Senate, 89th Congress (6 parts).

United Nations Department of Economic and Social Affairs, 1966. World population prospects as assessed in 1963. *Population Studies,* No. 41.

Pollution

Beeton, A. M., 1965. Eutrophication of the St. Lawrence Great Lakes. *Limnology and Oceanography* **10**: 240–254.

Darling, F. E. and J. P. Milton (eds.), 1966. *Future Environments of North America.* Garden City, New York: Natural History Press.

Ecological Society of America, 1966. Biological aspects of weather modification. *Bulletin of the Ecological Society of America* **47**: 39–78.

Egler, F. E., 1966. Pesticides in our ecosystem. *Ecology* **47**: 1077–1084.

Federal Water Pollution Control Administration, 1966. Statement on water pollution in the Lake Erie Basin. Appendix 8, pp. 683–736. Committee on Government Operations, House of Representatives, 89th Congress. Hearing on Water Pollution. Great Lakes, Part 3. September 1966.

Goldman, M. I. (ed.), 1967. *Controlling Pollution. The Economics of a Cleaner America.* Englewood Cliffs, New Jersey: Prentice-Hall, Inc.

Goodman, G. T., R. W. Edwards, and J. M. Lambert (eds.), 1965. *Ecology and the Industrial Society.* New York: John Wiley and Sons, Inc.

Hynes, H. B. N., 1963. *The Biology of Polluted Waters.* Liverpool: Liverpool University Press.

Marquis, R. W. (ed.), 1966. *Environmental Improvement (Air, Water, and Soil).* Washington, D. C.: Graduate School, U. S. Dept. of Agriculture.

Moore, N. W., 1967. A synopsis of the pesticide problem. *In* J. B. Cragg, *Advances in Ecological Research,* Vol. 4. New York: Academic Press.

National Academy of Sciences—National Research Council, 1966. *Waste Management and Control.* Publ. 1400. Washington, D. C.: National Academy of Sciences.

President's Science Advisory Committee—Environmental Pollution Panel, 1965. *Restoring the Quality of our Environment.* Washington, D. C.: U. S. Government Printing Office.

Rudd, R. L., 1964. *Pesticides and the Living Landscape.* Madison: University of Wisconsin Press.

Russell, R. S. (ed.), 1966. *Radioactivity and Human Diet.* Oxford: Pergamon Press.

Woodwell, G. M. (ed.), 1965. *Ecological Effects of Nuclear War.* Brookhaven National Laboratory Publ. 917 (C-43).

Woodwell, G. M., 1967. Toxic substances and ecological cycles. *Scientific American* **216** (March): 24–31.

index

a

Abies (Fir)	120, 161–162
Acer (Maple)	122, 137, 162
Achillea (Yarrow)	144–145
Adenostoma (Chamise)	126
Aerobacter	49
Age structure	80–84
Agricultural plants, net production	19
Agropyron spicatum (Wheatgrass)	100–102
Algae:	
bluegreen	45–46, 154
golden brown	68
stonewort	155, 157
Ammonification	46
Anabaena	45–46
Andropogon (Bluestem)	122
Arctostaphylos (Manzanita)	126
Artemisia tridentata (Sagebrush)	123
Ash (*Fraxinus*)	137
Aspen, quaking (*Populus*)	121
Aspergillus	49
Autotroph:	
definition	2
energy fixation by	10–21
Autotrophic ecosystems	22, 152–153, 158
Azotobacter	45

b

Bacteria:	
autotrophic	2
chemosynthetic	2
coliform	49, 185
decomposers	3
nitrogen cycle	43–48
sulfur cycle	49–50
Balanus balanoides	102–103
Barnacles	102–103
Basswood (*Tilia*)	122, 133
Beach ponds, succession in	154–158
Beech (*Fagus*)	122, 133, 162
Beetle, grain (*Tribolium*)	72
Beggiatoa	50
Betula (Birch)	121, 137
Biogeochemical cycles:	
carbon	40–43
definition	35
in ecosystems	54–60
gaseous	40–48
nitrogen	43–48
phosphorus	50–54
sedimentary	48–54
sulfur	49–50
types	35
Biomass:	
biome distributions	128

Biomass (*cont.*)
    conversion to energy   11
    pyramids   32–33
Biome:
    altitudinal distribution   115–116
    characterization   114–129
    climate   119
    major types in U. S. A.   118–127
    productivity   127–129
    world distribution   114
Biotic potential   63, 69, 71–73
Birch (*Betula*)   121, 137
Bluestem (*Andropogon*)   122
Bouteloua curtipendula (Side-oats grama)   144
Broad-sclerophyll biome   126
Bromacil   59
Bromus tectorum (Cheatgrass)   101–102
Buchloe dactyloides (Buffalo grass)   122
Buffalo grass (*Buchloe dactyloides*)   122
Bulrushes (*Scirpus*)   155, 157

C

Calandra oryzae (Rice weevil)   71
Calcium   41, 56, 58–59, 182–183
Carbon cycle   40–43
Carbon dioxide as productivity measurement   11–12
Carbonic acid, dissociation   42
Carex pensylvanica (Sedge)   189
Carnivore   2
Carrying capacity   66, 95–97, 176–178
Carya (Hickory)   122, 162
Castanea (Chestnut)   162
Cattail (*Typha*)   155, 157
Ceratostomella ulmi (Sac fungus)   91
Cesium:
    –134   55–56
    –137   189, 192
Chamaephytes   130–131
Chamise (*Adenostoma*)   126
Chaparral   80, 114
Chara (Stonewort algae)   155, 157
Cheatgrass (*Bromus tectorum*)   101–102
Chestnut (*Castanea*)   91, 162
Chlorides   182–183
Chlorophyll in productivity measurements   13
Chthamalus stellatus   102–103
Cladium jamaicensis (Sawgrass)   125
Cladonia (Reindeer moss)   2, 119, 192
Clams, finger-nail (Sphaeriidae)   186
Climate as population regulator   89–91
Climographs   119
Clostridium   45
Coliform bacteria (*Escherichia coli*)   45, 185
Community:
    classification based on metabolism   152–153

Community (*cont.*)	
climax	158
diversity	158–160
stability	158–159
Competition:	
interspecific	97–103
intraspecific	101, 103–110
Coniferous forest	114, 119–121, 128
Consumer	2
Continuum, vegetational	139–140
Coral reefs, gross production	21
Cornfield, energetics	14–15
Cornus florida (Dogwood)	137
Cottonwood (*Populus*)	122, 157
Creosote bush (*Larrea divaricata*)	123–124
Cryptophytes	129–131
Cushetunk Mountain	131, 137

d

Daphnia (Water flea)	79, 85, 104
Day length, variation in	143
DDT	193–195
Deciduous forest:	
climate	119
description	121–122
function	140–154
productivity	128
structure	129–140
succession	154–163
world distribution	114
Decomposer	3
Deer, black tail (*Odocoileus*)	75–77, 80
Denitrification	47–48
Desert	20–21, 114, 119, 123–124, 148
Desulfavibrio	49
Detritus-based ecosystems	27–29
Didinium nasutum	93
Dinobryon	68, 70
Diversity:	
community	158–160
effect of irradiation	190–191
Dogwood (*Cornus*)	137
Drosophila melanogaster (Fruit fly)	78–79

e

Ecosystem:	
autotrophic	22–27, 152–153, 158
components	1
definition	1
detritus-based	27–29
heterotrophic	152–153, 158
models	4
steady-state	152–153, 158
types	5–6

INDEX

Ecotypes 144–147
Efficiency, gross ecological 31
Elm (*Ulmus*) 91, 122
Elodea canadensis 41
Endothia parasitica 91
Energy:
    budgets 14–17, 28–29
    conversion to biomass 11
    efficiency of transfer 4, 14–15, 18
    fixation 10–21
    flow 4, 22–33
    pyramids 31–33
Energy flow models 4, 24, 25, 29–33
Environmental resistance 63, 70
Epilimnion 148–149
Equations:
    carbonic acid dissociation 42
    photosynthetic 10
Equilibrium in populations 84–86
Erithacus rubecula melophilus (British robin) 75–76
Erythroneura (Leafhoppers) 103
Escherichia (Coliform bacteria) 49, 185
Estuaries, gross production 21
Eutrophication 181–182, 187

f

Fagus (Beech) 122, 133, 162
Ficus aureus (Strangler fig) 125
Finches, Galapagos (*Geospizidae*) 100
Fir (*Abies*) 120, 162
Fish 182, 186, 188
Food chain 31
Forests:
    composition in time 162
    coniferous 114, 119–121, 128
    deciduous 114, 119, 121–122, 128–163
    effect of microclimate and soil 136
    gross production 21
    net production 19
    rain forest 114, 119, 128
Fraxinus americana (Ash) 137
Fungi, decomposers 3

g

Galium (Bedstraw) 100
Gastropoda 186
Gause's competitive exclusion principle 98, 103, 159
Gleotrichia echinulata 45
Glossina (Tsetse fly) 92
Grassland 21, 114, 119, 122–123, 128, 145–147
Great Lakes 180–182
Great Smoky Mountains 137–139
Gross production:
    definition 11
    world distribution 20–21, 127–129

Growth curve (*See also* Population):	
J-shaped	68–69
logistic	69–70
sigmoid	64–68
Growth rate curve (*See also* Population)	64–65
Gull (*Larus argentatus*)	75–76
Gymnorhina tibicen (Australian magpie)	109–110

h

Hamamelis virginiana (Witch hazel)	137
Hectare	14
Hemicryptophytes	130–131
Hemlock (*Tsuga*)	120, 162
Herbivore	2
Heterotroph	2
Heterotrophic ecosystems	152–153, 158
Hexagenia (Mayflies)	185–186
Hickory (*Carya*)	122, 162
Hubbard Brook Forest	57–60
Human population:	
growth	166–170
mortality	171–172
natality	172–175
regulation	175–178
world density	170
Hydra fusca (Hydra)	75–76
Hydrologic cycle	36–40
Hypolimnion	148–149, 183–184

i

Infrared gas analysis	11–12
Insecticides	193–195
Intrinsic rate of natural increase	72–73

k

Kaibab Plateau	95–97

l

Lake herring	186, 188
Lakes:	
Cedar Bog	17, 21–27, 29
Erie	154–158, 182–188
Great Lakes	180–182
gross production in	21
Mendota	16–17
Sanctuary Lake	45–46
Superior	48
Lapland	2, 192–193
Larix laricina (Tamarack)	120
Larrea divaricata (Creosote bush)	123–124
Larus argentatus (Gull)	75–76

Leafhoppers (*Erythroneura*) 103
Lemming "cycles" 108
Lemna (Duckweed) 99–100
Life forms 129–131
Life table 74
Liriodendron tulipfera (Tulip tree) 137
Long-day plants 143–147
Lucilia cuprina (Blowfly) 86
Lynx 96

m

Macrophytes, net production 19
Magnesium 56, 58–59
Magpie, Australian black-backed (*Gymnorhina tibicen*) 109
Mangrove (*Rhizopora*) 125
Manzanita (*Arctostaphylos*) 126
Maple (*Acer*) 122, 133–135, 137, 144, 162
Marshes, net production 19
Mayflies (*Hexagenia*) 185–186
Metabolism, community 151–154
Metalimnion 148–149
Microtus agrestis (English vole) 72
Microtus pennsylvanicus (Meadow vole) 87–88
Midges (Tendipedidae) 186
Mineral cycling 4
Moina macrocopa (Water flea) 67
Mortality 67, 73–80, 171–172
Mouse, house (*Mus*) 105, 107
Mus musculus (House mouse) 105, 107

n

Natality 67, 172–175
Net production:
    agricultural plants 19
    definition 11
    Scots pine 18–19
    total for earth 21
    various ecosystems 18–20
Neurospora 49
Nitrification 46–47
Nitrobacter 47
Nitrogen:
    budget 56
    cycle 43–48
    fixation 43–46
Nitrosocystis oceanus 47
Nitrosomonas 47
Number pyramids 32–33
Nuphar advena (Yellow water lily) 155, 157
Nutrient:
    budgets 54–60
    cycles (*See* Biogeochemical cycles)

o

Oak (*Quercus*)	122, 128, 161–162
Oceans, gross production	20–21
Odocoileus hemionus columbianus (Black tailed deer)	
	75–77, 80
Oligochaeta	186
Overturn	149
Ovis d. dalli (Mountain sheep)	74–76
Oxygen:	
dissolved	183–185
diurnal oxygen production	12
productivity measurement	12
Oxyria digyna (Alpine sorrel)	144

p

Paramecium	93–95, 98, 100
Parasitism	91–93
Pediculus humanis (Human louse)	72
Perch, yellow	186, 188
Periodism	140–154
Pesticides	191–195
Petrel, Bermuda	194
Phanerophytes	130–131
Phenology	142
Phosphates	88–89, 183
Phosphorus:	
budget	56
movement in lakes	50–54
turnover time	52–54
Photoperiodism	144–147
Photosynthesis:	
diurnal pattern	151–152
equation	10
Phytoplankton	19, 185
Phytosociologists	140
Picea (Spruce)	120, 161–162
Pike, blue	186, 188
Pine (*Pinus*) (*See also* Scots pine)	120, 124, 161–162
Pine-oak biome	124–125
Platanus (Sycamore)	122
Pollen diagram	161
Pollution:	
definition	178–180
Great Lakes	180–188
ionizing radiation	189–191
Lake Erie	182–188
pesticides	193–195
radioisotopes	191–193
Population:	
age structure	80–84
biotic potential	63, 69, 71–73
carrying capacity	66, 95–97, 176–178
competition	97–110
density	170
environmental resistance	63, 70

Population (*cont.*)
    equilibrium levels   84–86
    growth   62–68, 166–170
    growth curves   64–69, 85–86
    human (*See* Human population)
    intrinsic rate of natural increase   72–73
    life table   74
    mortality   67, 171–172
    natality   67, 172–175
    parasitism   91–93
    predation   93–97
    regulation:
        abiotic factors   86–91
        interspecific factors   91–104
        intraspecific factors   104–110
    self-governing systems   105–111
    survivorship curves   74–80
Populus (Aspen, Poplar)   121, 122
Potassium   56, 58–59, 182–183
Precipitation distribution:
    biomes   119
    Sierra Nevada   116
    United States   37–40
    world-wide   37–38
Predation   93–97
Presque Isle   154–158
Proales decipiens (Rotifer)   74–76
Producer   2
Production, measuring   10–13
Productivity (*See* Energy, Gross production, Net production)
Proteus   49
Pseudomonas   47
Pterodroma cahow (Bermuda petrel)   194
Pyramids   31–33

q

Quercus (Oak)   122, 128, 161–162

r

Radiation, ionizing   189–191
Radioisotopes:
    carbon   12–13
    cesium   55–56, 192–193
    iodine   191–192
    iron   192
    phosphorus   53
    pollution   191–195
    polonium   192
    strontium   188, 192–193
    zinc   192

Rattus norvegicus (Norway rat)	72
Reindeer moss (*Cladonia*)	2, 119, 192
Rhizobium	43–44
Rhizopora Mangle (Mangrove)	125
Rhus glabra (Sumac)	142
Robin, American and British	75–76
Rotifer (*Proales decipiens*)	74–76

S

Saccharomyces cerevisiae	66
Sagebrush (*Artemisia tridentata*)	123
Salix (Willow)	122
Sassafras albidum (Sassafras)	137
Sauger	186
Sawgrass (*Cladium jamaicensis*)	125
Scirpus (Bulrush)	155, 157
Scots pine (*Pinus sylvestris*)	18–19, 28–29, 56–57
Sea lamprey	186
Seas:	
Black	50
Sargasso	45
Sedge (*Carex*)	189
Sheep, mountain (*Ovis d. dalli*)	74–76
Shock disease	108
Short-day plants	143–147
Side-oats grama (*Bouteloua curtipendula*)	144
Snails (Gastropoda)	186
Snowshoe hare	95–96
Social organization	109–110
Sodium:	
budget	56, 58–59
pollution	182–183
population regulator	87–88
Solar radiation	7–9
Sorrel, Alpine (*Oxyria digyna*)	144
Sphaeriidae	186
Springs:	
gross production	21
Root Spring	27–28
Silver Springs	25–27, 32
Spruce (*Picea*)	120, 161–162
Steady-state ecosystems	152–153, 158
Strangler fig (*Ficus aureus*)	125
Subtropical biome	125
Succession:	
beach ponds	154–158
characteristics	158–159
in the past	161–163
Sulfates	182–183
Sulfur cycle	48–50
Sumac (*Rhus glabra*)	142
Survivorship curves	74–80
Swamps, net production	19
Sycamore (*Platanus*)	122

t

Tamarack (*Larix laricina*)	120
Temperature:	
climographs	119
cycles	148–151
Tendipedidae	186
Territoriality	109–110
Tetragoneuria cynosura (Dragonfly)	82–83
Thais lapillus (Whelk)	102–103
Thermocline	150
Thermodynamic principles	33
Therophytes	129–131
Thiobacillus	50
Thrips imaginis	89–91
Tilia (Basswood)	122, 133
Transplant garden	144–146
Tribolium castaneum (Grain beetle)	72
Trichodesmium	45
Trophic-dynamics	22
Tropical rain forest	114, 119, 128
Tsetse fly (*Glossina*)	92
Tsuga (Hemlock)	162
Tubificid worms (Oligochaeta)	186
Tulip tree (*Liriodendron tulipfera*)	137
Tundra	114, 118–120, 128
Turdus m. migratorius (American robin)	75–76
Turnover time	52–54
Turtle grass	154
2,4-D	193
Typha (Cattail)	155, 157

u

Ulmus (Elm)	91, 122
Urtica dioica (Nettle)	88

v

Vegetation:	
photoperiodic response	145–146
structure,	
description	132–134
variation	135–140

w

Walleye	186
Water content of Earth	37
Waterfleas:	
Daphnia	79, 85, 104
Moina	67
Water lily, yellow (*Nuphar advena*)	155, 157
Wheatgrass (*Agropyron spicatum*)	100–102

Whitefish	186
Willow (*Salix*)	122
Witch hazel (*Hamamelis virginiana*)	137

Y

Yarrow (*Achillea*)	144–145

Z

Zurich-Montpelier "school"	140